C000038506

Driven to the Brink

Alicia Micklethwait • Patricia Dimond

Driven to the Brink

Why Corporate Governance, Board Leadership and Culture Matter

Alicia Micklethwait
United Kingdom

Patricia Dimond
United Kingdom

ISBN 978-1-137-59051-0   ISBN 978-1-137-59053-4   (eBook)
DOI 10.1057/978-1-137-59053-4

Library of Congress Control Number: 2016956856

Cover illustration: © Eric Anthony Johnson / Alamy Stock Photo

Printed on acid-free paper

This Palgrave Macmillan imprint is published by Springer Nature
The registered company is Macmillan Publishers Ltd.
The registered company address is: The Campus, 4 Crinan Street, London, N1 9XW, United Kingdom

With fond memories of Professor Stewart Hamilton, his knowledge, generosity and dry wit, and to the IMD MBA class of 1993.
AM & PD

Foreword

Driven to the Brink: Why Corporate Governance, Board Leadership and Culture Matter was inspired initially as a tribute in memory of IMD Professor Stewart Hamilton. Stewart was a strong advocate of the value of economic history, although he also observed that few apparently took its lessons to heart. He had long been fascinated by stories of corporate disaster, writing several case studies about the most egregious ones, some in collaboration with Alicia Micklethwait. *Greed and Corporate Failure: The Lessons from Recent Disasters* (2006), which Stewart and Alicia wrote together, was a natural development of these two interests, relating the stories of recent disasters and drawing the conclusion that the causes of failure were small in number and common to most. Sadly, Professor Hamilton passed away in September 2014. This book is a tribute to Stewart and his work.

Driven to the Brink was originally conceived as a second edition of *Greed and Corporate Failure*. However, as Patricia Dimond and Alicia Micklethwait began to research content for the second edition, they were disappointed to discover that, in the decade after the first edition of this book, there had been a significant number of new failures, at both corporate and market level, and across several geographic regions. There was a need then to explore, in more depth, the over-arching causes of corporate failure and whether lessons had been learned since *Greed and Corporate*

Failure had been published. These considerations warranted a new book rather than a second edition.

Using a similar approach, *Driven to the Brink* identifies major recent cases of corporate failure in companies and organisations with origins in the USA, UK, Germany, China and Japan and individual case stories are developed around these incidents. Additionally, the authors look at market failures in the context of price rigging scandals in the global LIBOR and foreign exchange markets as well as causes and consequences of the US and European banking crises of 2008. The authors then draw insights from these experiences, review regulatory responses, and offer specific recommendations on how such corporate failures or market scandals could be avoided in the future.

The central thesis of the book is that the seeds of corporate failure are mostly rooted in inadequate board composition and practices which in turn are often associated with a flawed corporate culture as propagated by the board and senior management. The authors are critical of ill-chosen and poorly informed boards, board focus on short-term profits, lack of independent board thinking, board complacency, lack of board attention to risk management responsibilities, and a corporate culture of deference and excessive loyalty to senior management.

The book discusses steps and precautions that boards, individual board members and regulatory agencies can and should take to prevent similar corporate or market failures in the future. It is in these respects that *Driven to the Brink* most develops the work of Professor Hamilton and contributes in significant ways to the literature on corporate governance, corporate culture and the links between these two drivers of corporate failure or success.

The book has insights that will attract a readership of those who are looking to become, or are already, board members, especially non-executive directors and trustees of charitable organisations. *Driven to the Brink* should also encourage investors to look more closely at the boards, leadership, and corporate culture of companies they invest in and attract corporate leaders and more general readers who are interested in stories of recent corporate and financial market scandals and the reasons behind these failures.

Patricia Dimond and Alicia Micklethwait are to be highly commended for a well-researched, readable and insightful book on an important business topic which develops specific and practical recommendations for how corporate and market failures could be avoided in the future.

James C. Ellert
International Institute for Management Development
Lausanne, Switzerland

Acknowledgements

We would like to express our appreciation to IMD, the institution that brought us together so many years ago and that had a profound impact on shaping our future. We were inspired then by so many accomplished professors, four of whom contributed to the writing of this book.

First, thank you Stewart Hamilton for your friendship over the years. You remain in our thoughts. Thank you Jim Ellert, Bill Fischer and J. B. Kassarjian for the wonderful spirit in which you have all given your time: Jim, for your guidance on banking and for agreeing to write the foreword; Bill, for sharing your experiences and entertaining stories of China; and J. B., for your wisdom and patience as we gained a better understanding of how corporate culture evolves.

We would like to thank our family and friends for their support and input, with a special thanks to our 'editing team': Hana, Millie and Phoebe. We would like to thank Mairi Hamilton for allowing us to access some of the material in *Greed and Corporate Failure*. Last, we would like to thank the Deloitte Academy for its inspiration and many cups of coffee!

London, UK   Patricia Dimond
                                                                   Alicia Micklethwait

Contents

About the Authors

Patricia Dimond has 25-plus years of board-level experience in consumer markets in London, Geneva, New York and Toronto and is a McKinsey alumna. Today she spends a significant amount of her time investing in early stage businesses. She is a Chartered Financial Analyst (CFA), a member of the Institute of Chartered Financial Analysts (CFA Institute) and has served on the board of the Swiss CFA society. She graduated from Canada's Richard Ivy School of Business with an HBA and has an MBA from the International Institute for Management Development (IMD), Switzerland. She qualified as a chartered accountant working with Deloitte Haskins and Sells.

Alicia Micklethwait is a graduate of the University of Oxford, a member of the Chartered Institute of Management Accountants and has an MBA from IMD. She is Chief Financial Officer of a technology start-up company and has held senior accounting and commercial positions in multi-national manufacturing companies in London and Brussels. She has taught accounting and finance at several European business schools and in China, and she co-wrote *Greed and Corporate Failure* with Professor Stewart Hamilton.

Praise for *Driven to the Brink*

'Riveting and relevant'

Lord Myners CBE, Chancellor of the University of Exeter, UK Chairman of Cevian Capital AB, former Chairman Marks & Spencer and former HM Treasury Financial Services Secretary.

'Independence, independence, independence. *Driven to the Brink* gives us succinct illustrations of how companies don't fail on their own – the boards of directors and management teams jointly cause the problems. Classic cases ranging from Enron through the banking crisis, which is described very succinctly and identifies all the key players and fatal decisions, to Kids Company and Olympus illustrate the disastrous effect when directors or trustees aren't sufficiently independently minded to challenge senior management's corrosive culture or perverse incentives. There are lessons in this excellent book – if tough questions are not asked, boards will fail in their duties and organisations will collapse. Independence, integrity and above all the willingness to challenge the managing elite are essential if behavioural norms and decisions in conflict with the organisation's values are to be reversed.'

Sir David Tweedie, former Chairman of the International Accounting Standards Board

'This is a truly insightful book, with numerous and vivid examples of how things can go wrong, in any organisation around the world – and what boards can and should do about them. Required reading for every board member and interested stakeholders.'

Rita Clifton CBE. Chairman, BrandCap, former Chairman Interbrand UK, and portfolio non-executive director

'The case studies in *Driven to the Brink* clearly illustrate the consequences of the failure of governance and an unethical culture. It concludes that the Board has a responsibility to ensure that a strong culture of integrity is present in the company. To do this the Directors need to be independent and assertive yet close to the organisation. This requires time, engagement and the commitment to govern in the best interest of the shareholders. The book is invaluable reading for all Directors and Executives and will raise the question: Do I do enough to ensure the company has an uncompromising culture of integrity? Am I even close enough to know?'

Bo Risberg, Chairman of Valmet Corporation, Chairman of Piab Group Holding, Vice Chairman of GrundFos Holding, former CEO of Hilti Corporation

'*Driven to the Brink* helps to remind us that the fatal combination of inadequate governance and perverse incentives is not unique to banks, but can be found in organisations as diverse as co-operatives, charities and Japanese instrument-makers.

It gives lucid explanations of complex issues, and demonstrates how even the best governance structures will still fail if not accompanied by the necessary behaviour – in particular a determination by board members, auditors and regulators to challenge dominant executives.

Micklethwait and Dimond have provided a valuable service by reminding us of the many failures and scandals of the past decade that have briefly dominated the headlines and then passed out of sight, and by emphasising that if the number of these is to be reduced in future, both organisation and culture need to be put right.'

Joanna James, former Managing Partner Advent International

1

Introduction

'Co-op Group loses £2.5bn after "fundamental failings in management and governance"',[1] 'Co-operative Bank ex-Chairman could face criminal charges over drugs video',[2] '"Crystal Methodist" Paul Flowers admits drug charges'.[3] Such were the UK media headlines at the end of 2013 and into the first half of 2014. The Co-operative Group, a business spanning 150 years, once recognised as the largest co-operative on the globe and a household name in the UK, was under fire. How does an organisation that prided itself on strong ethical values and customer service end up with a crack-smoking chairman; a Methodist minister with no relevant experience? The conclusion, after a review of the group governance structure that was eventually mandated by the board, was that 'the Co-operative Group, which was dubbed "ungovernable" by its departing chief executive, had been run by a "failed" and underqualified board that took "breathtakingly value-destructive" decisions.'[4]

'Companies do not fail: boards do.'[5] We agree with this statement but would extend the culpability to include leadership teams. Over the course

© The Author(s) 2017
A. Micklethwait, P. Dimond, *Driven to the Brink*,
DOI 10.1057/978-1-137-59053-4_1

of the past decade, taxpayers and shareholders have paid dearly, through fines and collapsing share prices, for the errors of a relative few. Enron and WorldCom are epic examples of how inadequate corporate governance and cultures built on short-termism and greed can lead to disaster. More recently, we have been reminded of this by Lehman Brothers, Bear Stearns, Northern Rock and the Halifax Bank of Scotland (HBOS), among others. These disasters highlight why corporate governance, specifically board oversight, and a productive ethical culture matter.

Driven to the Brink is a collection of short stories about corporate disasters and the role that inadequate board oversight and a flawed culture played in the massive destruction of shareholder value. In 2006, Stewart Hamilton and Alicia Micklethwait published *Greed and Corporate Failure*, a timely book about why corporations fail. They postulated that the reasons why companies fail are few and common to most, and that the major causes of failure include poor strategic decisions; overexpansion and ill-judged acquisitions; dominant chief executive officers (CEOs); greed, hubris and the desire for power; the failure of internal controls at all levels from the top downwards; and ineffectual or ineffective boards.

We set out to write a second edition to this book but quickly realised that in the past decade there was, unfortunately, more than sufficient new material to write a stand-alone volume with a common theme: corporate disaster. We chose to focus on two major causes of failure: inadequate board oversight, largely due to a lack of board independence; and flawed culture, specifically the behaviours that resulted from the incentive systems and organisation structures that were in place and supported by the board. We believe that although many of the reasons outlined in *Greed and Corporate Failure* are still relevant, they could fall under these two major themes with a slovenly approach to risk management a red thread running through both.

We believe that much of the disaster we have written about could have been avoided with the appropriate level of board oversight. The board represents the interests of shareholders and larger stakeholders, so collectively it is responsible for ensuring the long-term health of an organisation. Its greatest value comes from its ability to remain independent and objective, and to challenge conventional wisdom in its duty of signing off strategy, monitoring performance and overseeing the management of risk.

Indeed, it is responsible to ensure the evolution of a productive ethical culture as a critical part of a risk-management strategy.

Companies Do not Fail, Corporate Boards and Leadership Teams Do

'Nine of them are retired. Four of them are over 75 years old. One is a theatre producer, another a former Navy admiral. Only two have direct experience in the financial-services industry. Meet the Lehman Brothers Holdings Inc. external board directors, a group of 10 people, who perhaps unknowingly, carried the health of the world's financial system on their shoulders.'[6]

There is much evidence to support the fact that companies with strong corporate governance structures and a well-performing board produce significantly superior results: an average return on equity more than 20 per cent higher than counterparts with poor corporate governance structures.[7] When companies require injections of capital, whether through public capital markets or through banks, investors should put these capital seekers and the governance practices they employ through a serious review, starting with the board. The Lehman example begs the question not whether it was an age appropriate board but whether the mix of the skills and experiences could together provide the appropriate level of oversight required in the complex environment where Lehman operated.

There are many definitions of corporate governance. We choose to use a variation of that provided by the CFA Institute: a global association of investment professionals and an organisation we consider to be a standard setter within the industry. The CFA Institute defines corporate governance as the system of internal controls and procedures by which individual companies are managed; a framework that defines the rights, roles and responsibilities of various groups. With respect to boards, good corporate governance practices seek to ensure that board members act in the best interest of shareholders, and that the board and its committees are structured to act independently of management. The company must act in a lawful and ethical manner, and have appropriate controls and procedures in place to cover management activities in running the operations of the company.[8]

The board of directors should act as an intermediary between shareholders and management. This does not imply that shareholders have no role to play. Once invested, shareholders do have the power to influence the direction and governance of a company but this is most effectively done through dialogue between themselves and the board. Yet the number of interventions by activist shareholders continue to rise. *Activist Insight* quoted an increase of almost 90 per cent of these interventions between 2010 and 2013.[9] The reason for the increase: the boards were not doing their jobs.

The role of the board is to represent shareholders and to support the CEO and senior leadership teams. Collectively, the board has a duty to act with independence and take decisions based on the long-term viability and health of the organisation. It needs to balance the company's short-term operations with its long-term strategic goals.

To be effective the board requires *independence* in order to adopt an unbiased approach and to challenge conventional wisdom; *experience* to be able to evaluate what is in the best interest of shareholders; *resources* to engage outside expertise when required; and an appropriate level of accurate and timely information to provide *transparency* with respect to the financial position and the underlying value drivers of the organisation.[10]

Independent Thinking is the Greatest Value the Board can Add

Independence is an essential trait of an effective board; ideally, independent board members will constitute a majority. This is a necessary precondition for the objective review and judgement of management practices and the decisions taken. Independence is defined as not having a material business or relationship with the company, individuals or entities that exert significant influence on the company's management. We believe that there are two further requirements for independence to exist.

To be truly independent, board members must have the necessary business experience and expertise. They must possess a thorough understanding of the business model, its strategy, its most significant operating practices together with the internal controls that surround them, and the risks faced by the organisation. When this is not present, board members are more likely to defer to management, sacrificing their independence. If they are faced with situations or issues where they do not feel adequately informed, they must have access to resources which allow them to engage independent third parties with the necessary expertise in areas such as strategy, acquisitions, risk or remuneration.

Independence is most importantly a state of mind: the ability to provide objective, constructive challenge, to be a 'positive disruptor' representing shareholders so as to ensure the long-term viability of an entity. Indeed, Warren Buffett, CEO of Berkshire Hathaway Inc. and one of the world's most respected investors, said, 'True independence—meaning the willingness to challenge a forceful CEO when something is wrong or foolish—is an enormously valuable trait in a director. It is also rare.'[11] The story of Olympus is one that illustrates a woeful lack of independence. When the CEO questioned unusual operating practices, the board fired him. Olympus' independent board directors, of which there were only three should have stepped in to investigate the allegations. They did not.

The Trouble with Dominant CEOs

The board of directors is responsible for the succession planning of the most senior executives and to choose the CEO. Equally important is its responsibility to establish an effective and productive relationship between it and the senior executives. In some jurisdictions the CEO also holds the role of chairman of the board. Combining these two positions gives undue influence to one individual and dilutes the impact of the board.

All too often, dominant CEOs emerge because of their ability to deliver revenue, which in turn sets the tone for aggressive growth and rewards the behaviours that produce it. Dominant CEOs are often surrounded by allies or like-minded senior executives who, due to loyalty, are unlikely to challenge them or their decisions. The tone of the board and its independence is impacted. Boards that are impressed by past performance may stop challenging strategic decisions and the risks associated with them. Unhealthy and unappreciated high levels of risk are thus taken on.

Board Oversees Strategy and Risk

The board is responsible for signing off strategy and major growth initiatives, and for managing the expectations of shareholders. Many of the stories we write about expose the behaviours that arose as an organisation chased growth to meet revenue and profit forecasts. In his article 'The Overvaluation Trap', Roger Martin[12] describes a problem that occurs when capital markets overvalue a company's equity. The basic assumption is that when a company's stock is overvalued because of overly aggressive growth assumptions, managers struggle to deliver the necessary performance to justify the price. This in turn can lead to irrational behaviour, such as ill-conceived acquisitions and excessive risk-taking. When Olympus felt the pressure to grow despite an appreciating currency, it turned to financial engineering, using instruments that were high risk and not well understood, which in turn led to illegal activities to conceal the resulting losses. Rather than be driven by them, the board, together with management, must actively work to set and manage the market's expectations of growth and performance.

In many of the cases we discuss, the board lacked expertise and independence. Moreover, it had a poor understanding of the underlying risk of the actions taken. Its lack of overall industry and company expertise resulted in inadequate risk management. The Co-operative Group was an extreme example of this: its board, just after the merger with United Co-operatives, had an unwieldy structure composed of more than 33 directors, with painfully few having the necessary experience and expertise. Indeed, it is questionable whether the board directors fully understood their obligations and the personal risk they had assumed by accepting the board role.

The Co-operative Group's board signed off acquisitions that would provide a short-term boost to its revenues and market share, giving it the title of the largest co-operative in the world. Ultimately this euphoria was short lived. Large write-offs were required and, the Co-op Bank had to be rescued and to give up its status as a co-operative. Despite much evidence to suggest that growth through acquisition is often unsuccessful—assets are overvalued, synergies are rarely achieved and cultures clash—this practice is too often fueled by pressure to deliver growth and market share. Given the lack of relevant experience on the Co-op board, it is hard to imagine that the members engaged in a robust discussion of the risks associated with the acquired company's balance sheet or indeed the risk associated with the integration of operations.

A Slovenly Approach to Risk Management is a Common Theme

Inadequate risk management is a common theme running through these stories, particularly within banking. The lack of appreciation and understanding of risk often results in an inappropriate level of risk management and excess risk-taking. This theme is widespread whether associated with the products that were traded, the capital funding strategies employed or the aggressive growth strategies pursued.

During the banking crisis the banks' boards failed to understand the level of risk associated with the derivative products that were being traded and held on their balance sheets. Indeed, did the boards discuss or appreciate the positive correlation between high risk loans and short-term borrowing, and the impact it would have on its ability to raise capital? Northern Rock and HBOS employed a capital funding strategy that leveraged short-term money markets to fund long-term assets, while the Royal Bank of Scotland (RBS) used an equally risky strategy in its acquisition of ABN Amro with a 90 per cent cash bid. The internal controls did not assist in highlighting the excessive risk.

Ineffective internal controls are a function of many issues, including an organisational structure which leaves gaps in reporting lines, under-resourced risk-management departments or underappreciated risk managers. As a consequence, risk managers have neither the authority nor the incentive to challenge. Enron and the banks were examples where all of these shortcomings relative to risk were present and resulted in huge financial costs or disaster.

The transparency of an organisation's performance through the fair representation of its current and future financial position should be the result of a well-performing audit and risk committee. This is a prerequisite for adequate risk management. The committee's primary objective is to ensure that reported financial information is complete, accurate, reliable, relevant and timely.[13] In particular the committee should be wholly independent with each member having the appropriate level of financial expertise. Complex accounting issues must be thoroughly understood. It must come to an informed view that internal controls are functioning adequately or otherwise demand that changes are made. To do so it must meet sufficiently often to be informed. According to Lehman's Securities and Exchange Commission (SEC) filings, in both 2006 and 2007 the risk committee of Lehman's board met only twice each year.[14] Lehman went into Chapter 11 bankruptcy on 15 September 2008.

Board Oversees Culture: Culture Defines Leadership

'Enron's unspoken message was, "Make the numbers, make the numbers, make the numbers—if you steal, if you cheat, just don't get caught. If you do, beg for a second chance, and you'll get one."'[15]

It is generally accepted that corporate culture is shaped by the actions, behaviours and values of the board, CEO and most senior executives. The organisational structures they create, the outcomes they reward and the behaviours they accept drive the culture. Leadership does not define the culture; rather, the reverse. Once the culture is formed it defines what leadership qualities are nurtured and rewarded. Often it develops organically; it may be implied without being defined. It follows behaviours and practices that are perceived to deliver the desired results. 'Culture is an outcome of successful adaptation.'[16]

Enron was an aggressive, deal-oriented, risk-taking organisation which approached the employee-assessment process as 'rank or yank'. How did this environment develop when it was founded by two people who professed to believe in organisational ethics and the need for controls?

Edgar Schein, professor at Massachusetts Institute of Technology, developed a model of organisational culture: a reverse pyramid that defines three distinct levels: those things that are *observable* (language, norms and customs), things that are *published* (values or rules of behaviour) and things that are *assumed* (unconscious behaviours that result from shared learning over time). Schein's research is based on the theory that culture is an outcome of successful adaptation: established behaviours that are reinforced through acceptance.[17]

Enron was founded by people who espoused ethical values and beliefs. Yet the structures, performance evaluations and incentives systems that were introduced all applauded and rewarded any behaviours that produced revenue growth. As these behaviours delivered the outcomes that defined success, they became accepted practices. Those who produced these results in this manner were rewarded and promoted. When the cycle was repeated and gained traction, it spread rot through the heart of the business.

A young organisation is often a profound illustration of the behaviours of its founder(s), behaviours that have led to the founders succeeding against the odds. The cultures of older established organisations evolve from visible and recognised success and through the hiring and retention of certain types of individuals. This process can also apply to a country's culture. Japan and China, for example, have very strong cultural norms that impact personal networks and relationships in business. *How much cultural training and awareness did Glaxo employees have of the unique behaviours and norms prior to launching in China? How did these impact its thinking about risk?*

A Productive Ethical Culture must be Part of a Risk-Management Strategy

Exploring the notion of behaviours and their impact on culture further, we reviewed an article in the McKinsey Quarterly entitled 'Bad to great: The path to scaling up excellence'.[18] Perhaps unsurprisingly, bad behaviours have a significantly greater impact on an organisation than constructive behaviour. As a consequence, in order to make room for the good, you must move out the bad behaviours. Thankfully there are warning signs: places where bad behaviour is likely to lurk. Feelings of injustice or help-lessness when people believe they are getting a raw deal or are powerless to stop events are dangerous. Enron had a risk-management department but it was understaffed. Its employees could not keep up with the workload and they did not believe that changes would be made if they raised an issue, so much of the documentation which flowed through the department was simply rubber stamped.

Anonymity is a dangerous feeling, creating the belief that no one is watching so you can do whatever you want. The LIBOR and FX scandals are illustrations of people and departments working in silos with estab-lished bad practices which had been reinforced by acceptance, and rewarded because they produced the results that fell within the banks' definition of success.

In the banking environment it has long been known that there are some inherent characteristics that traders exhibit. Many traders are gam-blers by nature: taking risks, beating the system and, better still, earning large bonuses give them a buzz. So much of this behaviour should not come as a surprise. As a consequence the need for appropriate controls, compliance reviews and reporting structures escalates. *How many of the banks had risk-management strategies that adequately acknowledged and addressed the differences in the inherent characteristics of employees across revenue/profit centres?*

When an organisation does not ensure appropriate controls or trans-parency through adequate and timely reporting, it is not demonstrating accountability for its actions—plausible deniability becomes, and is accepted as, a defence when things go terribly wrong. Sadly, all too often this is the case. Operating practices that threatened the integrity and financial health of the banks, and, indeed, the industry, were allowed to exist under the nose of senior management. As these practices produced results which continued to fall within the organisations' implied defini-tion of success, they were allowed to continue.

It is generally accepted that companies should publish an appropriate ethical framework, adopting a code of conduct that sets standards for ethical behaviour based on principles of integrity, trust and honesty. The *Journal of Business Ethics* published a few universal values that all companies should subscribe to: trustworthiness; respect for customers, employees and others; responsibility for the outcomes of a company's actions or inactions; fairness; caring; and citizenship.[19] To be accepted, the behaviours and actions of the board and senior executives must reflect these. Enron published an exhaustive 64-page Code of Ethics, yet its management actions were in conflict with it and a clear indication that the company had not embraced it. Without visible support from the board and senior executives, a written code is near worthless.

Values are merely things we place value on. When corporate values are published they suggest that these are things that the organisation values. Yet they only become strong signals if recognised by way of compensation and incentive systems. Indeed, organisational structures and reporting lines illustrate the functions that are valued and, of course, those that are not. One of the reasons Canadians believed that they fared relatively well in the financial crisis was because risk management was so much part of the culture that a CEO is considered to be the ultimate chief risk officer (CRO). Yet, often, audit and risk have little visibility or voice in organisations. *If each of the banks had deemed the risk function important enough to carry a board seat, would this have altered the outcome of the crisis?*

Boards have a significant role to play in defining success within an organisation and thereby shaping and reinforcing a company's culture. This can be achieved through board committees such as the remuneration and the nomination committee. These committees have an opportunity to influence how an organisation defines success by overseeing the reporting structures and reward systems that define what constitutes success. But it cannot stop there: it needs to ensure that the behaviours that result support the company's values. The board's objective must be to reinforce and incentivise behaviours that illustrate its values, such as respect for customers, employees and others.

Here again, it is important that the remuneration committee is composed of independent board members to ensure that executive incentives are in the best interest of shareholders. Together with the audit/risk committee, it should ensure that compensation does not encourage excessive risk-taking.

Its goal should be to link executive compensation to the long-term profitability of the company and long-term increases in share value relative to competitors or comparative companies. Ideally, individual performance is risk weighted and compensation adjusted accordingly.

Unfortunately, all too often we find that this is not the case. Rather, remuneration systems are often disconnected from the long-term strategic interests of the company and are determined by industry standards or have been set to attract specific individuals. In the case of the banking industry, remuneration too often incentivises the delivery of short-term profit. Share options often form a significant part of compensation package, yet they are a financial instrument whose value increases with risk.[20] Also, of course, they do not include a put option if the share values decline. So options can be incentives for risk-taking, particularly if they have short vesting periods. Where these norms exist, the remuneration committee has a difficult job. Today the banks have a significant challenge to address: examining the root causes that nurtured the prevailing culture. Only then will they make progress towards instilling meaningful respect for customers across all of the industry's profit centres, particularly the trading desks.

Excessive remuneration is not only a bank issue. There has been significant focus on the extraordinary pay packages of CEOs across industries. There was an outcry when Martin Sorrell, WPP's CEO and the highest paid CEO of a British public company, received a £43 million package in 2015.[21] The Pensions & Investment Research Consultants urged investors to vote against it at the annual general meeting. Yet too often the argument is used that the business will not secure the necessary talent if this level of excessive remuneration is not part of the package. We do not believe this argument is valid: it just leads to soaring remuneration levels for senior executives.

The Stories that Follow

In the stories that follow, corporate governance—specifically inadequate board oversight and flawed culture—led to disaster. Greed, short-termism and excessive risk-taking were present, and aggressive growth through acquisition was a dominant theme. Enron was certainly an example where all of these shortcomings played a significant role.

With the banking crisis we saw a combination of events: the markets had slowed, bank lending rates were very low and stocks were overvalued, reflecting future growth rates that were unachievable. This type of pressure, when not managed, can result in CEOs, supported by their board, across industries taking excessive risks to provide the desired levels of growth to maintain share prices.

Many of the following stories had a dominant CEO, or some combination of a few dominant executives. This was the case with Enron: asking questions to understand a constantly evolving strategy was not encouraged, and any challenges to existing practices were punished. In the case of Olympus, it was a very compliant culture: loyalty was rewarded, questions were not.

Of course, dominant CEOs do not always result in disaster. In the case of Alibaba, its Chairman, Jack Ma, is the lead founder and is recognised to have been a dominant CEO. Indeed, at one time he held the dual role of CEO/chairman, and today he is the *executive* chairman. He has also led the company through an extraordinary growth period. One of the biggest single differences between this story and the others is that Alibaba has a strong customer ethos and a productive culture. Its culture has developed from the behaviours of its dominant founder, its most senior executives and its focus on the customer. Its growth has been predominantly organic. Perhaps in Alibaba's case it could be said that the customer is dominant and Ma is influential. Is this strong customer ethos sufficiently entrenched in the organisation to ensure its survival if Ma were to leave?

We start with the Enron story because it is an epic example of a business which had an ineffective board, a dominant CEO and a culture which valued excessive risk and greed, and it chased growth at all costs to deliver its quarterly results. The Enron story is one whose lessons are still relevant and should not be forgotten.

Notes

1. Neate, R. (2014) Co-op Group loses £2.5bn after 'fundamental failings in management and governance', *The Guardian*, 17 April 2014.
2. Siddique, H. (2013) Co-operative Bank ex-Chairman could face criminal charges over drugs video, *The Guardian*, 17 November 2013.

3. Dixon, H. (2014) 'Crystal Methodist', Paul Flowers admits drug charges, *The Telegraph,* 7 May 2014.
4. Bounds, A. (2014) Myners proposes Co-op Group board shakeup, *Financial Times*, 14 March 2014.
5. Leblanc, R. (2015) Harvard University Summer 2015, MGMT S-5018 Corporate Governance.
6. Berman, D. (2008) Where was Lehman's Board? *The Wall Street Journal*, 15 September 2008.
7. Brown L. D. & M. L. Caylor (2004) Corporate Governance Study: The Correlation between Corporate Governance and Company Performance, *Institutional Shareholder Services.*
8. CFA Institute (2009) *The Corporate Governance of Listed Companies*, Centre for Financial Market Integrity, Second Edition 2009.
9. Barton, D. & M. Wiseman (2015) Where Boards Fall Short, *Harvard Business Review*, February 2015.
10. CFA Institute (2009) *The Corporate Governance of Listed Companies*, Centre for Financial Market Integrity, Second Edition 2009.
11. Connors, Richard (2009) *Warren Buffett on Business: Principles from the Sage of Omaha* (San Francisco: Wiley).
12. Martin, Roger (2015) The Overvaluation Trap, *Harvard Business Review*, December 2015.
13. CFA Institute (2009) *The Corporate Governance of Listed Companies*, Centre for Financial Market Integrity, Second Edition 2009.
14. Berman, Dennis (2008) Where was Lehman's Board, *The Wall Street Journal*, 15 September 2008.
15. www.cengage.com, Enron: What caused the Ethical collapse? A quote from Sherron Watkins.
16. Schein, Edgar (2006) *Organisational Culture and Leadership* (New Jersey: John Wiley & Sons).
17. Schein, Edgar (2006) *Organisational Culture and Leadership* (New Jersey: John Wiley & Sons).
18. Rao, H. & Sutton, R. (2014) Bad to great: The path to scaling up excellence, *McKinsey Quarterly*, February 2014.
19. Swartz, Mark (2005) Universal moral values for corporate codes of ethics, *Journal of Business Ethics*, June 2005, Volume 59, Issue 1.
20. Ellert, Jim (2015) Causes and consequences of financial crises, *IECD Bled School of Management*, May 2015.
21. Sweney, M. (2015) Sir Martin Sorrell's pay package labelled 'excessive' by investor advisory group, *The Guardian*, 3 June 2015.

2

Enron: Launch to Boom and Bust, 1985–2001

At the end of 2000 the world became better acquainted with Enron, a once unknown energy firm from Texas, when it became one of the largest companies on the New York Stock Exchange (NYSE), with a market capitalisation of $60 billion and a stock market price of 70 times earnings. However, the company's success was short lived. By December 2001 it had filed for bankruptcy protection, fired thousands of employees, whose pensions and life savings were lost, and headlines around the world were screaming fraud.

Enron went from launch to boom and bust within a mere 16 years ending in the biggest bankruptcy the world has ever seen; the demise of Arthur Andersen, one of the largest international accounting firms; and a shake-up of US corporate regulation, with the introduction of the Sarbanes–Oxley Act of 2002.

And since? The most senior executives and inner circle of Enron were found guilty of criminal acts including money laundering, fraud and conspiracy. Enron's founder, Ken Lay, died of heart failure six weeks after his trial ended; its chief operating officer (COO) and briefly its CEO, Jeff

---

This Enron story was updated from the Enron chapter in *Greed and Corporate Failure*.

© The Author(s) 2017
A. Micklethwait, P. Dimond, *Driven to the Brink*,
DOI 10.1057/978-1-137-59053-4_2

Skilling, received a 24-year jail sentence, reduced to 14 years in 2013; and its chief financial officer (CFO), Andrew Fastow, served a 5-year sentence. Today, more than 15 years after Enron's implosion, the impact is still felt and the lessons are still relevant.

During its heyday and over six consecutive years, Enron was voted by the readers of *Fortune* magazine as one of the most innovative companies in the USA. It had been written up as a glowing example of what we fondly refer to today as a 'disruptor'. Enron's performance had been lauded in the media and Harvard Business School case studies.[1] It was a story of the transformation of a conservative, domestic energy company into a global player. Other, more traditional, energy companies had been criticised for not producing the performance that Enron had apparently achieved.

The speed of Enron's collapse surprised many. In the months before, the rating agencies had not signalled any problems with credit risk, and most financial analysts following the stock were still rating it as a 'buy' or 'hold'. Only six months earlier an analyst with Goldman Sachs had described Enron as 'a world-class company', 'the clear leader in the energy industry'. While acknowledging that its 'transparency' was

> 'an investment in Enron shares right now represents one of the best risk/reward opportunities in the marketplace'

'pretty low' and that it had been indifferent to cash flow as it sought to build businesses, this analyst's view was that 'an investment in Enron shares right now represents one of the best risk/reward opportunities in the marketplace'.[2] A view that was not atypical.

However, as details of massive undisclosed debt emerged, it became clear that Enron had many elements of a Ponzi scheme.[3] The drive to maintain reported earnings growth, and the share price, led to the extensive use of aggressive accounting policies and practices to accelerate earnings with, at least, the tacit approval of Enron's auditors, Arthur Andersen. Of these practices, the use of special purpose entities (SPEs) to accelerate profits and hide debt initially attracted the most attention because of the financial involvement of Enron officers and employees. This in turn led to the widespread conclusion that the company had been brought down by accounting fraud. The reality, of course, is much more complex.

The story of Enron is a tale of how a group of senior executives, driven by greed and ambition, pursued flawed and poorly executed strategies, including ill-judged acquisitions. They recklessly expanded a company in areas far beyond its

> 'borrowing from Peter to pay Paul': definition of a Ponzi scheme, named after Charles Ponzi, 1920

competencies and capital base in the relentless pursuit of income to meet analysts' expectations for quarterly growth. To try to sustain the unsustainable they were prepared to fraudulently conceal the extent of the problems they had created while enriching themselves at the shareholders' expense. And, of course, it is a story of a complacent, ineffective board, staffed by cronies who were grossly overpaid and failed to exercise any meaningful oversight.

The Creation of Enron and Its First Ten Years

Energy deregulation began in the USA in the late 1970s. It started with open market prices for natural gas discoveries and led to a new wave of energy trading. Ken Lay, who at one point in his career had been an energy economist and Under Secretary at the US Department of the Interior, formed Enron in 1985. He merged two traditional gas pipeline companies—InterNorth and Houston Natural Gas—to create the largest natural gas pipeline system in the USA, and significant oil and gas exploration and production interests. Lay knew that, as deregulation progressed, commercial opportunities would be created. He became chairman and CEO and, with the help of Richard Kinder as COO, began to build the company through a series of new ventures and acquisitions, much of which was financed by debt, a theme which would become common for Enron.

Prior to deregulation, the industry was vertically integrated from sourcing to transportation, distribution and, finally, sale into a captive market. It was also capital intensive, heavily regulated and relatively low risk. Deregulation led to disaggregation: companies could choose what activities along the value chain they would participate in. Enron chose to focus on high value-added activities, with a particular emphasis on trading. This emphasis would increase in parallel with the speed of deregulation. So Enron began as a natural gas pipeline company and within ten years was transformed into a global energy provider and trader. Initially confined to contracts for physical delivery, the trading ultimately extended to gas futures, long-term supply contracts and hedges. By 1994 the company had begun buying and selling electricity.

Enron was an innovator: volumetric production payments (VPPs), launched in 1990, were an early illustration of this. VPPs would later form part of the 'gas bank', created to get round the problem in the gas industry of the large number of small producers who lacked access to capital to improve their facilities and to search for new reserves. Enron provided liquidity by prepaying for long-term fixed-price gas supplies, with the payment secured on the gas itself and not on the assets of the producer. The risk of default to Enron was reduced because it had first call on a proportion (usually half) of the gas from the field. This arrangement also meant that Enron had secure long-term natural gas supplies.

A major breakthrough came in December 1990 when Enron secured a 23-year, $1.3 billion supply contract for natural gas to the New York Power Authority (NYPA). The price was fixed for the first ten years and would thereafter be adjusted monthly to market rates. This arrangement

> Enron was an innovator: an early illustration of this was the creation of the 'gas bank' with volumetric production payments.

was mutually beneficial because it allowed the NYPA to finance the construction of a 150 MW power plant on Long Island. The possibility of being able to depend on long-term supplies of natural gas at predictable prices reduced the risk of building the very expensive but much cleaner, and more environmentally friendly, gas-fired power stations. To fulfil its end of the bargain, Enron would require the secure long-term sources of natural gas provided by the 'gas bank'.

At the same time, in its drive to become a global player, Enron increased its foreign activities. It made an investment in Dabhol, a power plant project in India, followed by others in energy plants in Brazil and Bolivia, and an interest in an Argentinian pipeline system. In 1993 it entered the European energy markets, building a gas turbine power plant on Teesside in England. By 1994 the company was operating power and pipeline projects in 15 countries and developing a number in several others.

As Enron proved innovative in its business model, so it was in its financial reporting, adopting its own approach to 'mark-to-market' accounting.[4] The VPPs were contracts that had a predictable future cash flow and could be treated as 'merchant assets'. Following this logic, Enron applied to the SEC to be allowed to mark these assets to market.

In 1991 the permission was granted, on an exceptional basis, allowing Enron to become the first company outside the financial sector to adopt this method. The financial reporting effect of this approach was to allow a company to take upfront most—if not all—of the anticipated profits on the contracts, with a requirement to recognise losses if their value diminished. Although the permission was meant to be temporary, there was no evidence that the SEC revisited its decision, so Enron continued to employ this accounting treatment in the ensuing years.

The basic methodology was simple. To monetise a deal the trader would forecast the future price curve for the product, calculate the future cash flows and apply a discount rate to compute the net present value (NPV), which could either be sold to a SPE created for that purpose or kept on the company's books as a merchant asset. Some products had market prices while

> Enron began to 'mark to market' its assets, leading to a practice referred to as 'mark to Enron'.

others, where Enron was the only supplier, required Enron to derive its own price curves. As one trader put it, it was more a case of 'marking to Enron'. In other words, the company could determine its own profits based on a forecast price which it alone provided: a recipe ripe for manipulation.

Introducing the Dream Team...?

To accomplish all of this, Lay had put together a 'dream team', starting with Richard Kinder, the COO. Kinder was a lawyer by training and a traditional oil and gas man who insisted on rigorous controls. He had a reputation for being a 'fair but tough' manager. He would be with Enron for its first ten years but then resign in November 1996 to form his own company. Another key member of the team was Rebecca Mark. She joined Enron in 1985 and was sponsored by the company to do a Harvard MBA. As CEO of Enron International, she was responsible for international power and pipeline development, and was instrumental in negotiating the Dabhol power project. At around $3 billion, this was the largest foreign direct investment in India at the time.

In 1990, Lay appointed Jeffrey Skilling as head of Enron Finance. In the mid-1980s, Skilling, a Harvard MBA and the partner in charge of McKinsey's energy practice in Houston, had advised Lay about how to take advantage of gas deregulation. He had been responsible for establishing Enron's 'gas bank'. Later, Richard Kinder's resignation paved the way for Skilling to become president and COO of

> Jeffrey Skilling's vision: making money through an 'asset light' strategy, concentrating on trading and disposing of traditional activities.

Enron, and free to pursue his vision: making money through an 'asset light' strategy, which involved concentrating on trading while disposing of traditional activities.

In the same year, Skilling hired Andrew Fastow from Continental Illinois Bank. Fastow's background was in asset securitisation and structured finance. His role was to develop the company's funding business, and to obtain and manage the debt and equity capital to fund its third-party finance business. Although not a certified public accountant (CPA), Fastow would become CFO in 1998 and in the following year be voted by (US) *CFO magazine* the 'most creative financial officer of the year'.

This team was complemented by traders from the investment banking and brokerage industries, and a highly paid army of financially literate lawyers and MBAs from high-ranking business schools. It also included a large risk-assessment and control group that would be hailed as using best-in-class procedures by Andersen. By 2001, Enron employed over 20,000 employees worldwide.

And then there was the Board

Enron's board included a long list of people with impressive qualifications, including former chairmen of oil and gas, and electric companies, as well as former deans and university presidents. A number of the non-executive directors appointed by Lay had made substantial contributions to Enron's progress as a global trading company prior to joining the board. They included Wendy Gramm, the outgoing chair of the US Commodity Futures Trading Commission (CFTC) and the wife of the senior US senator for Texas; and Lord John Wakeham, a former UK Secretary of State for Energy and member of the House of Lords. Prior to joining the board, Gramm, in her role as chairman of the US CFTC, had granted Enron an exemption from normal regulatory oversight. Wakeham joined the board after he granted Enron permission to build the gas turbine power plant on Teesside in England.

The Enron Culture: 'Rank or Yank'

The occupants of Enron's head office at 1400 Smith Street, Houston, regarded themselves as an elite: Enron had left behind the Texan 'good ol' boy' culture and embraced Lay's free-market vision. Encouraged by Skilling, the culture was driven by finding new and increasingly innovative ways to 'translate any deal into a mathematical formula' that could then be traded or sold, often to SPEs. By 2001, Enron had in excess of 3,000 subsidiaries and unconsolidated associates, including more than 400 registered in a well-known tax haven, the Cayman Islands.

Skilling introduced a rigorous employee performance-assessment process that became known as 'rank or yank'. Under this system the bottom 10–20 percent of employees were shown the door; so, of course, there was heavy pres-

sure to meet targets and 'do deals'.
Remuneration was linked to the
deals done and profits booked in
the previous quarter, which created stress peaks at quarter end
and gave rise to the expression
'Friday night specials'—deals put

> The Enron culture was driven by
> finding ways to 'translate any deal
> into a mathematical formula' that
> could be traded or sold.

together at the last moment, and often inadequately documented despite the
efforts of the 200 or so in-house lawyers.

Much of Enron's culture was a direct result of the accounting principles that it had adopted and the pressure it imposed to hit quarterly
targets. The deal-driven environment, fuelled by Skilling's desire to
accelerate revenue and earnings by using mark-to-market accounting,
inevitably led to a treadmill effect. If you took all the profit from a deal
in one quarter, you needed to find another, larger deal in the next.
Employees felt extreme pressure to do deals—often with little regard to
how they were to be managed—and to make the quarter by whatever
means necessary. The focus on earnings rather than cash led to some
crazy deals being done.

Those who worked at Enron were reluctant to challenge the deals. One
former employee described his experience:

> From a cultural perspective, what shocked me was that no one could
> explain to me what the fundamentals of the business were. As a new person
> I have always been used to asking questions—many might seem dumb, but
> it is part of the learning process. In Enron, questions were not encouraged
> and saying things like 'This doesn't make sense' was unofficially [punished].
> Further, I got the impression that many people did not understand what
> was going on, so asking questions would show this lack of knowledge.[5]

The accounting policies that Enron adopted, and which Andersen
sanctioned, were unusual for a non-financial company. As one employee
recounted,

> The issue, which was unnerving, was their focus on immediate earnings
> (accounting not cash). Whenever a transaction or business plan was

presented, the focus was on how much earnings the deal would bring rather than if it made business sense or made cash. Another example is the way they conducted their trading business: Enron would create forward price curves on commodities, based in many cases on rather sketchy data or pricing points. Using these curves, Enron would enter into long-term transactions with counter parties (ten years was usual in illiquid markets like bandwidth). For Enron, it did not matter if they lost money in years 1–5 of a deal, selling below current market values, as long as they recovered the investment and made a 'profit' on years 6–10. This occurred because Enron used mark-to-market accounting and would take the NPV of the ten-year deal on day one, using the sketchy curves mentioned before as price points for discounting and, therefore, making a 'profit'. The fact that the company was bleed- ing cash in years 1–5 in exchange for potential gains in years 6–10 was usually not considered in these transactions. The only thing that mattered was 'earnings'.[6]

> At Enron, questions were not encouraged and saying things like this 'does not make sense' was unofficially punished.

Enron had a large risk-assessment and control group headed by a chief risk officer, who had come from Bankers Trust. The trading department was supposed to ensure that the traders' pricing was appropriate for the risks being assumed. However, sometimes the level of activity was such that there was time to do little more than check the arithmetic rather than question the underlying assumptions.

> 'The fact that the company was bleeding cash in years 1–5 in exchange for potential gains in years 6–10 was usually not considered in these transactions. The only thing that mattered was "earnings"'.

Nevertheless, Andersen hailed Enron's risk-management procedures as an example to all.

Despite, or perhaps because of, all the pressure, Enron's senior employees were loyal and well rewarded. In 2000 the top 200 employees shared remuneration packages of salaries, bonuses, stock options and restricted stock totalling $1.4 billion (compared with reported profits of $970 million), up from $193 million in 1998. The board also enjoyed handsome benefits well in excess of the normal levels of remuneration paid to non-executive directors of public companies in the US at that time.

Global Energy Provider and Trader to Ponzi Scheme, 1994–2001

From the date of Skilling's arrival, Enron pursued dual strategies: continuing to invest heavily in the traditional core activities of energy generation and pipelines, but increasingly outside the USA, and developing a substantial energy trading business. Both strategies required a great deal of cash, something that was always in short supply.

Rebecca Mark drove international expansion. Her strategy in the international markets required substantial capital investment in projects that would take a long time to complete and even longer to become cash positive. It exposed Enron to substantial risk, particularly in Latin America: premiums were paid for acquisitions and the currencies were volatile. When the currencies collapsed against the dollar in the late 1990s, this compounded the financial loss that Enron suffered as a result of overpaying for the acquisitions.

In July 1998, Enron purchased UK's Wessex Water for £2.2 billion as part of its strategy to build a worldwide water utility company. It formed a new company, Azurix, which it intended to float separately. The idea was to develop and operate water and wastewater assets, including distribution systems, and treatment facilities and related infrastructures. Azurix pursued projects in Europe, Asia and Latin America. These large, long-term investments hastened Enron's cash drain and increased the debt burden when the proposed flotation failed to take place.

In India the Dabhol project in Maharashtra State was bedevilled from the start: it was a vast undertaking in proportion to Enron's capital base;

and it was subject to serious political problems, particularly after a change in the state government. The project was always going to be difficult. The World Bank had refused to fund it. Only after considerable effort and much political lobbying was the finance arranged with some US government assistance. It was plagued with problems and the entire exercise cost Enron something in the order of $3 billion. This sum was more than three times its reported profits for 2000.

Many of these investments turned out badly partly because Enron had entered areas outside its core competences, such as water utilities, or high-risk areas of the world, such as India and Latin America, with insufficient knowledge or due diligence.

In parallel, Skilling drove Enron's trading activity. By the mid-1990s, the pressure to deliver quarterly growth figures was building. The company's trading portfolio was gradually extended to more exotic items, including weather derivatives. It believed that an energy supplier concerned that the weather was going to be too warm—and that its customers would consequently consume less energy—would want to find a way of hedging this income shortfall. As markets for existing products matured and competition eroded margins, Enron had to find new and more innovative instruments to trade. These products eventually included things as diverse as wood pulp futures and oil tanker freight rates. Ultimately there were more than 1,200 separate trading 'books', including broadband capacity, a book with its own special problems.

In late 1999, EnronOnline was launched, creating an electronic trading floor for oil and gas in the USA and Canada. It quickly expanded to other products and countries. Although it was developed at the relatively low cost of $15 million, it required a large amount of working capital to fund the 'book'.

The trading side was initially profitable but, as Enron turned to increasingly exotic products in its search for profits, it was the only market-maker, placing great strains on its liquidity. Enron used the short-term paper market for this, one that was to dry up in the immediate aftermath of September 11 2001.

This dual strategy would have been trouble enough, but Enron added a third element of risk with its venture into broadband. This was more opportunistic than planned. In 1997 it had acquired Portland General

Electric, an Oregon electricity generator and distributor that had laid some 1,500 miles of fibre-optic cable along its transmission rights of way. Enron, through its subsidiary Enron Broadband Services (EBS), started to build its own network using its existing rights of way to add 4,000 miles in 1998 and a further 7,000 the following year. The intention was to sell capacity to heavy data users on long-term contracts which could then be marked-to-market, and to trade bandwidth in a manner similar to gas or electricity. Despite Enron's claim to be turning into an energy and communications company, a story much touted to the investment world, the reality was very different. Broadband lost money from its inception, placing even greater strains on Enron's highly precarious finances.

Enron pursued this business at a reckless pace without undertaking fundamental supply-and-demand analysis or understanding the changes in technology. It found itself competing with the likes of WorldCom and Global Crossing for customers in a market which had huge overcapacity and improvements in technology that were exponentially increasing the amount of data that could be carried by existing cable. Overhead costs increased materially and for 2000, EBS would report losses of $60 million on revenues of $415 million.

The only way to make profits from the cable was to get data flowing through it. EBS, in an attempt to generate traffic, announced that it had entered into a memorandum of understanding with Blockbuster Video to provide video on demand. EBS would provide the means of delivery and Blockbuster Video the content. Small trials in four parts of the USA proved that the technology worked, and the service was rolled out with much fanfare in Seattle, Portland and Salt Lake City just before Christmas 2000. However, it proved impossible to attract enough subscribers to make it pay. Fearful of the cannibalising effect the project would have on its existing business, Blockbuster walked away from the deal after only a few months. EBS was left to go it alone. Yet this did not prevent Enron from booking a mark-to-market profit, based on its predictions of the project's future cash flows of $100 million. The spreadsheet model used a 10-year projection and assumed an unsubstantiated increase from 400 paying subscribers to some 8 million.[7]

Despite this setback, by the end of the year, broadband was being hailed as a major part of the company's future. Lay promoted Enron's future in broadband to the financial markets, commenting in October 2000, 'we are an energy and broadband

> The spreadsheet model used a 10-year projection and assumed an unsubstantiated increase from 400 paying subscribers to some 8 million.

company that also does a lot of other stuff'.[8] This was little more than wishful thinking. For Enron, the broadband exercise was a disaster, losing large amounts of money and consuming more cash than the company could afford.

The Most Creative Financial Officer of the Year: Where there is Smoke there is Fire.

After the collapse, a former employee posted his thoughts on his MBA class website:

> OK, now that it's bust, I can tell you a little bit of what was going on—at least where I was. Imagine that you make a spreadsheet model of a business plan (in this case it was taking over the world). You discount it with Montecarlo simulations (more like Atlantic City, really), sensitise it to all possible shocks, but still make sure you obtain a huge NPV. Then you sell this 'idea' to a company that Enron does not consolidate and which finances the purchase with debt guaranteed by Enron's liquid stock (remember no consolidation). You book all the NPV (or profit) UPFRONT.

Fastow certainly was a creative Chief Financial Officer (CFO). This label in itself should have had the board on high alert—where there is smoke, there is fire. As a CFO, a compliment might include the words prudent, rigourous and insightful, but not creative. That particular adjective should be left for the marketing department. Enron engaged in creative accounting. Indeed, its CFO was crowned the most creative financial officer of the year. *Why did the external auditors, the board and the audit committee not flag this as a concern?*

In the five years from 1996 to 2000, Enron reported consolidated net income rising from $580 million to $970 million in marked contrast to the tax losses of $3 billion declared to the Internal Revenue Service for the four years to 1999. Over the four years to December 2000, while revenues from the traditional physical asset energy-generating business grew relatively slowly, reported revenues from trading grew exponentially to become 80 per cent of Enron's turnover, increasing from $40 billion in 1999 to $100 billion in 2000. Much of this increase was accounted for by empty trades of broadband capacity with WorldCom and others. These swap deals had no cash effect but served to inflate the top line.

There was no evidence that the board had questioned the substance or sustainability of this growth. And, despite earlier expressing some misgivings about the accounting policies being used by Enron, Andersen had signed off each year without qualification. Given this reported growth, the company's shares significantly outperformed the market. As previously discussed, performing well on the stock market brings its own set of challenges. With an inflated share price, Enron had put tremendous pressure on itself to maintain growth in its quarterly earnings per share (EPS), and to find new sources of revenue and capital.

Going Off-Balance Sheet

Above all else, Enron needed cash. The large investments in major capital projects would not generate earnings or positive cash flow in the short term. Funding new investments with debt was unattractive because these investments would not generate sufficient cash flow to service the underlying debt and would put pressure on credit ratings. In order to maintain its triple A debt rating, its debt to equity ratio had to stay within an acceptable range. If Enron lost its triple A status, the company's ability to issue further debt would be affected. It would trigger bank covenants and guarantees, and influence the perceptions of—and its credibility with—counter parties in its trading operations. A solution might have been to issue new equity, but this would have diluted the EPS and in turn affected the share price. So rather than the route of a more prudent CFO—to manage market expectations—Andrew Fastow opted for financial engineering and to manage the reported results.

His solution was to get assets and the related debt off the balance sheet by finding outside investors willing to take equity in separate entities, which, in turn, could borrow from third parties. However, this would only work if these SPEs did not have to be consolidated in Enron's results, otherwise it would defeat the objective. Finding truly independent investors proved difficult, so the company turned to related parties.

Enron got creative with off-balance sheet transactions. The first controversial deal using an SPE was Chewco. This limited liability partnership was formed in 1997 for the purpose of acquiring the California Public Employees Retirement Scheme's (CalPERS') interest in an earlier joint venture (JV) with Enron called the Joint Energy Development Investment. CalPERS' initial investment of $250 million in 1993 had been valued at $383 million, and Chewco was to borrow, on an unsecured basis, a similar amount to buy out CalPERS' investment. In a rather complicated deal, the loan would be guaranteed by Enron.

The debt was provided by BZW, a subsidiary of Barclays Bank in the UK. Enron charged Chewco a fee of $40 million for providing the guarantee and booked that sum as part of its profit for the quarter. This deal had many questionable issues surrounding it. The general partners in the SPE were Enron employees or associates, in particular Fastow's assistant, Michael Kopper, and his partner, William Dodson. Fastow had wanted to do this deal himself but the Enron board would not permit it, so Kopper, a graduate of the London School of Economics, who had joined Enron in 1994 from Toronto Dominion Bank and had become close to Fastow both professionally and privately, took his place. Kopper would later plead guilty to a number of criminal charges and agree to cooperate with the authorities in order to reduce a potential 15-year jail sentence.

The next significant event was the formation of LJM1 in June 1999, a Cayman Islands registered SPE. The name was derived from the first initials of Fastow's wife and two children. Aware that Enron was anxious to get more debt off its balance sheet, Fastow had taken to the board a proposal to raise $15 million. Two limited partners using an SPE would purchase from Enron certain assets and associated liabilities that the company wished to remove from its balance sheet. Although the Enron code of ethics prohibited Enron from having any dealings with an officer of the company because of the potential for conflicts of interests, the board gave special permission for this to proceed. Subject to certain checks being put in place to protect the company's interests, LJM1 entered into a number of transactions with Enron.

A few months later, Fastow put a more ambitious proposal to the board: he would raise $200 million of institutional private equity in order to purchase assets that Enron wanted to syndicate. At that level the leverage potential was huge. The board agreed that he should go ahead, so in October 1999, LJM2 was formed. Merrill Lynch prepared a private placement memorandum for a co-partnership with LJM2, which ultimately had some 50 limited partners, including some well-known financial institutions such as GE Capital, Citigroup, Deutsche Bank and JP Morgan.

Enron was a significant purchaser of investment banking services, and Fastow was the gatekeeper who had made it clear that participation was a prerequisite for continuing banking business. The memorandum clearly identified Andrew Fastow, together with Kopper and Ben Glisan, as the managers and, in an unusual twist, highlighted their use of inside information: making reference to the fact that their access to Enron's information pertaining to potential investments would contribute to superior returns. Glisan had joined Enron three years earlier from Andersen. He would become known for structuring the company's deals of highly complex non-recourse or limited recourse JV and asset-based financings.

Enron's own disclosure was less frank. In a note to the 2000 Annual Report, on page 48, it simply said that, in 2000 and 1999, 'Enron entered into transactions with limited partnerships (the Related Party) whose general partner's managing member is a senior officer of Enron'. The note then went on to outline some of the transactions.

At the end of the third and final quarters of 1999, Enron sold interests in seven assets to LJM1 and LJM2. It bought back five of the seven assets shortly after the close of the respective financial reporting periods. While the LJM partnerships made a profit on every transaction, Enron recorded earnings from them of $229 million in the second half of 1999.

In June 2000, Enron sold $100 million worth of dark fibre-optic cables to LJM, on which it booked a profit of $67 million. LJM sold on cable for $40 million to 'industry participants' and the remainder to another Enron-related partnership for $113 million that December. Between June and December, these deals suggested that the value of fibre had increased by 53 per cent, while the open market value had fallen by 67 per cent in the same period. Fastow is reported to have profited personally from these deals to the extent of $45 million.

The Beginning of the End

On 5 March 2001, a reporter in a *Fortune Magazine* article questioned the stock market value of Enron.[9] She had a number of issues: it was very difficult to ascertain how the company was making its profits; these profits did not seem to be generating a commensurate amount of cash; and there was a lack of transparency in Enron's reporting and handling of media questions. The company's share price, which had already begun to decline, fell further.

A real blow was struck on 14 August 2001 when Skilling resigned after only six months as CEO, citing 'personal reasons'. Lay resumed the role of CEO. Subsequently, in an interview with *Business Week*, he said, 'There's no other shoe to fall', and went on to add, 'There are absolutely no problems [...] There are no accounting issues, no trading issues, no reserve issues, no previously unknown problem issues. The company is probably in the strongest and best shape that it has ever been in.'[10] Enron watchers, fearing there was more to the story, were not convinced and the share price continued to slide. At the same time as Lay sought to reassure investors, he was cashing in his share options, netting himself more than $100 million in the process.

> 'There's no other shoe to fall [...] There are no accounting issues, no trading issues [...] The company is probably in the strongest and best shape it has ever been in.'

Finally, a whistleblower stepped forward. On 15 August, Sherron Watkins, an Enron employee, and also a former Andersen employee, sent a memo to Ken Lay expressing fears over the company's accounting practices and asking whether Enron had become a 'risky place to work'. It was her view that 'Skilling's abrupt departure will raise suspicions of accounting improprieties and valuation issues'.

Lay met with Watkins briefly a few days later before passing her memo to Enron's principal legal advisors, Vinson & Elkins. This well-respected Houston legal firm, which had advised on some of the transactions being questioned, concluded that there was no need to get a second opinion on the accounting policies. Watkins was not appeased, and rightly so—this firm was clearly not independent given its prior relationship with Enron. She called someone she knew at Andersen and voiced her concerns. Andersen, Enron's auditors since the group's formation in 1985, had been uncomfortable for some time about the accounting practices that it had previously accepted. Revisiting some of the SPEs, it decided that, at least in the case of Chewco, there had been a breach and that Chewco would have to be consolidated, resulting in a restatement of Enron's results. It advised Enron that the accounts would need to be restated.

On 16 October, in a conference call with analysts, Lay disclosed a $1.2 billion write-down of shareholders' equity, focusing attention on the SPEs. Fastow was fired on 24 October, and the SEC announced an investigation into Enron's accounting practices and related party transactions.

Little over a week later, Enron's board announced the establishment of a special investigation committee chaired by the newly and specially appointed William Powers Jr., Dean of the University of Texas School of Law, with existing board members Raymond S. Troubh and Herbert S. Winoker. The committee was given a very limited remit, which was 'to address transactions between Enron and investment partnerships created and managed by Andrew Fastow, Enron's former Executive Vice President and Chief Financial Officer, and by other Enron employees who worked with Fastow'.[11]

Meanwhile, Enron's management was in frantic discussions with their many bankers to try to win some breathing space, and with the rating agencies, trying to persuade them not to downgrade Enron's debt. All the while it was desperately seeking a 'white knight' to bail the company out. Enron's great local Houston rival, the much smaller Dynergy Inc., announced a bid to acquire Enron but withdrew it on 28 November, having done some due diligence.

The following day, Moody's, the rating agency, downgraded Enron's debt to 'junk' (Ca), with the inevitable result that Enron was forced to seek Chapter 11 protection from its creditors. Ultimately the company's examiner in bankruptcy would reveal that the undisclosed off-balance-sheet debts and other liabilities amounted to some $25 billion, much more than had originally been suspected and more than twice the amount of debt reported in Enron's latest filings.[12]

The Powers Committee Post-Mortem

Working with commendable speed, the Powers committee team interviewed a number of key Enron employees and examined numerous documents. It claimed that its enquiries had been limited because they were denied access to Andersen personnel and papers, an allegation strongly refuted by Andersen. The committee's report was published on 1 February 2002 and posted on the Internet.[13] It contained some damning criticisms of many involved, including the board. The report's principal conclusion was that 'many of the most significant transactions apparently were designed to accomplish favourable financial statement results, not to achieve bona fide economic objectives or to transfer risk'. It went on to say that 'the LJM partnerships functioned as a vehicle to accommodate Enron in the management of its reported financial results'.[14]

In the committee's summary it concluded:

The tragic consequences of the related-party transactions and accounting errors were the result of failures at many levels and by many people:

A flawed idea, self-enrichment by employees, inadequately-designed controls, poor implementation, inattentive oversight, simple (and not so simple) accounting mistakes, and overreaching in a culture that appears to have encouraged pushing the limits.[15]

In seeking to understand the plight of Enron, the Powers report was a good starting point, but only that. Restricted in its remit to examine Fastow's dealings with the company, the committee did not probe deeper into the underlying causes of the collapse.

As is the case with most corporate failures, there was no single cause, nor was it the fault of any one individual. Instead the reasons were complex and multiple, involving many people. However, it is possible to highlight the contributions to this disaster that were associated with an ineffective board and a greed-fuelled culture.

Ineffectual Board Oversight: Failure in Strategy, Risk Management and Culture

The wide-ranging report of the Permanent Subcommittee on Investigations of the Committee on Government Affairs, published on 8 July 2002 and based on Senate committee hearings and the examination of tens of thousands of documents, was heavily critical of Enron's board as a whole for its oversight failure. It accused the board of knowing about and authorising high-risk accounting policies, despite warnings from Andersen as early as January 1999, shortly after Fastow became CFO, that Enron's policies 'pushed the limits' and that another firm might take a different view. These warnings were not acted upon. The board also allowed excessive remuneration and it did not ask the tough questions—its lack of curiosity was underlined when it failed to query how Enron had managed to increase reported revenue from $40 billion in 1999 to a reported $100 billion in 2000.

Perhaps lulled by the rising share price, Enron's highly flattering media coverage and Skilling's 'poster boy' status, the board did not fulfil its primary role—to provide constructive challenge. It is likely that complacency and a high level of personal remuneration made its members unwilling to rock the boat. These non-executive directors were paid an average of $350,000 per annum in addition to stock options. In January 2005, ten former directors agreed to pay shareholders $13 million from their own pockets. This settlement was part of a $168 million legal suit brought by shareholders who had seen their investments wiped out.

The board failed horribly in its remit to sign off strategy. After Kinder's departure, there was conflict between Rebecca Mark and Jeff Skilling. Both were contenders to succeed Ken Lay as CEO and they were pulling in different directions pursuing dual strategies. The third leg to Enron's strategy was Lay's reckless pursuit of broadband. All of this expansion led to competing demands for a scarce resource: cash. The financial reporting and controls that underpin strategy were not in place. Fastow—who was not a qualified accountant—was not up to the task. It is doubtful if he had the skillset required of a CFO of a major corporation, let alone one as complex as Enron. In any event, he was Skilling's protégé and unlikely to be effective as an arbitrator. Companies with cash-flow problems need tight controls. Enron did not have this. Its ill-fated strategies led to borrowing, spending and cash commitments spiralling out of control.

The board also failed in its oversight of risk management. The audit committee oversaw an environment of poor risk management and control. In a deal-driven environment with a focus on quarterly earnings, a strong control system is necessary to prevent aberrant behaviour. This was absent from Enron. Although the company claimed to have a strong risk-management and control system, the reality was quite the reverse. Many of the deals being done and booked under mark-to-market accounting required complicated modelling and, sometimes, heroic assumptions about future prices and volumes, as with the video on demand story. Enron's risk managers were supposed to challenge and validate the assumptions upon which the calculations were based to ensure that they were reasonable, but they often failed to do so. As one recounted, 'at times we were so overwhelmed with work that we could do little more than check the arithmetic, and in any event, it was difficult to turn down deals that would directly affect a colleague's remuneration'.[16] On at least one occasion, a business unit bypassed internal risk management and cleared a major deal direct with Andersen.

Indeed, the board did not challenge the external auditors about their leniency with regard to accounting policies, their lack of independence or their egregious fees. While the misuse of accounting permitted by compliant auditors did not *cause* the collapse, it was certainly a contributing factor.

At Arthur Andersen, David Duncan was the client-engagement partner for Enron which, as one of Andersen's largest clients, generated audit fees of $25 million and additional consulting fees of $26 million for the firm in 2000. A large team of Andersen staffers was based in Enron's offices, and Enron had many employees who had joined from the audit firm.

'at times we were so overwhelmed with work that we could do little more than check the arithmetic, and in any event, it was difficult to turn down deals that would directly affect a colleague's remuneration'.

Skilling was on record saying that one of Andersen's most useful services was to provide a pool of accounting talent that it could tap—clearly a conflict of interest for a young audit staff member if they viewed Enron as a potential employer. Additionally, and unusually, Enron had subcontracted its internal audit function to Andersen. This was an example of another serious conflict of interest because it removed one of the essential checks and balances that are necessary in a robust system of internal control.

Andersen failed in its public duties. A more robust approach might have prevented the misuse of accounting practices, thus making the extent of Enron's problems clear at an earlier stage when action could have been taken to prevent the collapse. In August 2002, Andersen, by then an empty shell, agreed to pay $60 million to settle a number of lawsuits relating to the collapse.

The board failed in its oversight of an ethical culture. The lack of an ethical culture, no doubt, was a significant contributor to the downfall of Enron. When Ken Lay founded Enron, he was, by some accounts, a man who was well intentioned and believed in the need for a strong code of ethics. Indeed, he launched the business with Kinder, a COO who was a lawyer by training, came from a fairly low-risk background and believed in rigorous controls. One of Lay's early endeavours was a 64-page code of ethics based on the values of respect, integrity, communication and excellence. Despite the fact that something of this size would not be read, it was an indication of good intent. However, over time, the behaviours of the board and the executives did not support the code—in fact, they were in direct conflict with it. The culture that evolved was a reflection of the behaviours that were accepted and rewarded. Enron's board and leadership team reinforced values of 'booked' income and the 'appearance' of exceeding targets at any cost.

When Fastow received board approval for the first SPE, whose shareholders were employees and officers of the company, the board unofficially made a statement through its actions: the code of ethics did not apply and was unimportant. Had Enron adhered to its ethical code, the board might have probed deeper, Fastow would never have been permitted to enter into the SPE transactions and the collapse might have been averted. Standards must be set, and demonstrated, from the top, including intelligent inquiry and action where required.

It is not surprising that excessive remuneration based on short-term profit performance can lead to aberrant behaviour. The board should have been alert to the impact of the remuneration policies and insisted on rigorous controls; the incentives should have been aligned to long-term sustainable results. Enron's remuneration was significantly linked to stock options that could be exercised almost immediately. This increased the focus on meeting market expectations at the expense of shareholders' longer-term interests. In Enron's case the senior team misled the market, creating a horribly overinflated stock price, and then used trickery and creative accounting to keep the cycle going.

A Few Selected Highlights from the Enron Story

- *Independence is also a state of mind. Working as a team of equals, the board must remain independent, be willing to ask tough questions and challenge conventional wisdom as it oversees the long-term health of an organisation.*

- *The board is responsible not only for signing off strategy and overseeing performance but also for managing the associated expectations. It should actively set and manage the market's expectations rather than be driven by them.*

- *Bad behaviours should be identified and addressed before they become normalised through acceptance. An organisation's reporting structure and incentive systems should inspire behaviours that reflect its ethics.*

Notes

1. See, for example, Bartlett, C. A. *Enron's Transformation: From Gas Pipelines to New Economy Powerhouse,* Harvard Business School Publishing, case reference 9-301-064.
2. Fleischer, D. N., Goldman Sachs, Enron Corp. conference call transcript (12 July 2001).
3. A swindle, also known as a pyramid scheme, which involves 'borrowing from Peter to pay Paul'. It is named after Charles Ponzi who, in the 1920s, conned tens of thousands of people in Boston into investing in international postal reply coupons by offering to pay vast amounts of interest, which he did by using the later investments.
4. Market-to-market is an accounting term for the practice of revaluing assets to market value.
5. IMD interview.
6. E-mail to the authors.
7. Copy seen by authors.
8. Lay, K. Dain Rauscher Energy 2000 Conference.
9. McLean, B. (2001) Is Enron Overpriced? *Fortune Magazine*, 5 March 2001.
10. *Business Week Online* (24 August 2001).
11. *Business Week Online* (24 August 2001).
12. US Bankruptcy Court, Southern District of New York, Second Interim Report of Neal Batson, Court appointed Examiner in re: Enron Corp, et al. (21 January 2003).
13. Enron Special Committee Report (the Powers Report) (1 February 2002).
14. Enron Special Committee Report (the Powers Report) (1 February 2002), p. 4.
15. Enron Special Committee Report (the Powers Report) (1 February 2002), p. 1.
16. IMD interview.

3

The Banking Crisis: Born of Dreams, Fuelled by Bad Behaviours

'Major banking crises are not accidental. They are rooted in irresponsible and misguided behaviours.' Jim Ellert, Professor Emeritus Finance and Strategy, IMD

The International Monetary Fund (IMF) estimated that financial institutions around the globe would eventually write off more than $1 trillion of subprime mortgage-backed securities (MBSs); these losses would wipe out much of the capital of the world banking system.[1] Yet with the benefit of hindsight the banking crisis was predictable and events unfolded as one could have anticipated. The crisis was born of dreams. It started with the American dream—the pursuit of happiness and the right to own your own home, was followed by the entrepreneurs dream—new and untapped opportunity, and then picked up by the capital market dream—extraordinary profit.

© The Author(s) 2017
A. Micklethwait, P. Dimond, *Driven to the Brink*,
DOI 10.1057/978-1-137-59053-4_3

The banking crisis was fuelled by bad behaviours. Insatiable material-ism and greed resulted in unparalleled levels of personal and public debt. Unconscionable lending, a lack of transparency and understanding of the inherent risks associated with the products of 'innovative finance', and a slovenly approach to risk management raised risk to intolerable levels.

From 2003 through to 2005 the Western world, on the surface, was thriving; prosperity abounded. With low interest rates, rising house prices, booming housing markets and philanthropic giving at an all-time high, politicians were promising an end to boom and bust. Yet, under-neath, a tremor first felt in 2006 as US housing prices peaked and sales slowed was followed by a paralysing quake in 2007, when international financial markets froze.

Historically low interest rates in the USA encouraged consumers to buy, to pursue the dream that every US president, Bush and Clinton included, had promoted: own your own home. Relaxed lending regulations opened up the market to a new class of buyer: the low-income buyers in 'under-served' communities. Among more prosperous owners, rising housing prices increased the equity in their homes and allowed them to take on more leverage, to buy, buy, buy: second homes, holiday homes and homes to let. The housing market boomed and there was access to all, regardless of income or assets.

Financial institutions and mortgage lenders took advantage of the opportunity. Lending standards deteriorated, subprime mortgages bal-looned and new products were born, such as the NINJA (no income, no job, no assets) mortgage . In order to exploit this opportunity, the supply chain lengthened; mortgages were packaged together and jumped from local retail markets to the international capital market through securitisa-tion. The shadow banking system, not subject to traditional bank regula-tion, was heavily trading the derivative products from these mortgages. All the while, the credit-rating agencies gave the thumbs-up.

Then interest rates began to rise, the US housing market slowed, delinquencies increased to unparalleled levels and the derivative prod-ucts became worthless: the bubble had burst. The banks began to falter, one by one, some irreversibly. The crisis originated in the USA, but in a global economy its impact spread like a virus with no Western economy left untouched.

In September 2008, several major financial institutions collapsed, causing significant disruption to the flow of credit to businesses and consumers. It was the onset of a severe global recession. The crisis had multiple causes and there was much blame to spread: financial institutions, regulators, credit agencies, government housing policies and, of course, consumers themselves.

What role did corporate governance and culture play in this disaster? The banks' boards of directors failed in their duty to safeguard the long-term viability of their organisations. They approved strategies which led to intolerable levels of risk and ultimately placed the future of those banks in doubt. They failed to ensure that they had appropriate levels of control and reporting in place to cope with the increasing volume and complexity of the products they were trading. They oversaw cultures where greed and the pursuit of profit were rewarded, universally engaging in unconscionable lending, creating derivative products and trading securities of which the market had little understanding.

We have contrasted the experience of three countries: the USA, the UK and Canada. Ultimately this is a story about the danger and impact, on a global scale, of the lack of independent thinking, inadequate risk-management structures, and cultures where bad behaviours driven by greed flourished. Universally the incentives systems did not inspire behaviours reflecting respect for the customer or accountability for the actions and inactions of the individuals involved.

'The Blood of the Global Economy has Begun to Freeze Right from its Heart—The United States'[2]

From as early as 2003 the USA was caught up in a mood of exuberant optimistism. Its economy had made a quick recovery from the dot. com boom and bust of 2001 and had only a brief encounter with recession. Greenspan had slashed interest rates to a 45-year low of 1 per cent. The housing market was thriving: home ownership rose to an all-time high, hovering around 70 per cent, and house prices continued to rise. This rise was a ten-year trend which saw house prices double between 2000 and 2006. Warren Buffet referred to the housing market as the biggest bubble he had seen in his life. Property was thought to be an investment insulated from a material drop in value and the American public were caught up in the belief that housing prices could not drop, a fallacy that underpinned the banking crisis.[3]

The Pursuit of Happiness: Let the Good Times Roll

Loans were easy to obtain and consumers had an insatiable appetite for material goods. The ratio of debt to disposable income in the USA would hit 130 per cent before falling. Lending standards were relaxed and the number of subprime borrowers, who were originally shut out

> People overwhelmingly came to believe that house prices could not fall significantly.....it created....probably the biggest bubble in our history.[4]

from home ownership because of their poor credit rating or lack of earnings, exploded, rising to one in five. Mortgage products became more creative and accessible, referred to as 'liar loans', with no verifiable assets or income and little or no verifiable documentation.

Eventually more than 40 per cent of mortgages had no down payment and approximately 90 per cent were adjustable variable rate mortgages: teaser loans with very low initial payments and loans vulnerable to interest rate rises. The questions were, or should have been: What would happen when initial low payments converted to normal rates, or when interest rates rose? And did the mortgage sellers consider stress tests to understand the capacity of a borrower and whether they could support rising interest rates? The answers to these questions should have stopped the sale of these mortgages and broken the chain.[5]

The exuberance was contagious. The combination of low interest rates and a significant building pool of capital in low-yield fixed income product encouraged banks to look for higher yields. The search for yield led to 'financial innovation' in the form of derivative products—securities which derived their value from mortgages—and allowed international financial institutions to profit from the US housing market achieving the higher yields they sought.

These derivative products, which Warren Buffet once labelled 'weapons of mass destruction', changed mortgages from products previously referred to as 'originate and hold' to 'originate to trade',[6] allowing banks to go off-balance sheet lend more and take on more risk.[7] So the banks' non-interest income grew with these new products, earning fees from structuring and selling these products with significantly greater and unappreciated levels of risk. The shadow banking system became a significant antagonist in what followed.

The shadow banking system, essentially non-bank financial institutions, grew in response to regulation. When regulators of traditional banks limited the amount of credit that banks could extend to industry, other financial intermediaries moved in to fill the gap, most commonly employing short-term borrowing against long-term assets. These institutions became critical to the flow of capital. Not regulated as conventional depository banks, they were able to take on greater and more diverse risks and, of course, they did.

The additional risk they took on was in the form of derivative products: MBSs, collateralised debt obligations (CDOs) and credit default swaps (CDS). CDOs were first created by the corporate debt market in the 1980s to package and sell junk bonds. They are structured, asset-backed securities that essentially pool together cash flow or interest-bearing assets and repackage them to be sold in parcels called tranches. These tranches had different risk profiles depending on the underlying asset and the priority of its claim. They remained a niche product until 2003, when the US housing boom and the flood of new mortgages provided a ready supply of debt. Their annual sales grew from $30 billion in 2003 to $225 billion in 2006.[8]

The CDS contract was also invented. Essentially it was a derivative insurance product that paid out against default. It was intended to protect investors against default risk on the underlying asset, such as the MBS. The buyer paid an insurance premium which was dependent on the price of the asset and subject to mark to market accounting.[9] One of the largest US sellers was AIG, and the buyers were the banks. The global CDS market grew from $1 trillion in June 2001 to $57 trillion in June 2008.[10] The existence of these products increased the opaque view of the overall risk in the market. Although the banks believed that the existence of the CDS market spread risk over a wide base, thereby reducing the risk that any one institution bore, the banks would not have been so heavily exposed to derivative securities without this insurance product. The incredible growth of this market was a sign that there was significant sentiment in the market that the borrower would default. The total risk assigned to the insurer became unbearable.

Material layers of unappreciated risk existed. The banks were acquiring more and more subprime debt (mortgages), repackaging them and selling on the derivative products. The further the mortgage moved from origination and the more complex it became through securitisation, the more difficult it was to understand the underlying risk. This became particularly perilous in an environment where lending standards were falling. It was apparent that few were tracking or reviewing the individual mortgages that were packaged in these derivative products. The barometer of risk was the rating that the credit agencies assigned. Unfortunately, these agencies had a conflict: they were being paid by the very institutions whose products they were evaluating. And in any case, with the CDS, it was unclear who ultimately bore the risk.

As derivatives became more sophisticated, rather than understand or analyse the underlying risk in the bundled products, banks increased their reliance on credit-rating agencies. What further complicated the situation was the response of these agencies: the scores that were being assigned to increasingly opaque products of bundled mortgages. Low credit scores turned to high, subprime into triple A credits. Over a six-year period, one of the largest agencies, Moody's, rated nearly 45,000 mortgage-related securities and over half were initially rated as triple

A. By the end of 2008 an estimated 80 per cent of these securities had been downgraded to junk.[11]

Cracks Began to Form: The Unravelling

Long before the crisis actually hit there were warning signals for those who were prepared to listen. However, as most chose to ignore them, trading within this group continued. Famously, Citigroup's CEO said, 'as long as the music is playing, you've got to get up and dance'.[12] By the time the music stopped, subprime loans were collectively worth $1 trillion and the largest five investment banks had taken on an estimated $10 trillion of securitised debt within the credit system.

> 'as long as the music is playing, you've got to get up and dance'

An entire supply chain for mortgages benefited from the exuberant consumer, the euphoric mortgage broker, the depository banks, the credit agencies and the shadow banking system ... until it didn't, and then it busted apart.

Interest rates began rising as early as 2004, and by 2006 the federal fund rate had moved from a low of 1 per cent up to 5.25 per cent. Mortgages with variable interest rates or teaser mortgages became unmanageable when interest rates were reset. Interest payments rose significantly, in some cases 50–100 per cent higher than the rate owners had signed up to. Housing ownership peaked, and, in a saturated market with rising interest rates and slowing demand, house values fell. Over time, houses would lose on average 30 per cent of their value. As a result of the decline in house prices and lax lending standards, an estimated 11 per cent of householders had negative equity values. This would rise to more than one in five US homes having a mortgage greater than the value of their house.[13]

By 2007 an estimated $3 trillion in loans had been made to home buyers and owners with bad credit and undocumented incomes, bundled into MBSs and CDOs, and given top credit ratings to appeal to global investors. With negative equity and rising mortgage payments, mortgage delinquencies began to rise and then to soar as people began to hand back keys and walk away from their property, no longer willing or able to meet the payments. Others were forced out of their homes through foreclosures. By 2009 almost 15 per cent of all outstanding US mortgages were either delinquent or in foreclosure.[14]

When the market finally acknowledged that the mortgage values packaged within the derivative products were flawed, the MBS market faltered. CDO securities, backed by mortgages and widely held by international financial firms became worthless and trading in these securities dried up. Credit ratings tanked and the once-valued, innovative financial products essentially became junk. During 2007 the unbearable stress placed on the financial system took its toll. By the end of the first quarter, subprime lenders, one after another, were collapsing because of the avalanche of defaulting loans.[15]

In the spring of 2007, signs that Bear Stearns, a large player in the shadow banking system and Wall Street's largest underwriter of MBSs, had taken on too much risk could no longer be ignored. There were rumours in the media that hedge funds and financial institutions owned $1 trillion in securities backed by failing subprime mortgages. By August, two of Bear Stearns' hedge funds had failed and the bank was effectively bankrupt with almost $400 billion in liabilities against $12 billion of equity. By August 2007 the crisis had extended beyond the US borders and the interbank market, frightened of what might happen, virtually froze.[16] In March 2008, JP Morgan stepped in, backed by $29 billion of guarantees by the Federal Reserve Bank of New York, and bought the bank.[17]

The market was somewhat reassured by the Bear Stearns rescue and the stock exchanges gained some momentum. However, the recovery was shortlived and by the summer of 2008, the markets were in turmoil and rumours surfaced that the US government would need to bail out the mortgage giants: Freddie Mac and Fannie Mae. As this nightmare turned into reality, people looked at the next globally visible victim: Lehman Brothers. It had made billions in profit trading MBSs but was now caught holding these toxic assets.

Lehman Brothers filed for Chapter 11 bankruptcy proceedings on 16 September 2008. No one came to its rescue, and those that had historically traded with Lehman pulled their funds. For a brief moment the UK bank, Barclays, looked like it might be the white knight, but the UK government stepped in to stop the purchase. In an attempt to prevent the UK banks from experiencing the same fate, Lehman was allowed to fail. This event provoked widespread panic and the next stage of the crisis: a global crisis of confidence.

Shortly after, Merrill Lynch confirmed that it too was in trouble and would be acquired by the Bank of America. Its estimated write-downs and losses were over $50 billion, a significant portion of the profits that it had accumulated over a 36-year period as a listed company.[18] Three of the top five investment banks had now ceased to exist if only in name: two had changed ownership and one was lost to bankruptcy. The two remaining—Goldman Sachs and Morgan Stanley—applied for depository bank status and qualified for federal support. The share prices of banks around the world plunged.

The consequence of these failures was a liquidity crisis. Funding evaporated in a series of events that was to see the banking industry brought to its knees. The events of 2007/2008 would later be referred to as a 'run on the shadow banking system'.

The Aftermath

What followed in 2008/2009 was a succession of government bailouts. The first of grand significance was in September 2008, when the US government proposed a $700 billion emergency bailout. Initially this proposal was met with resistance. In a historic meeting in September 2008, Ben Bernanke and Henry Paulson, the treasury secretary, met with key legislators. Bernanke was reported as saying, 'If we don't do this today [$700 billion bailout] we won't have an economy on Monday.'[19] TARP (Troubled Asset Relief Program) was later signed on 3 October 2008.

> 'If we don't do this today [$700 billion bailout] we won't have an economy on Monday.'

On 17 February 2009, the American Recovery and Reinvestment Act—a further $700 billion-plus stimulus and relief package—was signed. And in March 2009 the US government bailed out the largest mortgage lenders, Fannie Mae and Freddie Mac, bringing them under federal control. AIG, the insurance provider, also required a $45 billion bailout with public funds.[20]

Unappreciated and misunderstood levels of risk, together with the rampant and unchecked behaviours that resulted from the reckless pursuit and reward of profit, had brought the system down.

> The crisis was avoidable and was caused in part by widespread failures in financial regulation.

The US financial crisis inquiry commission published its findings in January 2011. Its conclusion was that the crisis was avoidable and was caused in part by widespread failures in financial regulation; dramatic breakdowns in corporate governance; an explosive mix of excessive borrowing and assumed risk by households; a lack of comprehensive understanding from Wall Street, as well as key policy-makers, of the financial system; and systemic breaches of accountability and ethics at all levels.[21]

The credit-rating agencies were described as 'cogs in the wheels of financial destruction' and key enablers of the financial meltdown. Errors in credit ratings were later attributed to flawed assumptions in the models they relied on, pressure from financial firms that paid for ratings, a drive to increase market share and a lack of meaningful oversight.

Sadly, this crisis was not contained within US borders; the UK's banks would also fail. The first domino to fall was the short-term credit markets.

Crisis in the UK Started with the 'Run on the Rock'

The subprime mortgage crisis was a homegrown US issue exported through the shadow banking systems to other vulnerable countries. Nonetheless, with relatively low interest rates, rising housing prices and increasingly lax lending standards, the UK found itself with a housing bubble arguably more dangerously inflated than that in the USA due to the level of household debt and its status as the global financial centre. Northern Rock, one of the UK's largest and fastest-growing mortgage lenders and heavily dependent on short-term money markets, was the first to falter. However, it was to fail not from bad mortgages but rather from over-reliance on leverage and, specifically, short-term capital markets.

Although governance and financial regulatory environments differ significantly between the USA and the UK, neither a prescriptive nor a principled approach prevented the crisis. In common was the relentless pursuit of profits, while missing were the universal values of respect for customers, and accountability for actions and inactions.

A report from the UK's House of Lords on the banking crisis concluded that too few senior bankers operated in an environment of accountability and personal responsibility, and that this must change for crisis to be avoided in the future. The general consensus was that remuneration is excessive and encourages, even incentivises, bad behaviour and excessive risk-taking. This in turn creates a culture with rot at its core. The report went further to state, 'individuals dodged accountability for failings on their watch by claiming ignorance or hiding behind collective decision making'. Individual incentives were not in line with high collective standards and they were often, in fact, the opposite. Furthermore, individuals faced too little real possibility of a penalty for their actions, financial or otherwise.[22]

London's Financial Markets Transformed Through 'Big Bang'

During the mid-1980s, London's financial markets were reformed through 'Big Bang', a transformation that liberated the stock exchange and the way in which securities were traded, ensuring London's place as the global financial centre. This status, along with significant benefit, brought with it equally significant risk. The regulatory environment, known as a light touch, attracted capital from around the globe. The city experienced a change in culture from a cosy London club to a brash new world, awash with American bankers. An establishment once quite stuffy and old school became concerned with meritocracy, short-term performance, early starts and large bonuses. The ability and willingness of bankers to take on risk increased exponentially and London's appetite for derivatives—products that repackaged and sold on risk—grew. Although good regulation was recognised to be an important part of this brave new world, the prevailing belief was that regulation should be principle based rather than prescriptive.

Early in the sequence of events that marked the banking crisis, the regulators were alerted to the frailty of the situation, not only from watching the events unfolding in the USA but also from the increasing funding gap between loans and deposits in UK banks. In 2007 the weighted average loan to deposit ratio for UK banks was 172 per cent, significantly higher than in the USA.[23] The underlying problem that would lead to the collapse of the UK banks was not subprime mortgages but rather the funding strategy underlying the aggressive pursuit of growth.

The Good Times in the UK

Albeit not at the same low levels as the USA, where real rates had remained near zero, interest rates in the UK had come down. They hovered around 4 per cent until 2008, and when the banking crisis hit they dropped near zero. This favourable interest environment was combined with rising housing prices, which had increased by 140 per cent over the ten years to 2007. A report produced by the Organisation for Economic Co-operation and Development (OECD) indicated that UK households were the most indebted of any in the G7.[24]

In the UK, subprime lending was also very much in fashion, but there it was referred to as 'non-conforming' or 'adverse-credit lending' with interest rates typically 50 per cent higher than those charged to the most creditworthy clients. Volumes of these mortgages grew from 6 per cent of all new loans in 2005 to 10 per cent in 2006.[25] And as the number of new mortgages which were extended on a 'self-certified' basis (borrowers were not required to provide proof of income) continued to grow, so did the brokers' income as these mortgages attracted higher than average commissions. Borrowers were able to combine an unsecured loan with their mortgage, and together the total borrowing often exceeded the value of the property. Northern Rock was particularly active in this market.

To make things worse, one in every three mortgages issued to new buyers was interest only. The warning signs were present. The Financial Services Authority (FSA) revealed that these non-conforming mortgages were being taken out by people who were already financially stretched. One in three borrowers were unable to continue repayments if the interest rates increased by only 1 percentage point. Unsurprisingly, people taking out these mortgages were more likely to have poor credit ratings and be borrowing more than 90 per cent of the value of their homes. So why was this allowed to continue? Why didn't the regulators step in?

An important distinction between the UK and the USA was that UK house prices continued to rise for at least 18 months even after US prices began falling and the inflation in these prices ensured that repossessions were kept low. While US mortgages were 'no recourse' loans, the UK's were not—people preferred, and were encouraged, to sell their property rather than default.

However, similar to the USA, the credit-rating agencies in the UK relied too heavily on models with questionable assumptions. They seemed quite secure in the fact that models indicated that in order for anything to go horribly wrong, the interest rates would need to go up and the housing prices would need to come down. Of course, this was exactly the conditions they were witnessing in the USA, yet the models used by the credit-rating agencies did not account for a possible fall in house prices.

The Unravelling in the UK

Very early in the cycle, as early as 2003, there were concerns that mortgage lending among some providers showed dangerous signs of being too relaxed. In April 2003, HBOS came under fire for reckless lending into the UK mortgage market. Stories surfaced of people borrowing six times their annual salary to buy a house. Shane O'Riordain, the then CEO, downplayed the story, claiming, 'There's a theoretical possibility that customers could be offered six times their salary but there are stringent conditions attached.'[26] However, it was not until 2007 that significant cracks appeared and Northern Rock was the first casualty.

For the year end 2006, Northern Rock reported a healthy profit and a robust credit book. But by September 2007 this same institution, one of the UK's largest and fastest-

> 'There's a theoretical possibility that customers could be offered six times their salary but there are stringent conditions attached.'

growing mortgage banks, experienced a run on the bank with people queuing in orderly fashion to withdraw their savings: the first run on a UK bank since the 1800s. Northern Rock's demise was not due to mortgage books going bad but rather its capital structure and over-reliance on short-term debt. It had relied heavily on short- to medium-term money markets to fund its record growth. When this dried up, so did Northern Rock. And although its very risky capital structure was well known, the regulatory system had not intervened and demanded corrective action prior to the panic.

At the end of 2006 the value of Northern Rock's assets was £101 billion, mainly comprising (more than 85 per cent) secured lending on residential properties. A subsequent report by the House of Lords reported that the lending side of the bank was well handled and the number of high-risk loans kept low.[27] The trouble was caused by the way in which Northern Rock funded its strategy of aggressive growth. Its assets had grown by 15–20 per cent per annum for over 15 years. While the average UK bank had a loan to deposit ratio of 172 per cent, Northern Rock's was more than 320 per cent.[28] The excessive use of leverage and short- to medium-term funds in the capital markets, with up to 50 per cent securitised in off-balance sheet vehicles, led to its cry for help.

In August 2007, due to the trouble in the USA with Bear Stearns, the international capital markets froze. Northern Rock was able to limp along for a short time but by 8:30 p.m. on Thursday 13 September 2007, the British Broadcasting Company (BBC) reported that Northern Rock had asked for and received emergency financial support from the Bank of England.

Only when the run looked like it was getting out of control did the Bank of England concede to wade in and restart the short-term money market. The UK government would extend over £25 billion of taxpayers' money to the bank and guarantee more than £100 billion in deposits. The government became Northern Rock's biggest shareholder in February 2008, subsequently selling its share to Virgin Money in a £1 billion deal that reportedly cost taxpayers £400 million.[29]

What followed in 2008 was a complete collapse and a total loss of confidence in the UK banks and the banking system. The largest UK banks would all cease to exist, become nationalised or require significant capital injections. In September 2008, after the market opened on the Monday morning following the bankruptcy of Lehman Brothers, the wholesale funding markets were paralysed and HBOS's share price immediately collapsed, dropping 18 per cent. Investors recognised that HBOS, the UK's largest mortgage lender, was a dead man walking.

On 1 October 2008, then Prime Minister Gordon Brown reiterated his support for a deal between HBOS and Lloyds, which reassured some that a 'merger' might happen. Backing from Standard Life Investments and other institutional investors—apparently orchestrated by Brown and the Chancellor, Alistair Darling—pushed HBOS shares up by 21 per cent while Lloyds TSB ended 10 per cent higher. Over and above the emergency funding from the Federal Reserve, the Bank of England also provided HBOS with a £25.4 billion emergency loan, a move that was not made public until November 2009. Many wondered whether Lloyds shareholders would have agreed to take HBOS off the government's hands if they had been aware that the bank they were buying was effectively bankrupt and had only been kept afloat by these emergency loans. In January 2009, taxpayers would hold a 43 per cent interest in the combined entity.[30]

The fate of the Royal Bank of Scotland (RBS) was sealed in 2007. In May of that year it had led a consortium to buy ABN Amro in the pursuit of growth, failing to anticipate problems in the credit market. It made a £48 billion acquisition bid that it would later win in October, with a tender offer of over 90 per cent cash. In December 2007 the combined write-down of this group was £1.5 billion. In August 2008, RBS would declare its first loss in 40 years as a public company, and by November the government would step in. In late 2008, RBS would be nationalised through a 58 per cent government share, later to be increased to 84 per cent.[31]

In relative terms, Barclays and HSBC fared well during the crisis although they would both need to raise funds to preserve their capital ratio.

The Aftermath in the UK

The impact of Big Bang—increasing levels of innovation in products; unrelenting search for profit; and the role of the UK as an intermediary in global markets—had contributed to the complexity of the financial markets. The regulatory community, the UK government, financial institutions and, of course, the bankers were devastated. The overall impact on the UK was frozen credit markets (a huge burden on taxpayers as financial institutions were nationalised), decimated pensions and a prolonged recession.

The OECD's report on financial trends (2009) concluded that 'corporate governance arrangements did not safeguard against excessive risk'. The financial crisis was largely

> 'Corporate governance arrangements did not safeguard against excessive risk.'

due to the failures and weaknesses in corporate governance. In particular, the risk management processes and systems—including board oversight, risk assessment and controls, communication, reporting and internal environment—failed.[32]

The UK has a comply-or-explain approach, referred to as a light-touch regulatory environment. However, a successful, light-touch environment, one that is based on principles rather than prescription, relies on high ethical and professional standards of individuals, and the willingness of those participating to self-regulate and be willing to step up and ostracise those who cross ethical boundaries. The flaw in this approach is, in Hector Sants' memorable phrase, that 'a principles-based approach does not work with individuals who have no principles'.[33]

The UK was not the only market to be affected by frozen credit markets and excessive debt. Canada was impacted by both, but to a much lesser extent, so its banking system would become something of a poster child for the USA and others.

Canada: Obama Adviser Looks to Canada's Financial System[34]

Relatively speaking, Canada felt only the brush strokes of the banking crisis. It was spared the depths of despair, widespread in many other countries: no banks failed, none were nationalised, and the Canadian government did not have to step in to buy shares in financial institutions to keep them alive or print extraordinary sums of money to bump start the economy. By comparison, Canada avoided the worst and although it would fall into a recession, the pain was sharp and shortlived.

Why didn't the euphoria and crisis of its neighbours to the south take hold of the Canadian economy? Some refer to the willingness of the Canadian financial community to work together and to take decisions quickly once it hit. However, deep crisis was avoided primarily because of a more restrictive regulatory environment, where the majority of mortgages are insured, and a different culture—one that does not overly promote or incentivise excessive risk-taking. In contrast there is a significant focus throughout the Canadian banking culture to be proficient at managing risk. Mark Carney, Canada's Deputy Minister of Finance during the crisis, was asked about the resilience of the Canadian banks. He said, 'through the organisations and up to the top of the organisation—[all] are proficient at managing credit and market risk'.[35]

Canadians have long been known for a more conservative culture, one that has often been the brunt of humour for that very reason. The editor-in-chief of Bloomberg news noted, 'Canadians are like hobbits. They are just not as rapacious as Americans.'[36] Yet this cultural trait would serve it well through the crisis.

The Good Times in Canada

Similar to the USA and the UK, the good times were also very much part of the Canadian economy. During the years leading up to the crisis, Canada experienced prolonged low interest

> 'Canadians are like hobbits. They are just not as rapacious as Americans.'

rates, rising housing prices and a booming housing market. Canadians also had a hearty appetite for material goods, which led to accumulated debt at unprecedented levels. Indeed, the average personal level of debt to disposable income ratio would surpass that of the USA.

During this time, although lending standards in the mortgage market would relax and lending in general would be at its most lenient, the extent of subprime mortgages would hit only an estimated 5 per cent of the pre-crisis market compared with 22 per cent in the USA. In contrast to either the USA or the UK where new mortgages were often taken out by those on a low income, much of the growth in Canadian mortgage loans came from refinancing where mortgage holders took on longer or larger mortgages. Mortgage delinquencies barely rose above 1 per cent.

What made Canada unique? The Canadian Mortgage and Housing Corporation (CMHC), a government-owned body, insured eligible mortgages. Some mortgages would exist outside this environment, but the majority of mortgages were insured. Although the CMHC insured some non-prime mortgages, these borrowers were subject to higher than average minimum credit scores, so the quality of insured mortgages remained relatively constant throughout the crisis. Government-backed mortgage insurance through the CMHC allowed the government to maintain control over the underwriting standards and helped to limit the growth in subprime lending. So Canadian banks did not engage in this lending to the same extent as other countries. Canadian banks also held on to their mortgages rather than packaging and selling them on. Less than a third were securitised compared with twice that level in the USA.[37]

Unlike in the UK where the race for growth was a priority, Canadian banks did not have the same level of freedom to pursue growth. During the early days, when US and international banks were expanding and venturing into new territories, the general consensus was that Canadian banks were being held back. The shadow banking system played a much smaller role in Canada because the credit activities that gravitated towards shadow banking in other countries remained inside the depository banking and its regulatory system in Canada.

The regulatory environment prohibited the levels of risk that others were taking. This would remain unchanged even as the financial community growled and pressed for change. That is not to say that Canadian institutions did not have international reach, or pursue large deals. In 2007 the Ontario Teacher's Pension Plan won an auction for a $35 billion takeover, which was the largest private equity deal in history.[38] However, Canadian bank regulations provided constraints to a higher degree than elsewhere, with higher capital requirements, greater leverage restrictions and fewer permitted off-balance sheet activities. As a result of these more restrictive guidelines, many Canadian bankers were left feeling that they could not compete on a world scale and that the 'overly conservative', 'somewhat provincial' tags they were given were well deserved. Although difficult for some Canadian bankers at the time, these restrictions served them well.

Canada: Tripped but did not Fall

Where Canada did feel the pain was in the short-term credit market. In the early years of the crisis there was a thriving market for asset-backed commercial paper (ABCP), which was short-term 30–60-day notes that paid interest on the bundling of assets such as mortgages and auto loans. As the fears of subprime defaults increased, buyers backed off and, in 2007, this market froze. It effectively left an estimated $33 billion of securities untradeable.[39]

The Canadian Imperial Bank of Commerce, a bank known to be the greatest risk-taker of the five largest banks, found itself holding an excessive amount of derivative securities tied to US subprime mortgages. It would take significant write-downs, billions of dollars, against that portfolio and, in turn, would need to sell shares to shore up its balance sheet.

The experience in the ABCP market provided the Canadian banks with an early warning system. The inner circle of the banking community began to talk about the possibilities of a global crisis and the options that they would have in that eventuality. During the crisis, as the CDO market dried up, the Canadian government introduced the Insured Mortgage Purchase Program, which led to an injection of $125 billion to purchase and ring fence securitised mortgages from banks. This programme allowed banks to continue lending.[40]

As a result of its performance up to and through the crisis, the Canadian Banking community has been held in high esteem not only by the USA but on a global level. As the USA performed its post-mortem on the banking crisis, President Barack Obama publicly claimed that they could learn from their neighbours to the north.

Similar to the UK, Canada has a principle-based regime. However, the regulator is heavily involved and actively works with each of the banks to ensure compliance. Moreover, although Canada adopted the standards of the Basel II accord, it applied them to a higher standard then some other countries. The capital ratios were applied to Tier 1 loans only, and they went further to implement a leverage ratio.

> 'We are "peace, order and good government." They [the US] are into the pursuit of happiness.'

Generally there is a widespread idea that Canadians are more conservative and boring than their neighbours to the south. Roger Martin of the Rotman School of Business attributes this to the idea that Canadians are 'peace, order and good government', while Americans are 'into the pursuit of happiness".[41]

So What did We Learn from this GLOBAL Crisis: Highlights of Regulatory Reform

Overall, banks have operated a 'heads-I-win-tails-you-lose' system.[42]

In terms of the shadow banking system, 'an enormous part of what the banks did—the off-balance sheet vehicles, the derivatives and the shadow banking system itself—was to find a way around regulation'.[43]

Subsequently there was a general consensus that anything that does what a bank does, anything that needs to be rescued in a crisis, should be treated and regulated in the same way as a depository bank.

The Basel Committee on Banking Supervision, a committee of representatives from the world's most important financial markets, agreed the Basel III accord in 2011. The accord was aimed at strengthening capital requirements by increasing bank liquidity and decreasing bank leverage. and it is gradually being phased in, scheduled for completion by 2019. Critics argue that it has not gone far enough and still relies heavily on credit agencies for the risk assessment of financial products. This is a notable concern given that the failure of credit agencies to correctly rate CDOs was a significant contributor to the banking crisis.

The European Union chose, among other actions, to target bankers' remuneration, capping bonuses at twice base salary and requiring at least 40 per cent of bonuses to be deferred for three years. As might have been expected, banks have been creative in trying to bypass this law by, for example, awarding allowances to top-up base salaries—really just a 'renaming' rather than a change in total compensation.

The UK changed the regulatory regime for banks but also revised the UK's corporate governance code in 2010 and 2012. In February 2015, the UK Financial Conduct Association (FCA) announced the Senior Managers Regime, which is aimed at increasing the personal responsibility and accountability of senior managers in financial services firms. These firms are required to map out responsibilities for strategy, risk management and control, and to assign them to named individuals with significant influence over the organisations' decision-making or control functions. Although it relates primarily to board roles, it may also include heads of business areas and other key functions.

The aim is to ensure that whatever governance or control structures are in place, there is a senior person accountable to regulators for any failings. Senior managers have a new statutory duty of responsibility to take all reasonable measures to ensure that there are no conduct breaches, although it is up to regulators to prove non-compliance, a weaker proposition from the original proposal for the senior manager to assume the burden of proof. It is hoped that this will remove the defence of 'plausible deniability' which allowed senior managers to claim ignorance or hide behind collective decision-making.

Financial services firms are also required to certify that all employees performing roles that involve material risk-taking or potential harm to customers are 'fit and proper'. This category includes customer-facing roles such as traders and benchmark submitters. The code requires that employees act with integrity, skill, due care and diligence. *Will self-certification here be sufficient?*

What Role did Inadequate Corporate Governance and Flawed Culture Play?

We agree with the assessment that this was a woeful case of inadequate risk management and flawed culture. 'Innovative' financial products and the use of securitisation led to a dangerously common international situation where the CEO and boards, which are responsible for setting the levels of risk and overseeing risk management and processes, simply did not appreciate the underlying risk of the financial instruments that were being traded.

The Basel II accord, in place before the crisis, allowed banks, subject to approval, to substitute their own sophisticated credit models instead of standardised weightings. These models were severely limited in assessing the risk of portfolios. Inconsistencies and the resulting risk, obvious when applying common sense were not highlighted through the models. How is it that you package subprime mortgages, essentially junk grade, with prime mortgages and the entire package becomes prime? The senior executives and board members did not understand the deficiencies of these models. Given that the models had been approved, it may be fair to assume that neither did the Basel II committee. A 2010 McKinsey study provided evidence that a simple ratio of common equity to risk-weighted assets would have outperformed the value-at-risk models or other ratios as a predictor of future bank distress.[44]

Moreover, the boards of the banks that were first to fail did not acknowledge or appreciate the impact of the risk associated with their capital structure and funding strategy. Bear Stearns relied heavily on short-term capital, as did Northern Rock; Lehman Brothers on client stocks; and HBOS on dangerously high levels of leverage. Generally the report from the senior supervisors group found insufficient evidence of active board involvement.[45]

The lack of board oversight brings in to question how many of these non-executive board directors were adequately screened and whether they were sufficiently experienced or knowledgeable to undertake their responsibilities.

A fundamental tenet of effective risk management must be a culture with the appropriate level of respect for, and understanding of, risk. However, the banking environment provided incentives for, and nurtured cultures of, excess risk-taking. Unlike the Canadian banking culture where the head of the regulatory body refers to the CEO, as the chief risk officer, often, these environments hold precious the revenue producers while ostracising or creating administrative roles for those individuals managing and measuring risk. In a rather shocking turn of events, an illustration of this is the story of how HBOS appointed its head of risk. In 2005 the head of group regulatory risk issued a report warning that the bank was headed for collapse due to its sales-obsessed culture and inadequate internal controls. He was then fired by the group CEO and replaced by the head of retail sales, someone with little knowledge, experience or understanding of risk management.[46]

The findings from the banking crisis suggest that too rarely were risk measurements ever included on the board agenda. And, of course, the greatest illustration of the disparity of roles is the gap in remuneration and the lack of senior roles present on the organisational charts.

A former banker and colleague said that bankers are in the business of taking risks. Those words bring to life visions of individuals scaling high mountains, jumping out of planes or saving underlings in distress. And it is just that kind of glorified thinking that can lead to excessive risk-taking. Banks were traditionally in the business of providing liquidity and capital for the purpose of development and growth. In doing so they assumed significant levels of risk and as a consequence one of the most critical functions within a bank, which demands the greatest duty of care, is understanding and managing that risk through sufficient and alert oversight.

A Productive, Ethical Culture must be Part of a Risk Management Strategy

As we have mentioned, the regulatory environments differ noticeably between the USA and the UK. In common, however, was the continual pursuit of higher yield, profit and personal gain.

Just prior to the unravelling of the credit frenzy, the New York comptroller's office estimated that Wall Street executives took home bonuses totalling $33.9 billion in 2006.[47] The incentive compensation for traders was based on the fees generated from the sale of products rather than the time-weighted performance of the products. In other words, they were given short-term incentives—remuneration did not account for losses over the life of the products. If we acknowledge that culture is a derivative of behaviours encouraged and rewarded, undoubtedly the banking cultures were ones of excessive risk-taking and short-term profit.

Unfortunately the executives taking the risk were handsomely rewarded for the upside but not penalised for the downside of their actions. In fact, some would argue, the only real penalty was for not taking enough risk to keep up with one's colleagues.

Moving Forward

The USA, the UK and Canada have all undertaken a review of their participation in the crisis to understand how to strengthen their regulatory environments and prevent future disasters, resulting in an increasing number of rules in the USA and more guidelines in the UK's code of conduct. On a global level, Basel III has been introduced, calling for tighter controls on capital ratios and introducing leverage ratios similar to those found in Canada.

As we have seen in other industries, the internet, the speed at which information changes hands, the volume of consumption and our ability to be 'always connected' will give way to a transformation of financial institutions. To an extent we have begun to see a rebirth of community banking through alternative lending organisation: crowd funding, peer to peer lending and challenger banks.

But while the dangerous gap remains between the benefits and consequences of risk-taking, global banks, or, perhaps, global bankers, are likely to continue to push boundaries where and when they can. We think that in a global economy, with the knock-on consequences we have seen, standards should converge and best practices across countries should be used to set the global standard.

A Few Selected Highlights from the Banking Crisis Story

* *Independent thinking is the greatest value the board can add. This applies equally to the companies that it engages. Institutions that are required to form opinions, such as the credit-rating agencies, must be independent, and they should be regulated and overseen by an appropriate and unbiased third party.*

* *From Canada we can learn from that country's appreciation of and education regarding risk. Developing a culture that understands and appreciates risk requires relevant reward systems, and appropriate representation in the organisational structure and at the board level.*

* *An ethical culture is an important element of an effective risk-management framework. The universal values of respect for the customer and accountability for actions and inactions should be adopted by all companies that are serious about enabling ethical cultures.*

* *From the UK we can learn from its Code of Conduct specifically the Senior Managers Regime. First, the board needs to be selected with the*

appropriate level of experience—a non-executive director must be sufficiently informed to be able to provide an adequate level of constructive challenge. Having assumed this responsibility, individuals must be held accountable for their actions or inactions. This accountability should be cascaded down to the operating managers who execute on a daily basis.

Notes

1. Desmond, M. (2008) 'IMF: Subprime Losses Could Hit $1 Trillion', *Forbes Magazine*, 4 August 2008.
2. York, G. (2008) Financial chaos bites the dragon, A quote from Ha Jiming, Chief Economist at China International Capital Corp. *The Globe and Mail*, 10 October 2008.
3. Crippen, A. (2010) Transcript: Warren Buffett on Moody's & Credit Ratings Agencies, *CNBC*, 2 June 2010.
4. Buffett, W. (2010). Interview with the FCIC, 26 May 2010.
5. *The Economist* (2007) Briefing America's housing market, *The Economist*, 24 March 2007.
6. 'Originate to hold': assets originally 'brought' to remain on balance sheets to maturity.
7. BBC News (2003) Buffett warns on Investment 'time bomb', *BBC News*, 4 March 2003.
8. US Government, Financial Crisis Inquiry Commisson (2011), page 130, 30 May 2011.
9. 'Mark to market' is an accounting term used to describe a process of valuing assets at market value.
10. Ellert, J. (2010) Lessons learned from recurring financial crises, 20th Zagreb Stock Exchange Conference, 30 October 2010.
11. Financial Crisis Inquiry Commission, p. xxv, GPO, 25 February 2011.
12. Nakamoto, M. & Wighton, D. (2007) 'Citigroup chief stays bullish on buy-outs', *Financial Times*, 9 July 2007.
13. www.stat.unc.edu.com, *Subprime Mortgage Crisis*, page 7.
14. www.stat.unc.edu.com, *Subprime Mortgage Crisis*, page 4.
15. Jurow, K. (2010) Here's How Widespread Mortgage Fraud Created the Housing Bubble. *Business Insider*, 18 May 2010.
16. The interbank market is the market between banks essential to provide overall liquidity.

17. Bloomberg (2008) Seven days of shocks unnerve investors, *Bloomberg*, 15 March 2008.

18. *The Economist* (2008) Bank losses, Hall of Shame, *The Economist*, 7 August 2008.

19. Nocera, J. (2008) As credit crisis spiraled, crisis led to action, *The New York Times*, 1 October 2008.

20. www.whitehouse.org, American Recovery and Reinvestment Act.

21. US Financial Crisis Inquiry Commission (2011) 'FCIC Releases Report on the Causes of the Financial Crisis', January 2011.

22. House of Lords (2013) Changing banking for good, *Reports of the Parliamentary Commission on Banking Standards*, 12 June 2013.

23. Pytel, G. The largest Heist in History, www.parliament.uk, Table A UK Banks.

24. Wolf, M. (2010) The European Economy in the Global Financial Crisis, *2010 CFA Institute Publications*, March 2010.

25. *The Economist* (2007) When the tide goes out, *The Economist*, 22 March 2007.

26. Gill, C. 'Home Loans: six times income', *Daily Mail*, undated.

27. House of Lords (2013) Changing banking for good, *Reports of the Parliamentary Commission on Banking Standards*, 12 June 2013.

28. Pytel, G. The largest Heist in History, www.parliament.uk, Table A UK Banks.

29. Amistead, L. (2011) 'Northern Rock sold to Virgin Money "at a loss"', *The Telegraph*, 17 November 2011.

30. Barrow, B. (2009) 'Mugged over a £25bn loan: Lloyds shareholders' fury that they were kept in the dark about ailing HBOS, *mailonline*, 25 November 2009.

31. Jarrett, T. (2009) 'Taxpayers direct support to banks (Lloyds, RBS, Northern Rock, and Bradford & Bingley)', *House of Commons Library*, 3 June 2010.

32. Kirkpatrick, G. (2008) The Corporate Governance Lessons from the Financial Crisis, *Financial Market Trends*, OECD (2009).

33. Sants, H. (2009) Delivering Intensive Supervision and Credible Deterrence, Speech delivered to the *Reuters Newsmakers Event*, 12 March 2009.

34. Perkins, T. (2009) Obama adviser looks to Canada's financial system, *Globe and Mail*, 11 February 2009.

35. Freeland, C. (2010) 'What Toronto can teach New York and London', *Financial Times*, 29 January 2010.

36. Freeland, C. (2010) 'What Toronto can teach New York and London', *Financial Times*, 29 January 2010.

37. Bank of Canada (2013) The Residential Mortgage Market in Canada: A Primer, December 2013.

38. Report on Business (2013) 'The 2008 financial crisis: Through the eyes of some major players', *The Globe and Mail*, 14 September 2013.

39. Report on Business (2007) 'ABCP: Anatomy of a panic', *The Globe and Mail*, 17 November 2007.

40. McLister, R. 'IMPP expected to continue' *Canadian Mortgage Trends. com*, 28 September 2009.

41. Freeland, C. (2010) 'What Toronto can teach New York and London', *Financial Times*, 29 January 2010.

42. Carney, M. (2014) Governor of the Bank of England, 'Inclusive capitalism: creating a sense of the systemic', *Speech given at the conference on Inclusive Capitalism*, 27 May 2014.

43. Wolf, M. (2009) 'Reform of regulation has to start by altering incentives', *The Financial Times*, 23 June 2009.

44. McKinsey & Company (2010) 'Basel III and European banking: Its impact, how banks might respond, and the challenges of implementation. Study on VAR, *McKinsey Working Papers on Risk*, November 2010.

45. Senior Supervisors Group (2009) Risk Management Lessons from the Global Banking Crisis of 2008, 21 October 2009.

46. Fraser, I. (2010) 'The Worst Bank in the World? HBOS's Calamitous Seven Year Life' *ianfraser.org*, 27 February 2010.

47. Shnayerson, M. (2009) 'Wall Street's $18.4 Billion Bonus', *Vanity Fair*, 2 February 2009.

4

Global Banking: Will the Scandals Never End?

'Probity and honesty are essential, as is trust which is based upon it. The LIBOR[1] activities, in which you played a leading part, put all that in jeopardy.'[2]

Tom Hayes held his head in his hands as he listened to Mr Justice Cooke's remarks, stunned by the 14-year jail sentence he had just received for conspiracy to defraud.[3] Hayes was just the first of a series of bankers to be tried for LIBOR and EURIBOR (Euro Interbank Offered Rate) manipulation following the collective penance of the banks that were fined more than $9 billion for their part in the scandal.

However, LIBOR manipulation was only one of a series of scandals that has resulted in more than $235 billion of fines and compensation imposed on global banks in the eight years to May 2015.[4] Both retail and investment banks have been heavily fined for mis-selling. In the UK, in addition to fines, retail banks have paid more than £24 billion to customers in compensation for mis-selling payment protection insurance policies. The list goes on and on: market manipulation, benchmark rigging, dark pool trading, money laundering and sanctions busting, to name but a few.

© The Author(s) 2017
A. Micklethwait, P. Dimond, *Driven to the Brink*,
DOI 10.1057/978-1-137-59053-4_4

The headline banking scandals of the last ten years are distinct from the derivatives scandals of earlier times, such as Leeson (Barings), Kerviel (Société Générale) and Adoboli (UBS), where one rogue trader was primarily responsible for billions of dollars of losses to the banks in each case. The recent mis-selling and market-manipulation activities were performed by many different people, often involving more than one department, while the LIBOR and foreign exchange (FX) scandals also concerned employees at different banks acting in collusion. This was not just the result of a few rotten apples; the decay was more widespread.

The culture and behaviours of the trading floor are often portrayed as 'young', 'aggressive', 'male-dominated' and 'egotistical', where the drive for profit supersedes all other considerations. While this may be a gross generalisation, most would admit that it holds at least a kernel of truth. How did this culture evolve?

These are stories of inadequate, or poorly enforced, controls where traders created and perpetuated a culture of unfettered greed. Awareness of LIBOR and FX manipulation was widespread among traders and their managers. Boards and senior management who should have curbed such behaviour were either ill-informed or, in some instances, they turned a blind eye to the goings-on. Remuneration packages, sanctioned by senior management, rewarded risk-taking without respect for customers' interests.

LIBOR: Rigging Interest Rates on a Grand Scale

The LIBOR scandal exploded in June 2012 when Barclays admitted attempts to manipulate the LIBOR and Euribor reference interest rates. The bank had massaged the rates to improve the appearance of the bank's creditworthiness during the 2007/2008 banking crisis. For an even longer period, both before and after the crisis, Barclays' traders had also influenced the rates for their own profit. Other banks were soon drawn into the investigation, huge fines were imposed and civil suits abounded.

The public's belief in the probity of banks, virtually destroyed during the banking crisis, was dealt another blow by this latest scandal. As records of e-mails and chat-room conversations were released to the media, the flawed culture at the heart of the trading floor was revealed. Not only were the banks clearly unable to police themselves but, once again, they were proven to have treated customers with disdain.

Lenders use LIBOR to set the interest rate on many variable rate loans, such as adjustable rate mortgages and bonds, by setting the lending rate at LIBOR plus a fixed percentage rate. If traders can manipulate LIBOR above or below its true market level, both lenders and borrowers are affected and, of course, one is the loser. This was the basis on which large bondholders and mortgage financiers such as Fannie Mae and Freddie Mac sued the banks: they believed that LIBOR had been forced below its true rate and therefore the interest income they received was less than it should have been. One could say that there were as many winners as losers, but that was no consolation to the losers.

Early Days of LIBOR

LIBOR was born in 1969 when a Greek banker, Minos Zombanakis, from London-based Manufacturers Hanover, arranged an $80 million syndicated loan to the Shah of Iran. Zombanakis called up several key banks to ask what their funding rates were and pegged the loan to the average of these rates, which he named the London Interbank Offered Rate.[5] It was created as a tool to use and exploit the eurodollar market, which had grown rapidly from its inception in the late 1950s, fuelled by US current account deficits, and the attraction of escaping strict reserve requirements and interest rate limits imposed by the Federal Reserve.[6] The use of LIBOR as a reference rate expanded rapidly, and in 1986, after banks started to use it heavily not only to loan money but also to borrow, the British Bankers Association (BBA), a trade association supervised by the Bank of England, stepped in to formalise and regulate the setting process.[7]

LIBOR is set by asking a panel of large banks the question: 'At what rate could you borrow funds, were you to do so by asking for, and then accepting, interbank offers in a reasonable market size just prior to 11:00 a.m.?' The top and bottom 25 per cent of submissions—the outliers—are ignored and the average of the remainder is calculated. The value is published by

Thomson Reuters and regulated by the BBA. It is a key global reference and benchmark interest rate that is used to set interest rates on trillions of dollars of loans and across $300 trillion of derivative contracts.[8] Banks typically set their lending rates at a 'spread' above LIBOR calculated in relation to the perceived risk of the borrower and the term of the loan. This practice helps banks to ensure that their lending rates never fall too far below their funding rate, as implied by LIBOR.

It is important to note that LIBORS were not necessarily based on actual trades as member banks may not have trades in all the currency-maturity pairs that they are submitting. Therefore they depend, to a greater or lesser degree, on the 'expert judgement' of the submitter. The same applies to the key phrase 'reasonable market size'. This is unquantified and again can require the application of expert judgement. Prior to 2014, individual bank submissions were published the day they were submitted. The practice of excluding outliers and publishing submissions was intended to discourage an individual bank from trying to manipulate the rate: excessively high or low rates would be omitted from the final rate and obviously false submissions would be identified, leading to that bank's expulsion from the panel.

The London market for interest rate products exploded after Big Bang[9] with the creation of more complex derivative products, and it is now one of the largest markets in the world. In 1998 the definition of LIBOR was changed from a lending rate to its current definition—a borrowing rate—and its use continued to expand. By 2012 it was being set for twelve different currencies for up to fifteen maturity periods from overnight to one year.

EURIBOR is similar to LIBOR. It is the second most used reference rate after LIBOR and the most commonly used rate for euro-denominated contracts. It is managed by the European Banking Federation and is set in a similar manner to LIBOR, though with a broader panel of submitter banks.

Older bankers insist that there was no rigging of the rates in the early years.[10] The relatively small market and 'cosy' culture of a gentleman's club limited the scope for manipulation. After Big Bang in 1986 when deregulation hit London and competition increased, the temptation to manipulate LIBOR grew. Douglas Keenan, a bonds and derivatives trader working at Morgan Stanley in London in 1991, claimed that it was a widespread assumption at that time that LIBOR was being manipulated to increase profits.[11]

> 'LIBOR misreporting has been going on for decades.'
> Douglas Keenan

Credit Ratings Encouraged Banks to Lowball Submissions

Prior to mid-2007 LIBOR tended to move in tandem with other short-term interest rates, such as Treasury yields, but from August 2007, and increasingly so after Lehman Brothers' bankruptcy in September 2008, LIBOR became much more volatile. From 2005 to mid-2007 the LIBOR-OIS (overnight indexed swap [rate]) spread was less than ten basis points, but this climbed to more than 360 basis points, or 3.6 per cent, after news of Lehman Brothers' bankruptcy broke in 2008 and it remained high well into 2009.[12] Credit worries drove banks to reduce their lending and to demand higher returns, which in turn reduced the banks' ability to access funding and ultimately impacted perceptions of their creditworthiness. This reinforcing feedback loop increased the credit-risk component of LIBOR, driving spreads wider against other, less risky products. At the same time, because the money markets were virtually frozen for anything longer than 30-day loans, rate-setters had to rely more heavily on their expert judgement to make their submissions because data from trades was not readily available.

As the banking crisis developed, eyes were firmly fixed on the large banks, and any indicator that pointed to the instability and fall in credit-worthiness of individual banks was jumped on. One of these markers was LIBOR. As the banks struggled to secure sufficient funding, the temptation rose to keep LIBOR as low as possible in order to give the impression of financial strength. It also became important not to diverge significantly from the mean—not to stand out from the pack. As individual submissions for LIBOR were published on a daily basis, any bank that consistently published rates above the mean, sufficiently high to be excluded from the rate calculation as outliers, would be considered to be more risky than the other banks.

Barclays in particular was worried about negative media perception of its creditworthiness. In August 2007 it borrowed from the Bank of England's emergency reserves twice in just over a week, attracting negative headlines from the financial press. Concern mounted when, three days later, Bloomberg published an article entitled 'Barclays takes a money market

> 'Barclays takes a money market beating.'
> *'What the hell is happening at Barclays?'*

beating', noting that Barclays' three-month US dollar, sterling and euro LIBOR submissions were the highest of all contributing banks. The article asked, 'What the hell is happening at Barclays [...] that is prompting its peers to charge it premium interest rates in the money market?'[13] Barclays' submitters were already concerned that other panel banks were lowballing (submitting rates lower than those they could achieve in the market) and circulated e-mails to that effect: 'Today's USD LIBORS have come out and they look too low to me.'[14] But after the Bloomberg article, senior management became involved. They were very concerned about the negative connotations of being out of line with other banks' LIBOR submissions. In their turn, less senior management, believing that other banks were lowballing rates, instructed the submitters to reduce LIBOR submissions to avoid media attention. The submitters were told that Barclays should not 'stick its head above the parapet' in terms of LIBOR and 'to keep LIBORS within the group (pressure from above)'.[15]

Barclays communicated its worries about low LIBOR submissions to the regulators on several occasions. The Federal Reserve Bank of New York received mass-distribution e-mails from Barclays claiming that banks were lowballing rates: 'USD: 3 month LIBOR rose 1 bp (basis point) yesterday. It should have risen more. One LIBOR contributor set it 2 bps lower than where they were paying at 11 am!?'[16] Barclays also raised the issue with the BBA and it was discussed at the meeting of the Bank of England Sterling Money Markets Liaison Group in April 2008, which noted that 'US dollar LIBOR had at times appeared lower than actual traded interbank rates'.[17] However, despite blaming other banks for falsifying LIBORS, Barclays was rather coy about admitting its own activities. When it discussed LIBOR with the Financial Services Authority (FSA) in December 2007, a manager recalled, 'we didn't say anything along the lines of, you know, we're not posting where we think we should [...] because of. I just talked about dislocations, LIBORS [...] and kept it [...] simple, shall we say'.[18]

Barclays was not the only bank to reduce its LIBOR submissions during the worst of the financial crisis in order to improve its apparent creditworthiness. For instance, UBS managers issued guidance in August 2007 to 'err on the low side' in order to avoid what they saw as unfair media speculation about UBS's fundraising ability. A few months later, on 9 April 2008, UBS's three-month US dollar LIBOR submission was 2.71 per cent. The next day, Manager D queried with Manager C why this submission was so much lower than UBS's actual three-month commercial paper issuance at 2.81 per cent:

Manager D: Here is a mind fuck for you. If we are doing CP [commercial paper] at 2.81% and that is 3m usd LIBOR + 10, why aren't we putting our 3m rate in at 2.81% for LIBORS.

Manager C: We should.

Manager D: But then GT [group treasury] will rip our boys a new one for being the highest bank in the poll.[19]

When group treasury put pressure on the submitters to alter their LIBOR submissions, the submitters apparently did not approach the compliance department for advice or support. Had the department known of the manipulation, one would hope that it would have stopped it unless it was blocked by senior management. Even in this event, a respected compliance department could have taken the issue higher, to the Board Risk Committee if necessary.

On 16 April 2008, *The Wall Street Journal* published an article about LIBOR submissions claiming that 'one of the most important barometers of the world's financial health could be sending false signals'.[20] It claimed that banks had been lowballing their submissions in order to avoid suggesting that they were in difficulties. The following day the submissions of a number of panel banks increased and UBS's directive to submitters changed to be in 'the middle of the pack'.[21] The article prompted the BBA to undertake a review of

> 'one of the most important barometers of the world's financial health could be sending false signals'

LIBOR. Although it concluded that the methodology of calculating the rate did not need to change, the BBA did issue guidance to the panel banks on 5 August 2008, reminding them that 'the rate at which each bank submits must be formed from that bank's perception of its cost of funds in the interbank market'.[22] At this point the BBA was worried about banks lowballing rates to enhance the perception of their creditworthiness rather than the possibility that the rates were being influenced by traders for their own profit. The press, however, had reported suspicions that the latter might be happening.

In October 2008, Paul Tucker, Chairman of the Money Markets Liaison Group at the Bank of England, had a phone conversation with Bob Diamond, then Chief Executive of Barclays Capital, to discuss why Barclays' LIBOR submissions were consistently at the top end of the range of panel submissions for that month. Diamond explained that Barclays thought that other banks' submissions were unrealistically low, not reflecting rates that were achievable in the market. While the record of the conversation did not instruct Barclays to falsify its submissions, Jerry del Missier, then President of Barclays Capital, concluded that it was a direction to reduce rates and passed it down the line to submitters.[23] Barclays continued to submit skewed LIBOR submissions to avoid negative media comment until May 2009, despite signing up to the reiterated guidance from the BBA saying that submissions must be formed from the bank's perception of its borrowing rate on the interbank market.

Rigging Rates for Personal Profit

While submitters were being pressured to reduce LIBORS in order to boost the creditworthiness of their banks, they were also facing requests from traders to help them increase their own profit. This practice had started well before the banking crisis, as illustrated by the activities of Tom Hayes and others.

Derivatives traders make trades on behalf of clients who want to hedge their interest rate exposure. Offsetting trades can be executed to reduce traders' overall risk, but they can also build up a 'position', essentially betting on interest rate movements. The profit on these trades generally depends on movements in LIBOR or EURIBOR. So even very small adjustments to LIBOR can increase a trader's profits or losses significantly, particularly if this takes place on quarter day, International Money Market dates, when the majority of futures contracts are settled or reset.

Evidence gathered by the FSA[24] and the Commodities Futures Trading Commission (CFTC)[25] provides ample proof of attempts to influence LIBOR and EURIBOR submissions. Traders shouted across the trading floor, used internal e-mail and Bloomberg or Reuters chat rooms to ask submitters to alter their rates.

At RBS, for example, on 16 March 2009, a derivatives trader was recorded asking a primary submitter: 'Can we pls get a very very very low 3m and 6m fix today pls, we have rather large fixings!' The primary submitter responded, 'Perfect, if that's what you want.' The derivatives trader

> *Trader*: Can we pls get a very very very low 3m and 6m fix today pls, we have rather large fixings!
> *Submitter*: Perfect, if that's what you want.

then responded with a thank you and further instructions: 'tks [primary submitter], and then from tomorrow, we need them thru the roof!!!!:)'. The primary submitter replied, ':-)'. RBS's three-month LIBOR submissions did follow the derivatives trader's requests.[26] Knowledge of LIBOR rigging was widespread, at least at UBS, where Tom Hayes claimed, 'it was blatant'. During interviews with the UK Serious Fraud Office, Hayes said that he had discussed rigging the rate during a meeting attended by Kemgeter, a senior executive at UBS.[27]

Some submitters did not even wait to be asked to change their LIBORS, approaching traders to see what they wanted. For instance, a Deutsche Bank US dollar LIBOR submitter asked a trader on 22 March

2005, 'If you need something in particular in the LIBORS i.e. you have an interest in a high or a low fix let me know and there's a high chance i'll be able to go in a different level. Just give me a shout the day before or send an email from your blackberry first thing.'[28]

Of course, the fact that a single bank falsified its LIBOR submissions did not necessarily affect the resulting rate, or at least not to the degree that traders wanted. If traders could get other banks to move their rates in the same direction as they wanted, the effect would be correspondingly greater. So traders regularly requested their counterparts at other banks to ask for changed LIBOR submissions in return for favours. One trader (in a competing bank) sent a thank you message the day after asking a Barclays trader to use his influence to change Barclays' submissions: 'Dude. I owe you big time! Come over one day after work and I'm opening a bottle of Bollinger.'[29]

Another method of influencing the rate was to encourage cash traders to make bids in the money markets at rates which might affect banks' submissions for LIBOR/EURIBOR based on actual trades. In early 2007, a trader at Barclays built a position which would benefit from a low EURIBOR on 19 March 2007. As well as asking Barclays' submitter for a low rate he asked traders at three other panel banks to request low rates: 'Tell your cash to put the 3m fixing in the basement.' Then when he found out that Barclays was bidding for three-month cash on that date (which could potentially push up the rate), he requested the cash desk to cancel the bid, which it did. The Barclays trader, thrilled with the success of his scheme, commented to one of the external traders in the deal, 'This is the way you pull off deals like this chicken, don't talk about it too much, 2 months of preparation [...] the trick is you must not do this alone [...] this is between you and me but really don't tell ANYBODY.'[30]

> 'This is the way you pull off deals like this chicken, don't talk about it too much, 2 months of preparation [...] the trick is you must not do this alone [...] this is between you and me but really don't tell ANYBODY.'

Traders went even further by involving interdealer brokers in their schemes to manipulate LIBOR. Interdealer brokers sit between investment banks, helping to find buyers and sellers at other banks for large blocks of securities or derivatives in return for brokerage fees. As intermediaries they have access to information about deals with many different institutions, plus a stream of other inputs, such as internet-based chat rooms provided by Bloomberg or Reuters and conversations with clients. This wealth of data made them useful advisors to banks when compiling their LIBOR submissions, particularly during the banking crisis when lending dried up and banks had little evidence from their own trades on which to set their submissions. The brokers sent daily 'run-through' emails to LIBOR setters giving their opinion of where the rates should be set and, on many occasions, certain traders asked them to alter their run-through rates to help the trader's position.

Traders' relationships with their brokers could be very influential. The Japanese yen derivatives desk at ICAP, one of the world's largest inter-dealer brokers, did a great deal of business with UBS. Between 2006 and 2009 this business accounted for more than 22 per cent of the desk's revenue. Tom Hayes, while at UBS, provided between 12 and 20 per cent of the desk's revenue during this period and, in fact, was the only client of one of the brokers, Darrell Read.[31] Another ICAP broker, Colin Goodman, who worked on the cash desk, normally sent the daily run-through e-mails for Japanese yen and considered that he had so much influence on panel banks' LIBOR submissions that he referred to himself as 'Mr LIBOR'. Goodman's e-mail was well respected: for a long period, submitters at two banks just copied his predictions.[32] Hayes talked regularly to Read, asking him to get Goodman to alter his run-through rates, rewarding his apparent connivance with lavish meals and champagne.

After a time this was no longer enough: Goodman demanded a bigger share of the pie. On 18 April 2007, he e-mailed a colleague of Read's, stating, 'With [UBS] how much does [Hayes] appreciate the yen LIBOR scoop? It seems to me that he has all his glory etc and u guys get his support in other things. I get the dribs and drabs.' He then requested 'some form of performance bonus per quarter from your … bonus pool to me for the LIBOR service'. The following day, Goodman sent another e-mail to Read's colleague, threatening 'LIBORS no more' if he did not receive more compensation. He added that, 'As far as I was concerned [Hayes] was paying for the LIBOR assist for my assistance' and if he was not compensated properly there would be 'no more mr LIBOR'. The threat worked and the brokers arranged, with the agreement of Hayes, to pay

Goodman a £5,000 quarterly retainer out of a £15,000 quarterly payment that UBS made to ICAP for market information.[33] However, at the brokers' trial in late 2015, Goodman maintained that he very rarely actually changed his predictions to suit Hayes. Read said that while he passed on Hayes' requests to Goodman, it was all just a trick to keep Hayes happy; he claimed credit when LIBOR moved in Hayes' favour and made excuses when it did not. As one of the brokers explained, 'That's just how it was. Banks lie to brokers, brokers lie to banks, banks lie to each other, brokers lie to each other.' The brokers declared that they would never have jeopardised their relationship with other clients by favouring UBS, a defence that the jurors accepted, acquitting the brokers at their

> 'That's just how it was. Banks lie to brokers, brokers lie to banks, banks lie to each other, brokers lie to each other.'

trial in late 2015.[34] Despite Hayes being strung along by the brokers, he believed that they were influencing LIBOR submissions according to his instructions and rewarded them accordingly.

Meals and champagne did not satisfy the brokers for long. Brokers' bonuses were chiefly based on the revenue, or brokerage fees, they brought in. Building business with particular traders increased their revenue and thus their bonuses. But when liquidity plummeted during the banking crisis, deals were hard to find, affecting revenue and bonuses. So traders had to find a new way to compensate their brokers: wash trades or churning. A wash trade occurs when securities, or some other asset, are bought and then sold within a short period of time so that final ownership does not change. For derivatives brokers, wash trades meant extra brokerage, often on each leg of the trade. Hayes often employed this tactic when he wanted help to move the Japanese yen LIBOR. He suggested to his broker, 'Whatever the middle of the market is, I'll buy and sell 400 yards [billion].' The broker would need to find a willing counterparty to stand on the other side of the trade, but since the trade would go in both directions very rapidly it would involve minimal counterparty risk and no brokers' fees: 'you don't charge them bro[kerage] but I'll pay bro both sides obviously'. The £42,256 revenue the broker received from just these trades translated into a hefty bonus for the desk (the brokers received a 30 per cent cut of net revenue).[35]

Hayes was not the only trader at UBS who attempted to alter LIBOR submissions. It had become normal behaviour: several traders and managers were involved, and on at least one occasion a trader asked his junior colleague to continue his strategy of pushing LIBORS lower while he was on holiday.[36] Hayes was by no means a rogue trader operating on his own. At his trial in 2015, he said that 'The practice was tried and tested, it was so endemic within the bank [UBS], I just thought ... this can't be a big issue because everybody knows about it ... [it was] such an open secret.'[37]

Regulators Moved In

A whistleblower contacted the US regulator, the CFTC, in 2008, triggering an investigation into LIBOR. Meanwhile, in the UK, the focus was on reforming the procedures and regulation of setting LIBOR rather than investigating the banks for misbehaviour. It was not until early 2010, after the CFTC asked the FSA for help to gather information, that the FSA was eventually prodded into starting its own investigation and widened it to include EURIBOR. Two years later the first case was settled: Barclays was fined £59.5 million by the FSA and $200 million by the CFTC. Five more banks and two brokerage firms were fined a total of £3.9 billion by regulators in the UK, the USA and Switzerland, while 15 other banks across the globe also faced investigations. Tens of bank employees were fired and banks made gestures to claw back the bonuses that the disgraced traders had been awarded previously. Unfortunately this was impossible for those who had already moved on.

Few senior heads rolled, though Bob Diamond, CEO of Barclays, and his deputy, Jerry del Missier, were notable exceptions when they were 'encouraged' to leave. The draft audit report by the German regulator (BaFin) was critical of senior management but eventually decided not to institute prosecutions given the actions that had already been taken.[38] A few individuals were prosecuted and fined by the FCA and, after the successful Crown case against Tom Hayes, further actions ensued. At the time of writing, after the recent acquittal of six brokers, it is unsure whether other mooted trials will still go ahead. No senior managers have yet been indicted for LIBOR manipulation although regulatory bodies still have cases outstanding.

The administration of LIBOR was removed from the BBA and given to NYSE Euronext, now owned by Intercontinental Exchange Group, and regulated by the FCA. LIBOR procedures and regulation have been reformed in line with the Wheatley Review:[39] reducing the number of currencies and maturities it reports on; increasing the number of contributor banks; moving to setting the rates on reported trades rather than 'market sentiment'; and only publishing individual submissions three months after the rate is set. The range of trades on which LIBOR is based has widened from bank-to-bank lending to include other sources of funding, with the ultimate aim of eliminating human estimates. It is now a criminal offence in the UK to manipulate financial benchmarks, which may make it easier to prosecute guilty parties, and permit tougher penalties, in future.

New Scandal Emerges Hard on the Heels of LIBOR: FX Manipulation

One would have thought that the investigations into LIBOR fixing and the resulting fines and prosecutions would have forced compliance departments to crawl all over trading operations and to make traders very careful about what they were doing. Sadly, that was not the case as the subsequent investigation into FX rates manipulation proved. Just 18 months after the height of the LIBOR scandal, regulatory authorities worldwide opened investigations into FX rate fixing. Found guilty of collusion in fixing exchange rate benchmarks, banks were fined more than £6 billion and paid out £1.5 billion in civil lawsuits, brought by investors who had been ripped off by traders seeking to make more profit.

The FX market is huge. An estimated $5.3 trillion[40] worth of exchange rate contracts are traded every day, the vast majority in the decentralised, lightly regulated, over-the-counter (OTC) market. To put this in perspective, the *annual* economic output of the UK in 2013 was $2.5 trillion, less than 50 per cent of the FX contracts traded on a *daily* basis. A few large banks and dealers dominate the market, each with their own proprietary dealing and pricing platforms.

Without the pricing transparency of a significant independent exchange, outside clients usually preferred to set the price of their contracts at a daily reference rate. The two most commonly used reference rates (fixes) are the World Markets/Reuters (WMR) 4:00 p.m. London fix and the European Central Bank (ECB) 2:15 p.m. Central European time (CET) fix. The WMR fix is calculated based on trades within a one-minute window either side of the 4:00 p.m. London time, whereas the ECB fix is simply the rate at 2:15 p.m. CET.

The fixes are used to set the price in all kinds of currency trades, such as spots, swaps, forwards and options. Importantly, they are also used for valuing, transferring and rebalancing multi-currency asset portfolios. In particular, the WMR mid-rates are embodied in the construction of published indices used for tracking multi-country/currency portfolios of bonds, equities or credit instruments, and hence are implicit in many investment strategies, such as index tracking. Fund managers, trading in multi-currency assets throughout the day, like to trade their daily foreign currency exposure at the fix so that they can concentrate on the movements in local share prices and price all trades at the same exchange rate, avoiding any exchange loss due to intraday movements.

FX traders make money by quoting a buy and a sell rate and taking profit on the spread between the two rates. However, when traders offer to trade at the fix, they guarantee their clients the mid-market rate. The deal is often set hours before the fix, leaving the bank at risk of losing money if the exchange rate moves against it. Traders try to mitigate this risk by hedging or by trading in the market close to the fix time. Alternatively, traders can 'net off': matching the contract with another party with a client's order in the opposite direction. It is important to note that 'netting off' is not necessarily inappropriate as long as the client and counterparty are not disadvantaged: not the case in the schemes described below.

'The 3 Musketeers' and 'the Cartell' Formed to Manipulate the Fix

The trader will make money if the rate at which he buys a currency in the market is lower than the fix rate at which he sells to his client, and vice versa—hence the temptation to alter the fix. Since only a handful of global banks dominate FX trading, and the one-minute window to determine the fix is short, a few influential traders can alter the fix by transacting large orders in one direction during that period. Clearly this would be more effective if traders colluded.

Traders sought out fellow conspirators in Bloomberg/Reuters chat rooms, calling themselves 'the 3 Musketeers', '1 team' or 'the Cartell [*sic*]'. These exclusive clubs were careful who to admit. Traders in '1 team' had a discussion

> 'Don't want other numpty's in mkt to know [about information exchanged within the group], but not only that, is he gonna protect us like we protect each other…'

one day about admitting a new member as a UBS trader asked, 'Are we ok with keeping this as is [if the new trader joins] … ie info lvls [levels] & risk sharing?' A J. P. Morgan trader queried, 'Will he tell rest of desk stuff or god forbin his nyk [NewYork trading desk].' A Citibank trader followed up: 'Don't want other numpty's in mkt to know [about information exchanged within the group], but not only that, is he gonna protect us like we protect each other…'. The newcomer was eventually admitted for a month-long trial and told, 'mess this up and sleep with one eye open at night'.[41]

Traders in the emerging FX markets colluded to boycott local brokers in order to drive away competition. In the US dollar/Brazilian real market, for example, a Royal Bank of Canada trader wrote, 'everyone is in agreement in not accepting a local trader as a broker?'. A Barclays trader wrote back, 'yes, the less competition the better'.[42]

Traders had various strategies to help them influence the fix. Once traders in a chat room had decided in which direction they wanted to move the fix, anyone who had trades in the opposite direction would try to offload them by netting them off with unsuspecting traders outside the group (known as 'leaving you with the ammo'). If all members of the group had trades going in the same direction, they attempted to boost the impact of their trades. Just before the fix, they sought out external traders with large orders in the opposite direction and traded with them first ('taking out the filth'). Alternatively they transferred their own orders to another group member, giving him more control over the trades and thus more impact on the fix ('giving you the ammo'). Traders also built the volume of currency they needed to trade at the fix by doing deals with third-party traders ('building') or just by increasing the volume they traded at the fix beyond that necessary to cover their risk, ('overbuying' or 'overselling').

Traders used a combination of these strategies to boost their influence on the fix. In one scheme, Citi trades accounted for 73 per cent of all trades in one direction 30 seconds before the ECB fix, making $99,000 profit. Fellow team members congratulated the trader after the fix was announced: 'impressive', 'lovely' and 'cnt teach that'.[43]

Out in the Open

The Bank of England learnt of rumours that the WMR fix was being manipulated as early as 2006 during meetings of the Foreign Exchange Joint Standing Committee of the chief FX dealers of several major banks. More evidence emerged over the next few years as whistleblowers contacted regulators, but it was not until June 2013 that the FCA started to investigate. Global banks were fined nearly $10 billion and numerous traders were sacked, including middle managers, but no senior managers resigned. The UK regulators criminalised the manipulation of the most important FX benchmarks and investigators questioned some traders under caution, but no criminal prosecutions have been instigated to date. Some banks banned the use of multi-bank chat rooms while others increased monitoring activities. However, few believe that regulation is the cure for market manipulation.

Where were the Systems and Controls to Prevent this?

So how did traders' activities slip past internal controls? After all, the banks have three main lines of defence: senior management, compliance and internal audit. It could not have been any great secret that these suspect activities were going on, or that there was a strong potential for them to. So why were they not stopped or ultimately prevented?

In the case of LIBOR, the whole structure of the trading desks seemed designed to promote collusion and manipulation. At several of the panel banks there was a very close working relationship between LIBOR submitters and derivatives traders. In

> Deutsche Bank traders and LIBOR submitters were encouraged to communicate before setting rates.

2006, RBS merged the money market desk, where submitters worked, and the derivatives desk, and traders were encouraged to share information. Deutsche Bank's submitters sat on the pool trading desk where they traded cash and derivatives products and were encouraged to take trading positions to generate profit for the bank. The problem was compounded when, in 2006, the pool trading desk merged with the money markets derivatives desk, and submitters were encouraged by managers to communicate with derivatives traders before setting rates.[44] The draft BaFin report came to the conclusion that the reorganisation of the trading desks was at least an indirect cause of the substantially higher earnings reported by the money markets derivatives desk between 2007 and 2010: earnings higher than had previously, or subsequently, been achieved.[45]

All three main lines of defence failed either to spot what was going on or to stop it. Managers were, in some cases, complicit in these activities, particularly the manipulation of LIBOR, while others were either unaware or ignored what was going on. There were few systems and controls around the setting of LIBOR submissions and little, or no, formal training. The same was true concerning spot FX trading despite industry codes of practice which prohibited manipulating the fix.

The second line of defence—the compliance department—was inadequate to say the least and although, after the LIBOR scandal broke, the banks started to improve monitoring systems, they failed to stop FX fix manipulation or the sharing of confidential customer information. The ineffectiveness of the compliance role was particularly marked at the broker, Martin Brokers Ltd (Martins): the CEO ensured that the compliance officer 'had nothing to do with that [FX trading] front office' as he thought it would 'destabilise' the desks.[46] The banks' compliance departments had more teeth but, in the end, were equally ineffective. The third line of defence—internal audit—failed to expose bad behaviour even when it did perform audits in the relevant areas.

The compliance department was hampered by its perceived status within banks, being considered a cost burden that had to be supported by the revenue generated by the front office: traders and deal-makers. The

> Bankers look at the compliance department the way footballers look at linesmen: losers running back and forth along a line, stopping players from scoring or doing great things.

contribution of the department, such as the losses it prevents, is much more difficult to put a figure on, and less exciting, than the revenue that dealers bring in. The status of the compliance department is mostly easily illustrated by the names it is given: 'deal killers', 'show stoppers', 'box tickers' and 'cost centres', whereas top dealers are called 'rock stars', 'movers and shakers' or 'big swinging dicks'. One compliance officer described the attitude towards the department: 'Bankers look at the compliance department the way footballers look at linesmen: losers running back and forth along a line, stopping players from scoring or doing great things.'[47] Although in theory risk and compliance have the power to stop a deal going through, in practice it is more difficult. The low standing of the compliance department can make it hard to challenge the 'rock stars', and compliance employees may be reluctant to stop a trade because they feel expendable compared with traders. Many compliance staff have ambitions to move to a front-office position, a situation which probably affects their interactions with the front-office dealers they are required to monitor.

Spending on compliance has multiplied since the 2008 crash, and the role of the chief compliance officer has been enhanced with more than three-quarters now reporting directly to board level. However, in too many organisations, compliance was merely a box-ticking exercise with too little weight given to the intention behind regulations when this conflicted with existing practices. Control issues slipped between the cracks across the differing functions involved in compliance and risk management, and where rules did exist they were not always observed. Compliance and risk-management employees need a career track and remuneration structure that will give them the status and authority to challenge deal-makers successfully. Reporting lines must be clear to eliminate gaps in accountability.

Separate banking activities have different risk drivers, as do the people they attract. FX trading will have a risk profile distinct from that of structured finance, for example. Risk-management frameworks should not be applied equally across the bank but should recognise and account for differences between departments. The reporting and control systems applied to one area will need to be adjusted for another.

'When Bankers Become Detached from End-Users, Their only Reward Becomes Money'[48]

The LIBOR and FX scandals did have something in common with the 'lone wolf' derivatives disasters: they also took place in the trading operations of the banks. What was it about these operations that nurtured bad behaviour? This time it was not the complexity of the deals: the LIBOR and FX manipulations were relatively straightforward compared with the derivatives cases where billions were lost. Controls and compliance were weak in both cases but it was more than that. The fast-moving, testosterone-fuelled environment of trading operations encourages risk-taking. It is a highly competitive business where performance is measured by a simple number. Unlike in many jobs, the revenue attributed to individual traders is instantly visible and a large proportion of traders' remuneration is dependent on it. At the interbank brokers Martins, traders kept 30 percent of the brokerage commission as a bonus, larger than most banks but an indication of how traders were rewarded.[49]

Perverse Incentives

On the trading floor, traders working ten to twelve
hours a day became divorced
from the real world, working
on a 'financial archipelago'.
As a retired Bank of America
manager said, 'The fact is, after

> 'The fact is, after you start trad-
> ing in millions and now billions
> of dollars, you have difficulty in
> relating to real things.'

you start trading in millions and now billions of dollars, you have difficulty in relating to real things.'[50] In this highly competitive environment,
bankers can lose their sense of loyalty: 'You are very atomised—you are
on your own, trying to make money.'[51] It is tempting to say that traders are driven purely by greed, but that would be a mistake. Monetary
rewards are important, more so to some than others, but the challenge
and thrill of the job, and the camaraderie, are also key. The problem lies
not so much in the level of compensation but how it is structured. If
bonuses are based primarily on revenue, regardless of risk or customer
respect, then traders will do their utmost to increase their revenue, and if
that means taking on more risk, taking actions on the edge of legality, or
taking actions that are not in the best interests of their customers, then
that is what they will do.

Much has been written about the perverse incentives of the banking industry: rewards for risk-taking but no equivalent penalty if it all
goes wrong. This is compounded by the frequent movement of bankers
between different institutions. Banking in capital markets is no longer
a lifetime job. Bankers tend to hop employers after eighteen months to
three years, hunting for greater rewards. The banks themselves are complicit, with a hire-and-fire mentality. There is little notice of firings, with
employees called up one morning by human resources and out of the
office within an hour. A side-effect of this game of musical chairs is the
futility of deferred compensation. An employee who wants to leave but
who could lose huge deferred compensation by doing so will be given
a 'golden hello' or 'buy-out' by his new employer. This means that any
deferred bonus can no longer be clawed back. Some of the changes

introduced in the wake of the banking crisis sought to address the issues of short-term mentality. Rules were introduced regarding the proportion of bonuses that must be deferred; the length of the deferral; and claw-back in cases of employee misbehaviour, and for senior executives and major risk-takers. The rules vary between the different jurisdictions but have generally increased the deferred proportion and length of deferral. In addition, the FCA is consulting on how to claw back deferred compensation subject to buy-outs, but whether a practical solution can be found is open to question.

Amoral Focus on Profit

Mark Carney, Governor of the Bank of England, noted that 'when bankers become detached from end-users, their only reward becomes money'. Bankers talk about

> 'If I voiced an opinion based on moral considerations, I'd get looked at as if I were an alien.'

the amoral culture of the industry where as long as something is legal, it is acceptable. The terms 'right' and 'wrong' have no part in the decision-making process. One investment banker, new to the job, reflected, 'If I voiced an opinion based on moral considerations, I'd get looked at as if I were an alien.'[52]

A clear example of this was behaviour that the US authorities uncovered of actions less than sympathetic to the banks' clients. Part was illegal and contrary to the banks' policies, where traders disclosed confidential information about their clients' identities and trading activities. Other activities were not strictly illegal but were what many would regard as unethical. When customers asked for a quote, they might request that the phone line remained open so that they could hear the rate that the trader was offering. In some cases the salesman made hand signals to the trader, asking him to apply a mark-up to the trade without disclosing to the customer that he was charging commission. Salesmen would also accept limit orders[53] and then not fulfil them, when it was possible to do so but less profitable to the bank than not completing them.

The banks were not fined for these behaviours but were forced to write to their clients to tell them what they had been doing. However, they promptly followed up by writing another letter, essentially informing their clients that they would continue to act in this way in future, tempering this by saying that they 'will be truthful if [J. P. Morgan] agree to disclose such information'.[54] Clients dealing in OTC markets are considered to be professionals and therefore, unlike retail customers, generally do not fall into the category of clients who rely on the bank as agents to act in their best interests. Professional clients are deemed to be able to shop around for the best price, so J. P. Morgan's clients' letter, along with that from other banks, is perfectly legal and follows the principle of *caveat emptor* (buyer beware). However, bankers are also fully aware that there are different levels of financial knowledge among professional clients and a small regional bank or medium-sized company is often much more naïve than a large hedge fund or major central bank. Yet they are all subject to the same treatment.

The letters imply a certain detachment from clients. Banks have become accustomed to referring to 'counterparties' rather than 'customers', and to focusing on short-term opportunistic deals rather than long-term relationships. Salesmen and traders showed contempt for some of their customers, not always referring to them in the politest of terms, and these were not insignificant accounts but large corporates, pension funds and even central banks. Revenue and profit have become by far the most important drivers, with customer interests trailing far behind.

Although evident in trading operations in particular, this detachment is not true of all banking sectors: relationships with corporate finance clients, for example, are often close and long term, but here again customer interests have been downgraded. As one retired Citibank employee noted, 'to say we always put the interest of the clients first was not entirely correct. But there was certainly in the past far more emphasis on sustained and continued relationships with clients.'[55] Divisions within banks no longer had a sense of vocation, and no longer considered their part in promoting investment, innovation, growth and prosperity. When banks came to consider their primary purpose as money-maker, rather than service provider, compensation became purely financial, abandoning non-pecuniary rewards such as satisfaction in providing a good service or contributing to team success. It can also be said that distance from, or lack of respect for, the customer reduces the incentive to do the right thing.

In the banking industry, remuneration too often incentivises the delivery of short-term profit. A reward structure that includes other elements, such as customer respect, would change the measure of success and thus the behaviours to achieve it. If behaviours that reflect customer respect attract rewards, then banking culture will adapt to reflect these desired behaviours.

When Bad Behaviour is Ignored it will Become Entrenched

It was common knowledge among traders and their managers that LIBOR was being manipulated. It was seen as an accepted practice, not an unethical behaviour. When behaviours became normalised it is difficult for any individual to speak out against them. It is important that this sort of behaviour is identified early on before it becomes entrenched. Corrective action can then be taken before it becomes a major issue.

In the case of LIBOR and FX, a few traders have been severely punished, notably Tom Hayes with an 11-year sentence, but senior managers have escaped: pleading ignorance of their subordinates' activities has served them well. New regulatory controls such as the UK Senior Managers' Regime should make this more difficult in future as plausible deniability becomes a less reliable defence. Making an example of a senior employee is more effective than punishing the foot soldiers.

A Few Selected Highlights from the Global Banking Story

* *Risk-management frameworks should recognise and account for the fact that different activities across the bank, and the individuals that these activities attract, have different risk profiles. What is considered an appropriate level of reporting and control in one area will need to be adjusted in another.*

- *Compliance departments should be structured and remunerated appropriately to give them the status and authority to challenge and monitor bankers effectively. Reporting lines must be clear to eliminate gaps in accountability.*
- *Incentive schemes that merely reward increased profit will allow unethical behaviours to evolve. Remuneration policies should also reward core values, such as respect for customers, employees and others.*
- *Aberrant behaviours, however minor, should be identified quickly and sanctions applied to prevent them from becoming normalised.*

Notes

1. London InterBank Offered Rate.
2. Sentencing remarks of Mr Justice Cooke: R v Tom Hayes, 3 August 2015, https://www.judiciary.gov.uk/judgments/sentencing-remarks-of-mr-justice-cooke-r-v-tom-hayes/.
3. The sentence was reduced to 11 years on appeal.
4. Slater, S. (2015) Misconduct bill tops $235 billion as banks struggle to shake off past sins, *Reuters*, 21 May 2015.
5. Ridley, K. & H. Jones (2012) A Greek Banker Spills on the Early Days of the LIBOR and His First Deal with the Shah of Iran, *Reuters*, 8 August 2012.
6. US dollar-denominated deposits held by banks outside the USA and thus exempt from Federal Reserve regulations.
7. LIBOR then changed its name to BBA LIBOR but will be referred to as LIBOR throughout this chapter.
8. Brousseau, V., A. Chailloux & A. Durré (2009) Interbank Offered Rate: Effects of the Financial Crisis on the Information Content of the Fixing, Working paper series 2009-ECO-10, *Lille Economie & Management*, 4 December 2009.
9. Deregulation of London banks in 1986.
10. Ridley, K. & H. Jones (2012) A Greek Banker Spills on the Early Days of the LIBOR and His First Deal with the Shah of Iran, *Reuters*, 8 August 2012.
11. Keenan, D. (2012) My Thwarted Attempt to Tell of LIBOR Shenanigans, *Financial Times*, 26 July 2012.

12. Hou, D. & D. Skeie (2014) *LIBOR: Origins, Economics, Crisis, Scandal and Reform*, Federal Reserve Bank of New York, March 2014.

13. Gilbert, M. (2007) Barclays Takes a Money Market Beating, *Bloomberg*, 3 September 2007.

14. Financial Services Authority (2012) *Final Notice to Barclays Bank plc*, 27 June 2012. Mass email from Barclays employee dated 28 August 2007.

15. Financial Services Authority (2012) *Final Notice to Barclays Bank plc*, 27 June 2012.

16. New York Fed Responds to Congressional Request for Information on Barclays—LIBOR Matter. 13 July 2012. Mass email from Barclays employee dated 3 October 2007.

17. Minutes of the Bank of England Sterling Money Markets Liaison Group, 3 April 2008.

18. Financial Services Authority (2012) *Final Notice to Barclays Bank plc*, 27 June 2012.

19. Financial Services Authority (2012) *Final Notice to UBS AG*, 19 December 2012.

20. Mollenkamp, C. (2008) LIBOR fog: Bankers Cast Doubt on Key Rate Amid Crisis, *Wall Street Journal*, 16 April 2008.

21. Financial Services Authority (2012) *Final Notice to UBS AG*, 19 December 2012.

22. British Bankers Association (2008) BBA LIBOR review consultation feedback statement, 5 August 2008, http://www.bbatrent.com/archive/bba-libor-review-consultation-feedback-statement accessed 21 March 2016.

23. Barclays (2012) *Supplementary information regarding Barclays settlement with the Authorities in respect of their investigation into the submission of various interbank offered rates*, https://www.home.barclays/content/dam/barclayspublic/docs/InvestorRelations/IRNewsPresentations/2012News/03-july-supplementary-information-on-libor.pdf, 3 July 2012.

24. Regulator of all providers of financial services in the UK between 2001 and 2013. In 2013 its responsibilities were divided between two new agencies: the FCA and the Prudential Regulation Authority of the Bank of England.

25. US regulatory authority.

26. Financial Services Authority (2012) *Final Notice to Royal Bank of Scotland plc*, 6 February 2013.

27. Fortado, L. & L. Noonan (2015) Tom Hayes says senior UBS staff were 'aware' of LIBOR rigging, *Financial Times*, 3 June 2015.

28. Commodities Futures Trading Commission (2015) *Order Instituting Proceedings in the matter of Deutsche Bank AG*, 23 April 2015.
29. Financial Services Authority (2012) *Final Notice to Barclays Bank plc*, 27 June 2012.
30. Financial Services Authority (2012) *Final Notice to Barclays Bank plc*, 27 June 2012.
31. Financial Conduct Authority (2013) *Final Notice to ICAP Europe Ltd*, 25 September 2013.
32. Vaughan, L. (2016) These are the brokers cleared of helping Tom Hayes rig LIBOR, *Bloomberg*, 28 January 2016.
33. Financial Conduct Authority (2013) *Final Notice to ICAP Europe Ltd*, 25 September 2013.
34. Ridley, K. (2015) Broker in LIBOR trial says would have gone from 'hero to zero' if he had favoured Hayes, *Reuters*, 17 November 2015.
35. Campbell, A. (2015) LIBOR Trial Hears of 'Bribe' Wash Trades as Lehman Failed, www.Risk.net, 12 June 2015.
36. Financial Services Authority (2012) *Final Notice to UBS AG*, 19 December 2012.
37. Bloomberg and Telegraph Staff (2015) Tom Hayes LIBOR trial: The top quotes, *The Telegraph*, 4 August 2015.
38. Ernst & Young (2015), *Audit report for the IBOR special audit*, Bundesanstalt für Finanzdienstleistungsaufsicht, 13 May 2015.
39. Wheatley, M. (2012) The Wheatley review of LIBOR: Final report, available at http://cdn.hm-treasury.gov.uk/wheatley_review_libor_finalreport_280912, September 2012.
40. Bank of International Settlements (2013) *Triennial Central Bank Survey: Foreign Exchange Turnover in April 2013, preliminary global results*, September 2013.
41. Commodities Futures Trading Commission (2014) *Order Instituting Proceedings in the case of UBS AG*, 11 November 2014.
42. NYSDFS (2015) New York State Department of Financial Services Consent Order *to Barclays Bank plc*, 20 May 2015.
43. Financial Conduct Authority (2014) *Final Notice to Citibank NA*, 11 November 2014.
44. Commodities Futures Trading Commission (2015) *Order Instituting Proceedings in the matter of Deutsche Bank AG*, 23 April 2015.

45. *Audit report for the IBOR special audit by Ernst & Young*, Bundesanstalt für Finanzdienstleistungsaufsicht, 13 May 2015.
46. Financial Conduct Authority (2015) *Final Notice to David Caplin*, 22 January 2015.
47. Luyendijk, Joris (2015) *Swimming with sharks: My journey into the world of the bankers*, (London: Guardian Books and Faber & Faber).
48. Carney, M. (2014) *Inclusive capitalism: Creating a sense of the systemic*, Speech at the Conference on Inclusive Capitalism, 27 May 2014.
49. Financial Conduct Authority (2014) *Final Notice to Martin Brokers (UK) Ltd*, 15 May 2014.
50. De Freytas-Tamura, K. (2012) How banking culture transformed over the decades, *BBC News, Business*, 5 September 2012.
51. Luyendijk, Joris (2015) *Swimming with sharks: My journey into the world of the bankers*, (London: Guardian Books and Faber & Faber).
52. Luyendijk, Joris (2015) *Swimming with sharks: My journey into the world of the bankers*, (London: Guardian Books and Faber & Faber).
53. Order to buy or sell currency at a specified exchange rate. If it is not possible to execute the order at the specified price, the order lapses.
54. JP Morgan website (2015). Client Letter Regarding Spot FX Sales and Trading Practices, 20 May 2015 https://www.jpmorgan.com/country/GB/en/disclosures/cib_special_disclosure_fx accessed 21 March 2016.
55. De Freytas-Tamura, K. (2012) How banking culture transformed over the decades, *BBC News, Business*, 5 September 2012.

5

Olympus: Management was Corrupt at Its Core

Early on 14 October 2011, Michael Woodford stood in his office at Olympus Corporation, shocked and angry. Ten minutes before he had been the President and CEO of Olympus, the Japanese camera and medical instruments manufacturer. Now, summarily dismissed by the board, he was being hustled out of the building and had been ordered to leave his apartment by the weekend.

Three months prior to this date, Woodford had been alerted to large, questionable payments relating to Olympus' acquisition activities and had spent the intervening period trying to get clarification from the Chairman, Tsuyoshi Kikukawa. He had been summoned to an extraordinary board meeting at the Olympus head office that morning to discuss 'Governance concerns relating to the company's M&A [mergers and acquisitions] activities'.[1]

Kikukawa joined the meeting late and announced that the agenda had been changed to 'the dismissal of Mr Woodford as President and CEO'.

Third Party Committee (2011) Investigation Report, p. 179, *Olympus Corporation*, 6 December 2011.

© The Author(s) 2017
A. Micklethwait, P. Dimond, *Driven to the Brink*,
DOI 10.1057/978-1-137-59053-4_5

Following a swift and unanimous show of hands, Woodford was stripped of his titles and left the meeting. He had been praised for his actions since becoming president six months earlier and his dismissal shocked the markets, especially since it is almost unprecedented in Japan to forcibly remove a company president from office unless there is gross malfeasance. Two months later, despite stalling by the board, an independent committee uncovered a $1.7 billion fraud and a management 'corrupt' at its core.[2]

> 'The core of management was corrupted.'

The committee revealed evidence of a fraudulent cover-up operation which had been going on for over two decades. The original fault—losses on derivatives trades in the 1990s—was due to errors of judgement rather than fraud. It was management's refusal to own up to, and recognise, the losses that led to the cover-up. Olympus moved the losses off-balance sheet and then, when that was no longer tenable, it made overpriced acquisitions and disguised the losses as goodwill on the acquisitions. The goodwill could be written off over a number of years without causing Olympus a huge, one-off hit to profit. This was not a story of just a few maverick employees: three successive Olympus presidents were involved in the decades-long conspiracy.

The scandal at Olympus uncovered serious corporate governance failings in both the structure and the operation of the board. A culture of deference and misplaced loyalty permitted the concealment of losses in the first place, while a supine and ill-informed board failed to live up to its responsibilities. The Japanese system of corporate governance has several long-identified weaknesses, while some Japanese cultural traits prove to be obstacles to detecting fraud.

Early Days

Olympus was launched in 1919 as a manufacturer of microscopes. It was originally named Takachiho Seisakisho after Mount Takachiho, the mythical home of Japanese gods,[3] but used 'Olympus', home of the Greek gods, as its brand name. In 1949 it was renamed Olympus Optical Co. Ltd.[4] Known to consumers primarily as a camera manufacturer, in fact Olympus' most successful business is gastrointestinal endoscopy, which has captured 70 per cent of the world market and generates 20 per cent operating margins. The camera business has been more of a rollercoaster ride: fierce competition from fellow Japanese companies has led to lower margins.

Appreciation of the Yen Led to Financial Engineering

In normal times, Olympus used its excess cash to invest in low-risk financial products, such as government bonds, and shares in companies with promising prospects. This all changed in the mid-1980s when finance ministers of the Group of Five (G5)[5] met in the Plaza Hotel in New York to discuss the recent revaluation of the US dollar. The revaluation had resulted in a large US current account deficit and pressure from US manufacturers to introduce trade restrictions on imports. The resulting Plaza Accord committed central bankers to take action to depreciate the dollar over the following two years by intervening in currency markets and by implementing fiscal and monetary stimulus packages. It was remarkably successful in its stated aim, causing the yen to appreciate by over 40 per cent against the dollar by the end of 1986, with similar effects on the currencies of the other G5 nations.

Olympus, heavily dependent on exports, suffered severely. Its operating profits fell by more than half, to ¥3.1 billion in 1986.[6] When Toshiro Shimoyama took office as President of Olympus in 1984, he had announced an ambitious expansionary strategy to grow the company's revenues to ¥1 trillion, with 60 per cent of total sales coming from new businesses. The fall in profits after 1985 put this in jeopardy. Shimoyama decided that it was impossible to improve profits sufficiently in the short term by cutting costs so, like many other Japanese companies at the time, he opted for financial engineering. The treasury group was asked to change its investment strategy and to invest in financial products with higher returns, such as bonds and futures.

After the Plaza Accord, the Japanese economy, export driven as it was, fell into recession and the government responded by cutting interest rates sharply. Japan entered an asset price bubble. Land prices soared and the Nikkei 225 share index rose from 13,000 in 1985 to nearly 39,000 in December 1989. Olympus took advantage of the bull market, buying swaps, Nikkei stock futures and derivative products. These products carried much greater risks than the staid government bonds that it was accustomed to investing in but the higher returns that they offered were irresistible.

The bubble burst in 1990 after the central bank began raising interest rates, resulting in a 35 per cent fall in the Nikkei 225 that year alone. Olympus' financial investments began haemorrhaging cash.

Hiding Losses in *Tokkin*

Olympus was reluctant to recognise its losses, hoping that the market would recover. So, like other Japanese companies at that time, it took advantage of Japanese accounting standards to keep them hidden. Prior to 2000, Japanese accounting rules permitted companies to value financial assets at either cost or market value unless the value had deteriorated substantially (more than 50 per cent). Olympus used monetary trusts (*tokkin*) to manage its financial assets.[7] The advantage of *tokkin* trusts was that assets held within the trust could be valued on an aggregated basis rather than individually. By including assets in the *tokkin* with low levels of loss, Olympus was able to keep the percentage loss of the whole *tokkin* above the 50 per cent notifiable level. This move allowed the company to avoid recognising its losses in the hope that asset prices would eventually recover.

The core group of Olympus employees who managed financial assets in the 1980s continued their involvement right through to 2011. This continuity facilitated the long-term nature of the schemes that follow. The department responsible for financial assets changed designations and position in the company structure over the years. It moved from accounting to finance, and then to management planning. However, a small coterie continued working for, or was responsible for, the department until

2011. The most significant players were Hideo Yamada, Hisashi Mori and Makota Nakatsuka, who worked together in the accounting department in the 1980s. They gradually worked their way up through the company in the various departments responsible for financial assets. Mori was appointed to the board in 2007 as director in charge of management planning. Yamada first worked in finance and accounting, and then internal audit. He became a standing statutory auditor in 2011, responsible for monitoring board activities. Nakatsuka managed several of the departments involved, eventually being appointed to the board in 2011.

There was little job rotation within finance and accounting during these years due to the perception that these were specialist roles and required years of experience. The limited rotation, combined with the Japanese custom of a job for life, resulted in few appointments of outsiders at senior levels. In turn this reduced the visibility of the finance departments.

In 1993, Shimoyama, the initiator of the financial engineering process, handed over the presidency of Olympus to Masatoshi Kishimoto but remained on the board as Chairman. Kishimoto had been head of accounting from 1987 to 1990 and was therefore well aware of the financial engineering activities. Shimoyama and Yamada together briefed Kishimoto on the extent of the financial losses when he took over. Yamada recommended that the losses be recognised in the accounts, but Kishimoto's response was, 'We will wait, because the losses will decrease if the market recovers, and we can turn things around.'[8] Kishimoto's position was that the losses must be recovered and it was up to the finance department to come up with solutions.

> 'We will wait, because the losses will decrease if the market recovers, and we can turn things around.'

So instead of cutting its losses, Olympus 'doubled up', making more and more speculative investments. In particular, it invested in derivative products that prepaid years of interest. The downside: if they showed a loss at maturity, the interest payments only added to the loss. This backfired disastrously and, by 1998, unrealised losses, still on the balance sheet, had risen to nearly ¥100 billion.[9]

In 1997, Japan revised its accounting standards for reporting on financial instruments, effective as of April 2000. As a result, KPMG, Olympus'
auditor, requested that Olympus begin to dispose of loss-making *tokkin*
and other investments in preparation for the new standard.

Tobashi: 'Flying Away'

When Yamada and Mori pondered what they should do, they must have
been reminded of the recent scandal at Yamaichi Securities. In 1997 it was
revealed that Yamaichi had used *tobashi* schemes to conceal customers'
losses of as much as ¥165 billion,[10] hiding them away in dummy companies.[11] *Tobashi*, meaning 'flying away', were schemes that allowed losses to
be hidden by transferring the assets at cost to off-balance sheet vehicles,
causing the losses to 'fly away'. The losses are shuffled around between different companies, keeping them off the parent company's books.

Over the past few years, Yamada had built up a relationship with two
brokers who worked for a Wall Street bank in Japan. One of the brokers
set up his own brokerage firm, Axes America, in the USA in 1997, and
the other followed shortly thereafter. Now, with their help, Yamada and
Mori embarked on their own *tobashi* scheme for Olympus.

Yamada asked the brokers to set up off-balance sheet funds (receiver
funds) based in the Cayman Islands and the British Virgin Islands.[12]
Olympus then set up credit facilities for the receiver funds with banks in
Liechtenstein and Singapore, backed by collateral in the form of Japanese
government bonds. The banks loaned $535 million to the receiver funds,
which then bought loss-making financial assets from Olympus at their
historical cost. The $535 million was roughly the loss on the assets
purchased.[13] Additional losses were transferred into the receiver funds
through business investment funds that Yamada and Mori set up. The
three successive presidents—Shimoyama, Kishimoto and Kikukawa—
were all fully aware of the *tobashi* scheme and received regular updates
on its progress.[14]

A problem arose during the half-year audit to September 1999 when
the auditor, KPMG, received information that a *tobashi* scheme had been
set up. KPMG had enough detailed information to persuade Yamada,

Mori and Nakatsuka to own up eventually to some part of the scheme. The auditor then demanded that Olympus cancel the transfer and return the products to the fund immediately. If not, KPMG would have to point out the illegal nature of the transaction in its audit report. The trio prevaricated but eventually the transfers were reversed and the assets were written down by ¥14 billion. KPMG had only discovered a small part of the *tobashi* schemes and although it did investigate further, it failed to spot any more.

Final Leg of Tobashi Scheme: Three Small Companies

Olympus' troubles were not yet over; it still had to repay the loans it had negotiated and gradually absorb the losses in its accounts. Yamada devised a plan to make acquisitions at inflated values, use the excess value to pay off the loans, and book this to goodwill, which could be written off over a long period. Kikukawa, who became President in 2001, had just announced a five-year plan which included a requirement for Olympus to expand into new business areas in order to escape its dependence on the endoscopy business, a strategy that fitted well with Yamada's plan.

Yamada and his advisors found three companies which they thought would suit their purpose: Altis, which disposed of and recycled medical waste; Humalabo, which sold processed food made using shiitake mushroom extract; and News Chef, which developed and sold microwave cooking containers. In a simplified form, the scheme was as follows: use unconsolidated investment funds to buy the three companies; the funds then sell shares in the three companies to Olympus, via other funds, at vastly inflated prices; funnel the proceeds back to the receiver funds which had bought Olympus' distressed assets; the receiver funds then repay their bank loan; the banks return collateral to Olympus. The difference between the final purchase price and the net book value of the three companies was booked to goodwill in Olympus' books. The structure of the scheme was extremely convoluted, which goes some way towards explaining why KPMG never uncovered it.

The acquisitions had to be approved by the board, supported by a business plan provided by Mori. Yamada talked to Kikukawa before the

'Let's move ahead based on this … If things go well, the losses will decrease by a large amount?'

meeting to say that the valuation of the three companies was rather high. Kikukawa expressed his support, saying, 'Let's move ahead based on this [...] If things go well, the losses will decrease by a large amount, won't it [sic]?'[15] A few cautious questions were posed during the meeting but Kikukawa supported the plan and the motion to purchase was passed unanimously, contingent on a third-party valuation. The valuation was done by a consultancy that Mori had used previously and was based on the business plan and financial model provided by Yamada.

A valuation based on a given financial model is essentially just a mathematical exercise—a question of applying a formula. The skill is in deciding what assumptions to use to create the model, given the actual performance of the company and its realistic prospects. As the consultancy did not challenge any of the underlying assumptions, its valuation was in the same range as Mori's, allowing the purchase to be completed soon after, in 2008. Olympus paid ¥73 billion[16] for the three companies, a dramatic jump up from the original cost of the investment (plus a capital increase) of ¥1.7 billion. In reality the companies were worthless, racking up significant losses over the following three years.

In December 2008, KPMG questioned the valuation of the three companies considering their poor performance in comparison with the business plan. The auditor requested that Olympus supply a third-party valuation but clearly did not believe it, requesting another one and eventually doing its own in-house analysis. This resulted in a ¥56 billion[17] impairment charge for that year. KPMG also wrote to the board, questioning whether or not it had adequately examined the economic rationale for the acquisitions. The members of the board of auditors, themselves non-voting members of the board, commissioned a third party to look into the issue but they were unable to find any impropriety.[18]

Gyrus Acquisition: Record-Breaking Advisory Fees

A large proportion of the losses had now been recycled back into the accounts, although as a result of the goodwill write-down required by KPMG, some of the losses had been recognised in Olympus' accounts more quickly than the conspirators had planned. Together with the fees from financial and legal advisors, the losses had increased significantly and another substantial plan had to be devised. Yamada asked Axes America to find another acquisition target. The plan was to make a large acquisition and pay a higher than normal success fee, a proportion of which would be transferred to the receiver funds in order to repay their bank loans.

Axes, commissioned to do the search, identified two possible targets, both manufacturers of medical devices. After these purchases fell through, Olympus identified another desirable acquisition, Gyrus Group plc, a UK manufacturer of endoscopes. Olympus acquired Gyrus for $1.9 billion (¥206 billion) in February 2008 at a hefty 58 per cent premium to the share price. The original agreement with Axes was for $5 million of fixed-rate fees, plus a success fee worth 0.2 per cent of the value of the target paid in cash and share options in the acquired company equivalent to 4.9 per cent of the share capital. Although the success fee originated as 1 per cent of the value of the company, its actual value would depend on how the options increased over time. Yamada and Mori came to an agreement with Axes that any increase in the value of the options would flow back to the receiver funds to recover the losses. Yamada and Mori hoped that the options would increase so substantially that the remaining losses would be wiped out.

However, Gyrus was too small a company: the success fee, based on the original criteria, would not be sufficient to cover the losses. So after discussions with Axes, the agreement was changed. For a company the size of Gyrus, the completion fee would be 5 per cent, 15 per cent of which would be paid in cash and the remainder in share options, the equivalent of 9.9 per cent of outstanding shares. The original and the final financial advisor fees were authorised by Yamada, Mori and Kikukawa without discussion or approval by the board. After the purchase was concluded, Olympus paid Axes $12 million and transferred $177 million of preferred shares to its Cayman Island company, Axam Investment Ltd (Axam), in exchange for the options it had been granted as part of its fee. The preferred shares attracted a dividend worth 85 per cent of Gyrus' after-tax income.

The time had come to activate the loss-recovery scheme. In November 2008, Mori arranged for Axam to ask Olympus to buy back the preferred shares and put a value on them of between $530 million and $590 million. Mori elaborated on the request by saying that Axam had been hit by losses related to the banking crisis and needed the cash. Olympus commissioned a securities firm to value the preferred shares, which they did on the basis of the 85 per cent dividend and came up with a valuation of $557 million.

This valuation meant that the success fee was now worth 30 per cent of the acquisition price, an extraordinarily high fee to pay compared with standard advisory fees of 1 per cent or less. Despite the high price, the board approved the transaction, concerned that if Olympus did not purchase the shares they would be bought by a third party. The board had very little time to consider the transaction. As was common with acquisition deals at Olympus, board papers relating to the purchase were only circulated on the day of the meeting and were returned by the directors the same day.[19] Executive board members of Olympus tended to focus solely on their own businesses and have only limited interest in other areas. This 'silo' thinking, combined with a limited level of financial expertise among board members, meant that a detailed and objective discussion was unlikely.

During its audit, KPMG discovered the fee and talked through its concerns with the board of auditors. Despite much discussion, KPMG's concerns were not allayed and, as a result, the board of auditors requested a third-party report on the matter. The report was completed a week later and concluded that the transaction was legal and that the board of directors had acted correctly. This was hardly an in-depth investigation, based purely on paperwork supplied by Olympus. However, it was enough to satisfy KPMG, which signed off the accounts without qualification. The auditor's only request was that Olympus cancel the resolution to buy the preferred shares. Extraordinarily, the other directors were never told of the discussions with the board of auditors and KPMG's concerns. They passed a board proposal to cancel the purchase but did not question why it was necessary.

Shortly after, in May 1999, Kikukawa announced to the stock exchange that Olympus' contract with KPMG had come to an end and that Ernst & Young ShinNihon LLC (E&Y) would be its new auditor. Kikukawa wrote to senior executives explaining that the real reason why KPMG had been replaced was because of disagreements over the goodwill impairment charge of some consolidated companies and the purchase of Gyrus.[20] Information regarding these disagreements should have been released to the stock exchange but Kikukawa wanted to avoid any awkward questioning, so it was kept secret.

With KPMG out of the way, Mori restarted the process to purchase the preferred shares. He contacted Axam and requested an e-mail stating that the dividends had not been paid. Mori knew that he needed $620 million in order to close the last of the receiver funds, and he hoped that by performing a revaluation of the preferred shares and by adding the unpaid dividend he could arrive at this figure. At the board meeting to approve the payment, it was reported that Axam claimed that the shares were worth $724 million, while Olympus thought they were worth $519 million. Mori offered a compromise amount of $620 million, an average of the two figures. Mori justified the price by saying that Axam held veto rights over some activities that were important to Gyrus and that the price included a 30 per cent control premium. After dismissing a question concerning the level of the control premium, the resolution was passed unanimously.

The final total of the success fee came to $682 million, or 36 per cent of the purchase price, while a further $12 million was paid in fees to other advisors. $670 million of the success fee was used to repay the loans used to fund the purchase of the dud assets. The final destination of the remainder of the fee is unknown. Olympus converted the preferred shares to equity, which allowed the difference between the repurchase cost of the preferred shares and their original $177 million valuation at the time of the deal to be booked to goodwill. E&Y signed off on the goodwill allocation but did query the size of the purchase, although it allowed it to pass.

> The total success fee amounted to 36 per cent of the purchase price of Gyrus.

News Crept Out

The conspirators must have breathed a sigh of relief when the Axam payment was made in March 2010 and the last of the loans repaid. So they

> 'Olympus "reckless M&A": mystery of huge losses.'

would have been horrified when Woodford raised the issue a year later. A whistleblower within Olympus had contacted *Facta*, an obscure Japanese magazine, resulting in an article claiming 'huge losses' on 'reckless M&A'.[21] A Japanese friend of Woodford sent him the piece when it was published in August 2011 and Woodford was determined to get to the bottom of it.

Woodford was an Olympus lifer who had worked his way up the ranks, culminating in his appointment as President in April 2011. He was the first *gaijin*—foreigner—to be appointed President, and one of very few foreigners heading up Japanese companies. He took office at a difficult time for the organisation. Operating profit had slumped, down from $1 billion in 2008 to around $400 million in 2011. The advance of smartphones had decimated the compact camera market. Sales at Olympus' Imaging Division had fallen by 50 per cent over the previous three years, leading to an operating loss of $175 million in 2011. To make matters worse, the Fukushima nuclear disaster in March 2011 had severely disrupted the supply chain.

Although Woodford was now president, his predecessor, Kikukawa, remained as chairman and created a new position for himself as CEO. Previously the president had acted as CEO with the chairman being a more honorary role. It seemed that Kikukawa did not want to relinquish total control although, as president, Woodford had legal responsibility for signing off the company accounts and duties of care towards shareholders. Woodford had a close relationship with Kikukawa, who had promoted him throughout his career, so he was particularly concerned that the *Facta* article seemed to point to Kikukawa's involvement.

At the first board meeting after the *Facta* article was published in July 2011, Woodford was surprised to find that no mention was made of it.

Concerned that he did not have all the facts and thinking that it was more an issue of incompetence than fraud, he made no comment himself, waiting until he had a full translation of the article. The translation disabused him of that notion. The article's sources seemed credible and it contained considerable detail of the transactions. It also mentioned that Olympus had refused to reply to *Facta*'s requests for clarification. Clearly people within Olympus were fully aware of the accusations, but apparently Kikukawa had issued a general instruction that Woodford was to be kept in the dark. No other Japanese or foreign paper had picked up on it and if Woodford's friend had not sent him a copy, he might never have discovered the scandal.

Armed with the translation of the article, Woodford demanded a meeting with Kikukawa and Mori. Kikukawa explained that he had instructed colleagues not to concern Woodford with the article because he

> 'There are life-long relationships between superiors and juniors. You often place your loyalty for the whole of your career with the person who showed you around when you first entered the company.'

'was much too busy to be bothered by domestic issues', an explanation that Woodford received with bemusement.[22] When Woodford pressed for more clarification, Kikukawa admitted that some of the article was correct but he refused to elaborate. A meeting with Mori later that day went nowhere. Exasperated, Woodford asked Mori who he worked for, expecting him to say, 'Olympus'. The response was unexpected: 'I work for Mr Kikukawa. I am loyal to Mr Kikukawa.'[23] Woodford was shocked but then realised that this was just an example of the importance of personal loyalty in Japanese culture. As Simon Wong, a visiting fellow at the London School of Economics, explained, 'There are life-long relationships between superiors and juniors. You often place your loyalty for the whole of your career with the person who showed you around when you first entered the company.'[24]

Woodford had a dilemma: as a loyal company man he did not want to do anything to damage Olympus' reputation or performance, but on the other hand he absolutely could not tolerate any kind of malfeasance. He discussed the issue with many Olympus managers. Most of them urged him to push ahead and uncover the truth. Woodford, aware of the support that Kikukawa had on the board, knew that it would be a bruising fight. However, when *Facta* published a follow-up article with more details, hinting at a connection to organised crime, Woodford knew he had to act.

He wrote a series of letters to Mori and Kikukawa, copying in other board members, demanding specific details about the transactions and explaining that, as president, he had a responsibility to understand the issues involved. Mori's replies provided little clarity, so Woodford upped the stakes, threatening to resign if he did not receive satisfactory answers. He also copied the letters to senior partners at Olympus' auditor, E&Y. Once back in Japan, he met with Kikukawa and Mori, and requested that he be given the CEO role so that he could get to the bottom of the issue. When Kikukawa claimed that the shareholders would never accept such a course of action, Woodford again threatened to resign. Later that day, Kikukawa seemingly caved in, offering Woodford the post of CEO and sole responsibility for nominating future directors, a role that Kikukawa had previously held.

At the board meeting the following day, Woodford was voted in as CEO but faced hostile questioning from his fellow board members, including criticism from a non-executive director for writing to the auditor: bringing in 'outsiders'. Woodford used his new authority to request an independent auditor, PricewaterhouseCoopers (PwC), to review the Gyrus payment. The report, when Woodford received it eight days later, gave him all the ammunition he required: PwC stressed the importance of investigating the transaction and the possibility of offences such as false accounting and breach of directors' duties. Woodford provided a copy of the report to the board, accompanying it with a copy of a letter to Kikukawa in which he requested Kikukawa's and Mori's resignation.

At the emergency board meeting the following day, Kikukawa put forward a motion to sack Woodford. The motion was passed unanimously with no discussion. Woodford was not permitted to comment or to explain his concerns. The other directors showed no desire to investigate the issue.

Having anticipated his dismissal, and spooked by the references to 'antisocial forces' (a Japanese euphemism for *Yakusa*, or organised crime) in *Facta*'s articles, Woodford contacted a journalist from *The Financial Times* and handed him all the information he had gathered before rapidly leaving the country. Meanwhile, Kikukawa gave a press conference to announce Woodford's departure, stating that he had been fired because he 'couldn't understand Japanese-style management' and

> The reason given for Woodfords' dismissal: 'he [was] causing problems for decision making.'

was 'causing problems for decision making'.[25] He also announced that he would replace Woodford as president and CEO.

The Olympus share price fell 18 per cent following the announcement, and then a further 75 per cent during the next few months as information about the scandal trickled out. Olympus put out press releases that justified its actions, but Western newspapers splashed the story over their front pages and refused to let the rumours die away. In contrast, Japanese newspapers were slow to pursue the subject, confining any comment to the back pages. Journalists were perhaps hampered by language barriers and difficulty in contacting Woodford during the first few days after he was dismissed, but they had refused to cover the story when the *Facta* journalist tried to interest them in it earlier. Japanese mainstream business media does not have a reputation for investigative journalism, depending more on a series of small scoops, such as publishing company earnings the day before they are announced, sources that could dry up if they angered the bosses. *Facta*'s editor, Shigeo Abe, speculated that the risk of libel lawsuits and worry about losing advertisers made them even more cautious.[26]

Woodford piled on the pressure, talking to the media and giving evidence to the Serious Fraud Office in London and the Federal Bureau of Investigation in New York, both of which initiated investigations. He also wrote to Japan's Securities and Exchange Surveillance Commission, asking it to investigate. Meanwhile the Olympus board was issuing misleading statements in an attempt to make the story go away: admitting to a few errors of judgement but initially stating that the cost for the Gyrus fee was only half that claimed by *Facta*. Then Olympus' Western institutional shareholders joined the fray, demanding an independent investigation into the allegations. Nippon Life issued a rare challenge, seeking 'swift measures to give sufficient accountability'. Other Japanese shareholders followed tradition by remaining silent.

'Despite one of the biggest scandals in history, Japanese institutional investors have not spoken one single word of criticism, in complete and utter contrast to overseas shareholders who demanded accountability [from] directors,' said Michael Woodford at a press conference in Tokyo

After a week of relentless demands for information, Olympus bowed to the pressure and announced that a Third Party Committee of lawyers and accountants would examine the claims. The Tokyo Stock Exchange (TSE) also urged more disclosure, and a few days later Kikukawa finally gave in and resigned his posts, taking responsibility for the fall in the share price. Board member and Olympus veteran Shuichi Takayama became president and continued to defend the acquisitions.

The composition of the Third Party Committee was announced at the beginning of November. Following pressure from the TSE and shareholders, it was composed of a bevy of independent members; five lawyers, including a former Japan Supreme Court justice; and an accountant. A week after the investigation started, nervous about where the Third Party Committee investigation was going, Mori confessed to Takayama.[27] He and Yamada were dismissed, and Takayama released the bare bones of the cover-up to the press, admitting to 'inappropriate dealings'. However, he was still adamant that Woodford's dismissal was due to his aggressive Western-style management rather than his inquiries into the acquisitions.[28]

A month later the Third Party Committee published a hard-hitting report: 'the core of management was corrupted, and the periphery was also contaminated'.[29] Losses, plus fees to advisors to keep them off the books, eventually amounted to ¥135 billion ($1.7 billion). They had been concealed for more than two decades through the connivance of 'officers [with mindsets] stunted to the extent that the management and transfer of enormous amount of funds and the incurring of enormous losses were not considered to be an issue [... with mindsets] to sail through their duties [...] without rocking the boat, whenever they sensed that there might be a problem'.[30] It recommended the replacement of all directors who were in office when the cover-up took place.

> Losses had been concealed through the connivance of 'officers [with mindsets] stunted to the extent that the management and transfer of enormous amount of funds and the incurring of enormous losses were not considered to be an issue.'

The Fallout

The report was published just in time for Olympus to restate previous years' financial statements and to file them with the TSE before the deadline, avoiding an automatic delisting. The TSE fined Olympus the maximum amount of $100,000 for false accounting. However, because it avoided a delisting, Olympus still had access to sources of equity. The Third Party Committee was unable to trace all the money to its final destinations because its terms of reference did not allow it to employ forensic accountants, but it did determine that antisocial organisations were not involved.

Kikukawa, Mori and Yamada were found guilty of fraud and given suspended sentences. Olympus filed suits against 24 existing and past executives and statutory auditors, including its president, Takayama. This was a bizarre situation resulting in the board of auditors, in whose name the complaint was issued, suing its current members and directors, who mostly remained in employment. The board of directors eventually resigned in April 2012 but two of its members were reappointed as executives, to the disappointment of some commentators. The new board had a majority of outside directors: 6 out of 11. The chairman and senior director came from Olympus' main creditors, Sumitomo Bank and the Bank of Tokyo-Mitsubishi, rather to the disappointment of shareholders, who feared undue influence from creditors, which would adversely affect their own interests. Woodford abandoned his attempt to be reinstated as CEO and sued Olympus for breach of contract, eventually settling for a reputed £10 million.

The $1.7 billion write-off left Olympus with a dangerously low equity ratio of only 4.5 per cent. Rather than risk increasing the influence of independent institutional investors, the company chose to do a deal with Sony, which bought a 10 per cent stake in Olympus in December 2012. Ripples from the scandal were felt as far afield as Singapore and the USA. One of the banks was found guilty of enabling Olympus to commit fraud, and one of its ex-employees was found guilty of wire fraud: both cases related to the transfer of funds connected with the Gyrus advisor fees. One of the Axes brokers was given a lifetime ban from operating in the financial services industry. Shareholders sued Olympus, and one group received a settlement of £50 million.

Corporate Governance Failings

The case threw a spotlight onto Japan's corporate governance system. A 2014 study by KPMG and the Association of Chartered Certified Accountants (ACCA) found that Japan's corporate governance code ranked 21st out of 25 countries surveyed, behind countries such as the Philippines and Indonesia.[31] A lack of independent directors, limited powers of the commonly used corporate auditor system and the power of the president to appoint directors were key weaknesses.

Most Japanese companies operate under the corporate auditor system where a management board is monitored by a board of corporate auditors, of which at least one member must be independent. The board of corporate auditors has a similar role to that of the board audit committee in Western-style governance systems. However, although members of the board of corporate auditors attend board meetings, they have no voting rights. Neither do they have the power to dismiss directors or the president, which leaves them in a weaker position than their Western audit committee counterparts.

In 2010, while only 48 per cent of companies listed on the Tokyo stock market had one or more independent directors, Olympus had three.[32] The effectiveness of the independent directors was limited. One outside director hardly attended any board meetings between 2005 and 2008 while another, Yasuo Hayashida, was appointed purely for his medical expertise. As he told reporters, 'I do attend board meetings but I have no idea about their content. I only provide medical advice.'[33] Effectively, the outside directors were mere window dressing.

> 'I do attend board meetings but I have no idea about their content. I only provide medical expertise.'

The president had the power to nominate all directors and corporate auditors, and to decide their compensation.[34] This took away the power of the directors to monitor the performance of the president. Unfortunately the president's prerogative to choose directors is fiercely guarded in Japan, and the government has failed to reform this matter. The patronage of a president with the power to control directors' promotion and remuneration cannot be beneficial. Combined with the Japanese culture not to question superiors, the result is a board dominated and controlled by the president. The strongest rein on the president usually comes from the chairman, normally the previous president. At Olympus, Shimoyama, president, then chairman, went a step further. When Kishimoto became chairman in 2001, he appointed himself as lifetime supreme advisor. As the chairman is the patron of the president and still holds considerable influence, the likelihood of exposing faults committed under the chairman's watch is minimal.

The Olympus board of auditors had four members, two of whom were employees, or ex-employees, and two of whom were nominally independent: one was an old classmate of Kikukawa and one was from a supplier to Olympus, and neither had experience in financial matters. In fact, since the late 1980s, only one of the standing auditors, Yamada and before that his predecessor, had any professional financial experience at all. While the board of auditors is not required merely to monitor financial affairs, the lack of financial expertise on the main board should have made it essential for most of the corporate auditors to have financial experience.

Olympus reformed its corporate governance system as a result of the scandal. It still uses the corporate auditor system but now has a majority of independent directors on the board, and it has set up nominating and compensation committees, both comprising a majority of outside directors. The board of auditors has been strengthened with the appointment of two outside corporate auditors with legal and financial expertise.

On paper, Olympus appeared to have adequate risk-management systems, but the reality was different. The corporate auditor system, the internal audit and the general attitude towards financial impropriety all had serious flaws. A risk-evaluation exercise was performed at Olympus every three years from 2004, in line with accepted practice. The exercise identified that risks such as false accounting or concealment of information could have serious effects, but, since no one believed that any manager could possibly engage in, or cover up, such activities, little was done to prevent them.

The effectiveness of the internal audit function was severely compromised by its lack of independence. Yamada was in charge of the corporate centre, supervising finance, accounting, legal, IT and human resources, in conjunction with being head of the internal audit. This dual responsibility seriously affected the independence of audits of these departments.

This failure to segregate duties was visible further down the organisation. The root cause of the scandal—gambling on financial markets—was enabled by combining front-office and middle-office functions for financial transactions which were performed within the same department.

Olympus introduced a whistleblower system in 2005 with the aim of uncovering misconduct at an early stage. It was an internal system, with employees reporting to the compliance office. Six cases a year were submitted on average, and these dwindled to virtually zero once it became known that whistleblowers would have to identify themselves before an investigation could be initiated. The compliance office and the board of auditors proposed on several occasions that whistleblowers should be able to report to an outside agency, but Yamada strongly opposed this suggestion, not without cause, and it was never implemented.

Japanese culture rewards consensus and deference to authority. A Japanese proverb, 'the nail that sticks out will be hammered', is usually taken to mean that everyone is expected to conform and follow the rules: if you are going to stand out you need to be strong because you can expect to be heavily criticised. When Woodford asked for the *Facta* claims to be investigated, none of the directors was prepared to cast a shadow of doubt over Kikukawa by raising questions. They all followed Kikukawa's lead and, until Mori confessed, refused to believe that anything was wrong.

The report into the Fukushima nuclear disaster came to a similar conclusion, putting a large part of the blame onto the 'ingrained conventions of Japanese culture; [its] reflexive obedience; [its] reluctance to question authority; [its] devotion to "sticking with the programme"'.[35] Japan's discipline has helped it to rise to a position of great wealth and technological success, but, in Olympus' case, some of these qualities contributed to its downfall.

> The Fukushima nuclear disaster was blamed on the 'ingrained conventions of Japanese culture; reflexive obedience; reluctance to question authority; devotion to "sticking with the programme"'.

There also appeared to be a feeling, at least among Kikukawa, Yamada and Mori, that although the cover-up was unfortunate, no employees were benefiting directly from it. As public exposure could only harm the company, they believed it was better to cover up the scandal. The directors had turned inwards, concerned solely with the management of the business and with little recognition of their duties towards shareholders.

Japan's Corporate Governance

The government of Shinzo Abe is determined to bring corporate governance closer in line with OECD norms. Several attempts have been made over the last 20 years to reform the commercial code and introduce independent directors. While some progress has been made, the big business lobby has blocked serious change. However, partly as a result of the Olympus scandal, a new corporate governance code was introduced in 2015, requiring public companies to have a minimum of two independent directors or explain why they do not. Much more remains to be done but this small step is encouraging.

Independence is critical for non-executive directors—they must be able to provide constructive challenge. Developing this quality will be particularly difficult in Japan's corporate culture with its reluctance to question authority and where young executives pledge lifelong allegiance to their bosses. Market discipline in Japan is too weak to challenge complacent boards due to cross-shareholdings, a dearth of shareholder activism and an acquiescent press, which all fail to hold the board to account.

A Few Selected Highlights from the Olympus Story

- *To avoid a concentration of power, the roles of chairman and CEO should be separate. Normally retiring CEOs should not step up to the chairman's role because the presence of a CEO-turned-chairman risks undermining the CEO. It can also prevent or delay the disclosure of prior mistakes or malfeasance.*

- *Whistleblowers should be able to report to an external party and the system must provide anonymity if at all possible. Informers will only speak out if they are confident that their voice will be heard and that they will receive protection.*

- *A majority of the board should be independent. Board directors should be appointed and remuneration decided on by a committee of independent directors rather than by the president/CEO.*

Notes

1. Woodford, Michael (2012) *Exposure: From President to Whistleblower at Olympus*, (London: Penguin Books).
2. Third Party Committee (2011) Investigation Report, p. 179, *Olympus Corporation*, 6 December 2011.
3. *Kami*, or spirits, worshipped in the Shinto religion.
4. In 2003 it was renamed Olympus Corporation.
5. The USA, Japan, the UK, France and Germany.

6. Third Party Committee (2011) Investigation Report, p. 8, *Olympus Corporation*, 6 December 2011.

7. A *tokkin* trust is a trust created under Japanese law in which a registered investment advisor appointed by the trustor instructs the trustee regarding the investment of the trust's assets.

8. Third Party Committee (2011) Investigation Report, p. 75, *Olympus Corporation*, 6 December 2011.

9. Nearly $900 million.

10. Nearly $1.3 billion.

11. Strom, S (1997) Big Japanese Securities Firm Falls, Putting System on Trial, *The New York Times*, 24 November 1997.

12. Third Party Committee (2011) Investigation Report, p. 15, *Olympus Corporation*, 6 December 2011.

13. Securities and Exchange Commission in the Matter of Hajime Sagawa, 27 February 2015.

14. Third Party Committee (2011) Investigation Report, p. 19, *Olympus Corporation*, 6 December 2011.

15. Third Party Committee (2011) Investigation Report, p. 76, *Olympus Corporation*, 6 December 2011.

16. More than $800 million.

17. More than $600 million.

18. Third Party Committee (2011) Investigation Report, p. 153, *Olympus Corporation*, 6 December 2011.

19. Third Party Committee (2011) Investigation Report, p. 125, *Olympus Corporation*, 6 December 2011.

20. Layne, N. & K. Ridley (2011) Exclusive: Olympus removed auditor after accounting, *Reuters*, 4 November 2011.

21. Yoshimasa, Y. (2011) Olympus 'reckless M&A': Mystery of huge losses, *Facta,* August 2011.

22. Woodford, Michael (2012) *Exposure: From President to Whistleblower at Olympus*, (London: Penguin Books).

23. Woodford, Michael (2012) *Exposure: From President to Whistleblower at Olympus*, (London: Penguin Books).

24. Gapper, J. (2015) Japan will gain from Toshiba's humiliation, *Financial Times*, 22 July 2015.

25. Woodford, Michael (2012) *Exposure: From President to Whistleblower at Olympus*, (London: Penguin Books).

26. Soble, J. (2011) Japan's timid media in the spotlight, *Financial Times*, 28 October 2011.

27. Wakabayashi, D. (2011) Live blog at Olympus press conference, *Wall Street Journal*, 8 November 2011.
28. Tabuchi, H. (2011) Olympus hid investing losses in big merger payouts, *New York Times*, 7 November 2011.
29. Third Party Committee (2011) Investigation Report, p. 179, *Olympus Corporation*, 6 December 2011.
30. Third Party Committee (2011) Investigation Report, p. 180, *Olympus Corporation*, 6 December 2011.
31. ACCA-KPMG Study. *Balancing rules and flexibility: A study of corporate governance requirements across 25 markets*, November 2014.
32. Nagata, K. (2015) New rules are pushing Japanese corporations to tap more outside directors, *Japan Times*, 27 April 2015.
33. Simms, J. (2011) Japan can learn from Olympus ills, *Wall Street Journal*, 19 November 2011.
34. The president of a Japanese company usually acts as the CEO.
35. Fukushima Nuclear Accident Independent Investigation Commission (2012) The official report of the Fukushima Nuclear Accident Independent Investigation Commission, *The National Diet of Japan*.

6

The Co-operative: CEO Resigns amid Turmoil and Calls for Reform

Euan Sutherland, Chief Executive of the Co-operative Group, resigned after a short but difficult ten months at the helm. His parting conclusion: the group was 'ungovernable'.[1] Sutherland's resignation triggered an upheaval in the structure and composition of the group board. The directors met that evening in an emergency session to discuss a much needed review of the group's governance structure.

Soon after Sutherland's departure, Lord Myners, appointed to the board as senior independent director (SID) only four months earlier, also stepped down, stating that there was too much opposition and open hostility to his presence. Originally appointed to the board to review its governance, Myners would go on to publish a comprehensive and damning review of its governance structure and a set of recommendations for change.

The Co-operative Group is a diverse holding of companies from grocery and financial services to travel and funeral services. Owned by its more than 8 million members and referred to as the Co-op, it employs more than 70,000 people and generates in excess of £9 billion in revenues. It has been a formidable competitor: at one time it held an enviable share of the UK grocery market (more than 30 per cent) and had a respectable retail banking presence. Today its future is uncertain. Its grocery share is less than

© The Author(s) 2017
A. Micklethwait, P. Dimond, *Driven to the Brink*,
DOI 10.1057/978-1-137-59053-4_6

5 per cent and it no longer owns The Co-operative Bank (Co-op Bank). There has been much value destroyed over the years.

In 2013, media stories about the Co-op Bank's 'crack smoking' Chairman, Reverend Paul Flowers, provided entertainment and amusement for the UK: 'Former chairman of the Co-op bank uses crystal meth and crack cocaine'.[2] Flowers was asked to step down earlier that same year after reporting a £700 million loss and the discovery of a £1.5 billion black hole in the accounts which led to the near collapse of the bank. Flowers' original appointment was credited to his understanding of the Co-op, and his ability to 'manage the politics' and act as a chairman. With his background as a Methodist minister and a Labour councillor, and with a mere four years' experience in banking directly after university, this appointment was not an example of meritocracy but perhaps cronyism.

The story of the Co-operative Group is about the devastating impact that an inadequate governance structure and an ill-equipped board can have. The unsuitability of many of its board members, with a lack of relevant experience and expertise, for a company of its size and complexity, is unparalleled. The board presided over a flawed strategy of growth through acquisition in its goal to become the world's largest co-operative. This pursuit placed the group under significant financial strain and, together with its unwieldly governance structure, led to an untenable situation and a cry for reform.

The Co-operative Movement has International Significance

Internationally the co-operative movement is widespread and successful. A press release from the 2014 International Co-operative Summit announced that the top 300 co-operatives globally employ over 250 million people, grew at 11.6 per cent and produced revenues of more than $2.2 trillion.[3] In the UK the movement remains an important ownership structure. In 2014 the sector was reported to be worth £37 billion a year, and growing.[4]

The co-operative movement dates back prior to the 1800s, with 1830 seeing the first gathering of the national co-operative congress and 1852 the first legislation for co-operatives being passed. Although differences exist, the central premise of a co-operative is that it is collectively owned by its members, who have a voice in setting strategy and overseeing the operation of the busi-

> 'The top 300 co-operatives globally employ over 250 million people and produce revenues in excess of \$2.2 trillion.'

ness. It is a member-owned, member-run and member-serving business. The terms 'mutual' and 'co-operative' are often used interchangeably. However, a co-operative is expected to subscribe to a statement of identity published by the International Co-operative Alliance. That statement outlines its values and principles.[5]

The Co-operative Group Dates Back to Rochdale, 1844

The Co-operative Group evolved from the Co-operative Wholesale Society (CWS), originally formed by several hundred co-operatives that joined together to benefit from wholesale services that would be made available to them through association. The CWS was owned collectively by the co-operative societies within it. It sourced products from around the world, such as manufactured textiles, biscuits and soap, and distributed them through its own shipping line. In order to secure the loyalty of retail societies and its members, it extended its reach into financial services. The CWS bank provided the funds for expansion and development, as well as insurance and legal services.

The CWS continued to evolve in response to economic and social developments. It changed from the role of a wholesaler to become a buying group, before becoming a retailer. In the 1980s, when many co-operatives began to fail, the CWS took advantage of this trend and acquired independent co-operatives. In 1997 a botched takeover attempt led to the merger of the CWS and Co-operative Retail Services, giving birth to The Co-operative Group.

Its membership widened: originally made up of co-operative societies it would expand to include individuals as members. Eventually, membership was opened up to anyone professing to share its values and principles of self-help, self-responsibility, democracy, equality, equity and solidarity. Membership within the group provided the ability to trade, to share in its profits and to have a voice in the group through a vote or an elected representative

> The values and principles of co-operatives: self-help, self-responsibility, democracy, equality, equity and solidarity.

position. In short, the Co-op was more than a commercial entity; it held community appeal and was a beacon for the social goals that it stood for.

Over time the governance structure expanded in number but its philosophy remained the same. The group remained owned by its members, organised by area committees, regional boards and a group board, and it carried on business in accordance with co-operative values and principles. The boards were elected from and represented its members. Each member director was elected by its respective region for a specified term and each individual board elected its own chairman and CEO.

The responsibility of the group board remained similar to that of a publicly listed company. It was responsible for setting strategic aims, monitoring financial and non-financial performance against leading indicators, and overseeing risk management and governance.

As mentioned, the strategy of growth through merger or acquisition was a theme present throughout the Co-op's history. However, many of these historical acquisitions were small, and the entities were similar in nature. Today there is much evidence to suggest that growth through acquisition is often unsuccessful because assets are often overvalued, synergies are not achieved and organisational cultures are hard to merge. The Co-operative Group learned this first hand in both of its significant businesses. The board oversaw a five-year period, between 2009 and 2014, when more than half of its net asset value was destroyed.

Food Retailing: Our Coverage is Incredible, with a Food Store in Every UK Postal Area[6]

Today Co-op Food is the UK's fifth largest food retailer, with a market share of only 5 per cent. Historically the Co-op had been a formidable grocer. Once the largest food retailer in the UK, it had a 30 per cent market share. However, over the years, as Tesco grew and the other large grocers maintained their share, the Co-op's was seriously eroded.

The group was desperate to reverse this trend. In 2007, the world's largest consumer co-operative was created through the merger of the Co-operative Group and United Co-operatives. After years in decline, the merger would increase the Co-op's food retail sales by almost 50 per cent; double its profit; add more than 500 outlets to its store footprint; and increase its total membership base by more than 25 per cent. This merger propelled the Co-op into the position of the largest consumer co-operative in the world and created an organisation responsible for more than 80 per cent of the co-operative retail trade in the UK.[7]

At the time of the transaction, United Co-operatives' turnover was £2.2 billion, it had an operating margin of 2.8 per cent, and its revenues were split between food retailing and a combination of travel, motor dealerships and healthcare. The new CEO of Co-op Food came from United Co-operatives, even though the food business acquired was half that of the Co-op's. Needless to say, this was a significant transaction: one that would take much internal resource, time and focus to integrate well.

As part of this union the group chairman welcomed new members to the board, including eight from United Co-operatives' board, and simultaneously announced the need for a constitutional review referring to the need to develop a 'fit for purpose' governance structure and to refresh the Co-op's values and principles. The group board had 33 directors including two retired teachers, a councillor, a photographer, a book publisher, a farmer, a university professor, a carer, two engineers, a plasterer and a lecturer. It took until June 2009 to bring the number of board directors down to 20.

And then Co-op Buys its Rival Somerfield for £1.57 Billion

Less than two years later, on the tail of the merger with United Co-operatives, the Co-operative Group went on to acquire a rival. In February 2009 it bought Somerfield, paying £1.57 billion to a consortium of private equity firms. At the time of the acquisition, the research analyst, TNS, indicated that the Co-op had a 4.2 per cent share of the

UK market while Somerfield had 3.7 per cent, so the combined market share was just short of 8 per cent.

Peter Marks, the Group CEO, suggested that it was a transformational deal and that the acquisition would provide rocket fuel for the group's growth plans. He believed that the acquisition would help to double the organisation's profits over three years.

Some suggested that this would secure Co-op Food a position in the 'big league' even though it still trailed the four largest food retailers significantly: Tesco led the pack with a 31 per cent market share.[8] Although the price paid may have been reasonable at the time, considerably below the £2.2 billion that the consortium had originally asked for, and it provided scale for the group, the acquisition was not aligned with the strategy that Co-op Food had continued to espouse: a focus on local community convenience formats. Somerfield had a footprint of 880 supermarkets, a model that Co-op Food was not pursuing.

In March 2009 the Co-op welcomed Somerfield's colleagues and customers to the mix. The integration was estimated to take two years to complete and lead to the doubling of food profit within three years, but this was not to be. In less than two years the Co-op Group board had approved two very significant food retail acquisitions.

The board should have had long and difficult discussions considering the strain that transactions of this size would have on the business; the resources and skills it would require to manage the integration and gain any synergies available; and the impact it would have on the culture given the large number of employees impacted. Yet this board was unwieldly, with 33 members but few with the relevant experience and knowledge to contribute to such a discussion.

The financial year 2011 suffered a 20 per cent drop in underlying profit of the food retailing business, the reasons cited were pricing pressure and investment in the business. In 2012, three years after the acquisition of Somerfield, instead of the profits doubling, those for food retailing were merely flat compared with 2009. The Co-op Food business struggled with the integration and suffered significant damage to its brand. The number of customer complaints soared, citing rudeness, poor staff attitude, overcharging and food safety concerns.

Its acquisition issues continued, and in 2013 the food business wrote off £226 million of goodwill on the purchase of Somerfield. Along with this, during 2013 the Co-op brand was hit by the scandal in its associated business, concerning the bank's chairman, Paul Flowers. Yet the push for excessive growth continued. The CEO for the food business acknowledged the damage to the brand but said that the Co-op was recovering. His ambition was to expand and double its estate of 2,000 convenience stores over the following five years.[9]

In Paul Myners' *Report of the Independent Governance Review*, the Somerfield acquisition was referred to in a statement that accused the group board of spending too much time on transactions such as Somerfield, which had destroyed value. In an earlier interview, Myners spoke about the Co-op's careless pursuit of growth, stating that it was undermined by reckless deal-making and shocking levels of debt.[10]

The Co-op Bank: Focused on Future Growth,
financial statement cover, 2010

The other primary segment for the Co-operative Group was financial services and its bank. However, in 2013 the Co-op Bank lost its status as a mutual. Today, the Co-operative Group owns only 20 per cent of the bank; hedge funds own the balance.

> 'The Co-operative Bank, good with money'.
> 'We are a bank famous for our ethical stance and our standards of customer service.'

The series of events which led to this outcome began in 2008. The Co-op Bank was a complex organisation: it had an ambitious growth agenda but lacked the necessary strength in governance and leadership to navigate through the challenging times.

The 2008 annual report indicated good progress at both the group and the bank level. It outlined a very respectable 15 per cent increase in group revenues, exceeding £10 billion for the first time, and the completion of a constitutional review, resulting in what it believed would be a governance structure that would provide greater scrutiny. The tag line on the cover of the bank's 2008 annual report was 'The Co-operative Bank, good with money'. The CEO announced that great progress had been made towards a vision of the UK's most admired financial services business with an emphasis on customers, colleagues and social responsibility.

At the same time, the Chairman, Bob Boulton, introduced a board-approved proposal to merge with the Britannia Building Society. On paper there was much to be positive about: adding value to the community was a core principle, and growth initiatives appeared to be moving well.

The group announced 2009 as a historic year: gross sales increased by 30 per cent to more than £13 billion with profits up 20 per cent.[11] Financial services accounted for 15 per cent of the revenues and more than 35 per cent of the operating profits. In August of that year the merger with Britannia Building Society was agreed. This brought together, for the first time, a co-operative and a mutual society, both organisations owned by their members.

The marriage was thought to be sound because the two were successful member-run businesses with complementary customer-centred values.[12] The combined entity produced a solid performance, contributing 25 per cent of the group's operating profit, primarily through corporate banking. The retail side produced only a small loss but maintained the capital ratio that it required.

It later emerged, in a report commissioned by the Co-op, referred to as the Kelly Report, that the acquisition of Britannia was a significant contributor to the downfall of the Co-op Bank. Britannia was the UK's second-largest building society. It had moved beyond conventional residential mortgages and more than half of its lending was commercial real estate loans. Although Britannia was attractive because of its personal customers and retail branches, its commercial real estate book was outside the Co-op Bank's knowledge, experience and risk appetite.[13] A report by the House of Commons Treasury Select Committee claimed that the acquisition was improperly scrutinised by KPMG, the group's auditor, and by the bank itself.[14]

After the acquisition, Neville Richardson was given the role of CEO of the combined entity. He had come across from Britannia but had no prior banking experience and had never worked for the Co-op. Bob Burlton remained Chairman of the bank until the following year, when after a six-year term he stepped down. In April 2010, Paul Flowers was appointed Chairman of the bank and a Deputy Chairman of the group. Flowers was not an obvious choice: a Methodist minister with no real banking experience overseeing the bank during a time when the impact of the banking crisis and the global recession was still being felt. So neither the CEO nor the chairman of the bank had relevant experience or expertise.

Flowers' experience would be scrutinised, but only years later. During its review, the Treasury Select Committee asked Flowers whether there was anything in his background to qualify him for a job at the Co-op Bank. It would later report that

> The deficient composition of Co-op Bank's governance was embodied in Paul Flowers, who lacked any of the requisite financial services experience to act as Chairman of a bank. Mr Flowers lacked both the desirable experience and the minimum essential skills. He should not have been put forward for the role. The Co-op should not have selected him. The regulator should not have permitted his appointment.[15]

'The deficient composition of Co-op Bank's governance was embodied in Paul Flowers, who lacked any of the requisite financial services experience to act as a Chairman of a bank.'

The bank produced strong operating results for 2010 from its corporate banking and market group. However, its retail/personal banking results showed an operating loss of £3.2 million after an impairment charge of approximately £64 million. This was cited as a 'considerably improved position'.

The unravelling of the Co-op Bank began in 2011. In August of that year the bank was named the frontrunner in a bid to acquire Lloyds' bank branches. Lloyds, as a condition of its rescue package in the banking crisis, was required to sell 632 of its branches. Although its retail banking division had recently posted significant impairment charges and the regulator warned against it, the Co-op was keen to acquire these assets.

Following this news, the bank's CEO, Richardson, stepped down amid speculation that he was not in favour of the bid. He left with a package estimated to be £4.6 million, including £1.3 million for loss of office. His replacement was Barry Tootell, a fellow chartered accountant, a long time 'Co-oper' and the former CFO. For Flowers it was a good appointment: no obvious opposition to the growth strategy already set in motion, and someone who knew the group and was a strong supporter of the merger with Britannia. Although the loss of Richardson slowed the progress of the bid with the regulators, six months later it had received approval from the Lloyds' board.

During the same year the financial statements indicated a strong balance sheet but a year-on-year decline in operating profits before significant items. A provision of £90 million for mis-selling payment protection insurance (PPI) was booked, accompanied by an apology from Flowers and a promise to do better. PPI was an industry-wide issue that the regulator had prioritised to resolve.

PPI had been sold to individuals alongside mortgages, loans and credit cards. The policies were intended to pay interest charges if earnings were stopped due to illness or loss of employment. However, as the regulators later determined, only a small percentage of the insurance premiums was paid out to claimants. Many of the policies had been sold to people who could never benefit, so the balance was essentially profit to the banks. Consequently the banks were encouraging employees to aggressively sell this insurance product. Although Flowers had reassured the Co-op Bank's members that claims would be fairly handled, the bank was later fined more than £100,000 for not progressing claims in a timely fashion: the Co-op Bank had unfairly put on hold more than 1,600 complaints the same year.[16]

The cover of 2012's *Financial Statements* no longer claimed 'The Co-operative, Good with money' but instead 'The Co-operative, Here for you for life'. The chairman's statement opened with: 'I should start by saying that we recognise our reported loss for 2012 is disappointing.'[17] The loss that Paul Flowers was referring to was £642 million—more than disappointing by any standards. Year on year, income was down by 6 per cent while costs were up by 4 per cent. Write-offs, including provisions and losses, were greater than £800 million.

> 'I should start by saying that we recognise our reported loss for 2012 [£642 million] is disappointing.'

Tootell, the Co-op Bank's CEO, went on to point out that non-core activities, primarily from the Britannia business which was acquired in 2009, comprised the majority of the impairment risk. Apparently it was Britannia and non-core assets to blame, assets defined as disposable—areas that would not be pursued. Yet the Co-op had purchased these assets just three years earlier. The group accounts announced that Peter Marks would be stepping down and that Euan Sutherland would be taking the group CEO role, joining in May of the following year.

In April 2012, the FSA notified the group that it was not allowed to purchase the Lloyds' branches—it did not have enough capital. However, less than three months later, in July 2012, the heads of terms—a summary of terms that would define the deal—were confirmed. This happened amid some speculation that political pressure was being applied to encourage the group to proceed: the Chancellor, George Osborne was quoted as saying, 'the deal would help create a new banking system that gave real choice to customers'.[18] The government was keen to create competition for big banks. However, the deal was not to close. After the Co-op Bank disclosed its losses for 2012, it would prepare to sell a number of its non-core businesses—life assurance, asset management and general insurance—to help its cash-flow position.

A Disastrous Year, 2013

In April 2013, almost two years after its initial bid for Lloyds' branches, the Co-op Bank withdrew its offer. It was not financially able to pursue the bid. That May, Moody's downgraded the Co-op Bank's credit rating six ranks with an explanation: in Moody's assessment the Co-op

Bank faced risk of further substantial losses; it had made insufficient provisions against its lending portfolio; and the bank had been too slow to realise merger revenue and cost benefits which affected its earnings potential.[19]

The Co-op Bank then discovered a black hole on its balance sheet to the tune of £1.5 billion. Regrettably a recapitalisation was required. The global financial crisis had prompted the regulator to increase the quantity and quality of capital requirements of banks. Between 2009 and January 2013 the Co-op Bank's capital requirements increased from £1.9 billion to £3.4 billion. The timing of this increase coincided with impairment charges resulting from the write-down of Britannia's commercial real estate portfolio, a failed IT project and significant provisions required for the mis-selling of PPI.[20] The group, including the bank, experienced a significant shake-up. In June the Treasury Select Committee launched an inquiry into the collapse of the Co-op's bid and Paul Flowers stepped down as Chairman. News of Flowers' indiscretions—buying illicit drugs and picking up young men—began to fill the media.

The Group Experiences a Significant Shake-Up

In April 2013, Euan Sutherland joined as Group CEO in place of Peter Marks, and the bank's CEO, Barry Tootell, was also replaced. The bank, near collapse, required an injection of funds from institutional investors to remain operating. Effectively it would no longer be owned by the Co-operative Group or be considered a mutual as hedge funds moved in to keep it afloat. The first recapitalisation would reduce the group's ownership to 30 per cent and then to 20 per cent.

> 'Former chairman of the Co-op bank uses crystal meth and crack cocaine.'

Sutherland's challenge was to put the group back together amid the turmoil. The key events are listed below:

August 2013: Co-op Bank announced its largest loss in history: £700 million

October 2013: The Bank of England launched an inquiry into the circumstances leading to the discovery of the £1.5 billion black hole

November 2013: *The Mail on Sunday* published video footage of Paul Flowers, allegedly spending £300 on cocaine and boasting about his use of illegal drugs;[21] and Len Wardle, Group Chairman, offered his resignation with deep regret that he had led the board that had approved the appointment of Flowers

December 2013: At last some good news: Lord Myners was appointed to the group board as the SID and to chair a governance review; shortly after, the terms of reference for an independent governance review were announced.

Less than nine months after he joined, in March 2014, Sutherland resigned, declaring the group 'ungovernable'. In the annual report released shortly after, Richard Pennycock, the interim CEO,

> 'Today's results [...] also highlight fundamental failings in management and governance at the group over many years.'

stated, '2013 was a disastrous year for the Co-operative Group, the worst in our 150-year history. Today's results demonstrate that but they also highlight fundamental failings in management and governance at the group over many years.'[22] The statutory comprehensive loss of the bank, including discontinued operations, was £2.5 billion.

The unravelling of the Co-op Bank began in 2011, not long after Paul Flowers was appointed as Chairman. Was his lack of banking experience and questionable character responsible for the bank's demise, or were the boards of both the group and the bank ultimately responsible? Wardle, the Group Chairman, certainly felt that he bore significant responsibility when he stepped down.

The Co-op Bank under the Microscope

The group commissioned a number of reports, one of which was an independent review of the events leading to the Co-op Bank's capital shortfall. Sir Christopher Kelly delivered *Failings in Management and Governance* in April 2014. The report starts with a quote picked up by *The Financial Times*: 'the cost of mismanagement at the lender has finally washed ashore … the bank needs £1.5 bn to stay in business.' Kelly went on to say that the state of the firm was a sorry story of failings in management and governance at so many levels.

The conclusion of the report was that a number of factors had caused the capital shortfall, including a governance structure which led to serious failures in the oversight of the group's board. It referenced the way

> 'the cost of mismanagement at the lender has finally washed ashore … the bank needs £1.5bn to stay in business'

in which board directors were nominated, a democratic process of election, but acknowledged that this could still exist and be compatible with the election of duly qualified and experienced directors. However, in this instance the system had failed, letting the members down when unqualified and inexperienced individuals were elected to positions beyond their competence.

Kelly did not criticise co-operative ideals or the model but rather the method of governance adopted by the Co-op Bank and the group. His list of root causes for the crisis included the merger with Britannia in 2009; fundamental weaknesses in the governance and management of risk; material capability gaps leading to a serious mismatch between aspirations and the ability to deliver; and a flawed culture.

A commission led by the Financial Conduct Authority (FCA) would later conclude that at the time of the bid for the Lloyds bank branches, investors were misled and growth was pursued at the expense of financial stability. It listed a number of failings, and at the top was the duration and seriousness of risk management and control deficiencies. It quoted a lack of openness with the regulators as well as an overall lack of transparency and insufficient communication with the board, the investors and the regulators. Specifically, there were management and control failings, a lack of communication regarding the changes in senior management between April 2012 and May 2013, plus false and misleading claims. In 2012 the Co-op Bank had said that it had enough capital to pursue its growth agenda when it did not. It had gone on to report an approximate loss of £700 million, including a £474 million write-off of bad debts.

The commission did not stop there. It cited a culture of short-term gain, with unjustified optimism about bad debts and a failure of management to notify the board when the deal with Britannia was jeopardised. The Co-op Banks's capital had deteriorated to a point which would have given the bank an opportunity to back out of the deal. However, with all these failings in the pursuit of growth, the Co-op, whose vision it was to be the UK's most admired financial services business, was now owned by US hedge funds.

In both of its major businesses—food retailing and financial services—the Co-operative Group had pursued growth through acquisition at its peril. It did not have the necessary skills, experience or leadership in its executive team or at board level to support the transactions that it had entered into. The Co-operative Group was dubbed 'ungovernable' by its departing chief executive and described by Lord Myners as being run by a 'failed' and underqualified board that took 'breathtakingly value-destructive' decisions'.[23]

Independent Review of Governance, May 2014

The *Report of the Independent Review of Governance*, written by Lord Myners and published in May 2014, was commissioned by the Co-operative board and was to be a comprehensive review of the group's governance. Myners' intent was to be 'for-

> 'The Co-operative Group, which was dubbed "ungovernable" by its departing chief executive, has been run by a "failed" and underqualified board that took "breathtakingly value-destructive" decisions.'

ward thinking and provide the Group with a robust governance framework to replace the [then] current flawed system'. Its primary emphasis was the effectiveness of the group board. The resulting report outlined a recommended reform of the board and of the entire electoral system.

Principle among the findings and recommendations was the need for a competent board with individuals who have the necessary skills and experience to understand fully the scope of their duties. The report stated, 'It is the directors who are accountable to the entire membership for discharging their responsibilities with proper care, with skill and with serious effort. Their competence in providing constructive challenge, guidance and support to the Executive team is the essential foundation for future success. But such competence has been sorely lacking.'[24]

Myners also challenged the board structure and the number of board directors. The proposal recommended a structure with fewer appointments, and that those appointments made should be done to fill skill gaps. This is the current accepted practice for boards of publicly traded companies and is in line

> 'Radical decisions on governance structure need to be taken very soon—and with resolution—if the Co-op, as my mother knew it, is to be saved.' Paul Myners, *The Independent Review of Governance*, May 2014

with research conducted by Co-operative UK on successful co-ops around the world.

The author of the research, Professor Johnston Birchall, said,

> The participative model of the co-operative governance does work at scale, and governance in co-operatives worldwide is as good if not better, than anything we find in the plc realms. The structure and composition of the board also affects its ability to operate professionally with collective responsibility, a responsibility that is necessary for effective board governance and the assurance of mutual trust.

Myners' findings indicated that the board did not act professionally nor in accordance with its own code of conduct. He referenced the damaging impact of leaks of confidential information.

Finally, Myners' report refers to the need for appropriate regulatory regimes, particularly for co-operatives that have reached the size and complexity of the Co-operative Group. It questions whether the FCA might wish to conduct its own investigation. The FCA did go on to undertake a full investigation, releasing its results in 2015.

In summary, Myners' report suggests that a co-operative model can, and has, produced superior results: it does not advocate the adoption of a public limited company model. However, it emphasises that these results need to be earned on an ongoing basis with a focus on the customer, and a compelling strategy supported by tightly disciplined financial management and overseen by a governance structure that works. Furthermore, not only does the board need to possess the appropriate skills and experience but it needs to be committed to co-operative values. In the highly competitive markets where the Co-op operates, such as food, this is a prerequisite for success.

The report goes further and suggests that if the elected members do not have the appetite or discipline to undertake the necessary reform, they should consider selling the businesses and forming a tax-exempt charity foundation that would fund the group's social purpose. Indeed, 'If the Group cannot govern its businesses to the same standard as those with whom it competes, it would make more sense to put these businesses into the ownership of others who could more effectively create value than it is able itself to achieve.'[25]

The Co-operative Group: Here for You for Life?

The Co-operative Group is an example of a purpose-led organisation which over time found that its values and principles had become diluted. Individuals, indeed the leadership, with reference to the board and a handful of executives, had a sense of misplaced entitlement and self-interest, placing their personal gain ahead of the interests of the members as a whole. The governance structure and the inexperience of the board directors and senior executives had a pivotal role in the value destruction of the group.

Today, after being under the microscope with a series of reviews which were commissioned by the business, as well as the Treasury Select Committee, the FCA and the Financial Stability Board (FSB), the structure, governance and leadership have undergone significant reform and modernisation. The result is a much stronger, 'fit for purpose' organisation that is formidable by the standards of the very competitive markets in which it operates.

The interim CEO, Pennycock, assumed the full-time position and the group's first independent chairman was appointed in February 2015. Both individuals are veterans of the food industry with successful track records. The entire board has been reconstituted. At the time of writing it has nine directors—five are independent, three are member nominated and only one, the group CEO, is an executive board director. The member-nominated directors are required to have the relevant business experience to understand a complex organisation and the challenges faced by the Co-operative Group's various business interests. The results for 2014 announced a three-year recovery programme with a new statement of purpose: 'Championing a better way of doing business for you and your communities'.

The fact remains that the Co-op operates in one of the toughest industries in the UK. Food retailing is undergoing significant change, driven by consumer choice and delivered by retailers who are recognised to be some of the best in the UK, if not the world. As is the case with many industries, the rate of change and disruption is unrelenting. Consumer channels are rapidly evolving, with new store formats, sizes, locations and offerings. Margins are slim, with pricing pressures created by new entrants, such as the likes of Lidl and Aldi. Success requires a forward view, agility, and a unique and deep understanding of customer needs. There is no room for the weak of heart. Today the Co-operative Group is again a purpose-driven organisation, with community and customers at its core and what appears to be the necessary skills and experience governing it.

A Few Selected Highlights from the Co-operative Group Story

* *A SID is a necessary role on the board to prevent a concentration of power. It provides a sounding board for the chairman, and a conduit for other directors and shareholders to express sensitive concerns.*

- *Ideally the board should be made up of a majority of independent directors. Collectively it should have a broad range of experience and expertise to guide and oversee the long-term health of the company.*

- *Risk management is the responsibility of all directors. Every director needs to have sufficient knowledge and understanding of a company's risks to contribute to a robust framework and ensure that it is in place to manage these risks.*

Notes

1. Goff, S. (2014) 'Co-op's Euan Sutherland resigns amid turmoil and calls for reform, *Financial Times*, 11 March 2014.
2. Dixon, H. & H. Wilson (2013) 'Former Chairman of the Co-op Bank uses crystal meth and crack cocaine.' *The Telegraph*, 17 November 2013.
3. Press Release (2014) International Co-operative Alliance, 10 October 2014.
4. The Telegraph (2015) 'John Lewis is UK's biggest mutual after Co-op falls from top spot', *The Telegraph*, 24 June 2015.
5. www.parliament.uk, publication and records, co-operative models.
6. The Co-operative Group, Annual Report, 2010.
7. *BBC News* (2007) 'Top UK co-ops agree merger terms', *BBC News*, 17 February 2007.
8. *BBC News* (2008) 'Co-op buys Somerfield for £1.57 bn', *BBC News*, 16 July 2008.
9. Felsted, A. (2014) 'Co-op to double its 2000 convenience store base', *Financial Times*, 5 March 2014.
10. Farrell, S. & J. Treanor (2014) Extent of Co-op Shambles laid bare by Lord Myners, *The Guardian*, 14 March 2014.
11. The Co-operative Group, Annual Report and Accounts 2009.
12. The Co-operative Bank, Financial Statements 2009.
13. Sir Christopher Kelly (2014) *Failings in Management and Governance: Report of the Independent review into the events leading to the Co-operative Bank's capital shortfall*, 30 April 2014, paragraph 2.13.
14. Titcomb, J. (2014) Treasury Committee conclusion on year-long inquiry, *The Telegraph*, October 2014.
15. House of Commons Treasury Select Committee Report.

16. The Telegraph (2013) 'Co-op Bank to close 37 branches and lose Britannia name', *The Telegraph*, 24 January 2013.
17. The Co-operative Bank PLC, Financial Statement, 2012.
18. *BBC News* (2012) 'Co-op to buy 632 Lloyds bank branches', *BBC News*, 19 July 2012.
19. Moody's Investor Services, Global Credit Research, 9 May 2013.
20. Sir Christopher Kelly, *Report of the Independent review into the events leading to the Co-operative Bank's capital shortfall*, 30 April 2014, paragraph 2.9.
21. *BBC NewsBBC*, (2014) 'Timeline: Flowers, Labour and the Co-op', *BBC NewsBBC*, 07 May 2014.
22. The Co-operative Group, Annual Report, January 2014.
23. Bounds, A. (2014) Myners Proposes Co-op board shakeup, *The Financial Times*, 14 March 2014.
24. Myners, P. (2014) *The Co-operative Group, Report of the Independent Governance Review*, May 2014, p. 7.
25. Myners, P. (2014) *The Co-operative Group, Report of the Independent Governance Review*, May 2014, p. 98.

7

Kids Company: Passion Overruled Reason

It was July 2015 and panic was mounting at the offices of Kids Company, the charity for vulnerable children, because there was not enough cash to pay salaries that month. Within a few days, management heaved a collective sigh of relief as a long-negotiated £3 million grant from central government arrived and the wages were paid. But just hours later allegations of child abuse at Kids Company were handed to the BBC, which set off an investigation by the Metropolitan Police. Donors withdrew their support. The charity was forced to close as tearful children gathered outside the drop-in centres and staff distributed whatever food and goods were left.

The charity, led by its colourful and charismatic CEO, Camila Batmanghelidjh, had always operated hand to mouth, without reserves to cope with emergencies. The trustees and CFO had tried to persuade Batmanghelidjh to build reserves, but her response was that the children came first. As soon as donations came in, they were spent. Allegations had surfaced over the preceding few months accusing the charity of financial mismanagement: adults as well as children were attracting help;

© The Author(s) 2017
A. Micklethwait, P. Dimond, *Driven to the Brink*,
DOI 10.1057/978-1-137-59053-4_7

cash payments were made on a weekly basis to its clients; and many fewer children had been helped than had previously been claimed. Statutory accounts and reports had been published on a regular basis, and trustees met almost monthly to discuss issues as they arose. However, ultimately the trustees failed to ensure that the charity was being run on a sustainable basis or could survive an extraneous shock, such as severe damage to its reputation.

Although Kids Company is a story about a charity and its board of trustees, it should be read bearing in mind that the duties of trustees are similar to those of company directors. The Charity Commission, the UK's statutory body which regulates and oversees all UK charities, clearly lays out the duties of trustees: acting in the charity's best interests; managing the charity's resources responsibly; and complying with the charity's governing document and the law.[1] The board of trustees is also responsible for setting the strategy of the charity within certain constraints, such as funding. Similar to our other examples, Kids Company is an illustration of inadequate corporate governance and poor risk management.

The Charismatic Founder and CEO

Camilla Batmanghelidjh, born in Tehran into a wealthy professional family, was sent to boarding school in England at the age of 11. After the Iranian Revolution, having been misled to believe that her father had been executed by the revolutionaries, she received political asylum in the UK. Batmanghelidjh studied theatre and dramatic arts at university and later was reunited with her father, who had managed to escape Iran. Interested in psychiatry, she then studied for a masters degree in the psychology and therapy of counselling at a private college. Both during and after studying for her masters, Batmanghelidjh provided therapeutic support for abused and troubled children, and worked as a psychotherapist at a family support unit (FSU) in Camberwell, South London. While working at the FSU, Batmanghelidjh initiated a project called The Place to Be, a counselling service for troubled children within primary schools. An admirer of the project, who was also a trained counsellor and impressed with the idea of providing counselling to children at an early age, established The Place to Be[2] as a charity, taking over the project that Batmanghelidjh had set up. Batmanghelidjh worked for the charity until she resigned in 1995.

The Foundation of Kids Company: Meeting an Urgent Need

In 1996, Batmanghelidjh founded Kids Company, a charity registered under the name of Keeping Kids Company and based under the railway arches in Camberwell, a south

> Large numbers of the most vulnerable and challenging young people are currently falling through the gaps in the statutory system.

London suburb. The project's original target was children under the age of 11 who needed a place to go after school and during the holidays. It was meant to be a sanctuary from their often chaotic home lives where they could receive practical, emotional and educational support. However, within weeks it was invaded by groups of local youths intent on destruction. The charity found it impossible to turn these young people away. It was evident that they too desperately needed help, so the target was raised to include young adults up to the age of 23.

Kids Company outlined the need it saw:

> Large numbers of the most vulnerable and challenging young people are currently falling through the gaps in the statutory system. These young people have generally suffered abuse, been out of education for many years, have complex emotional and social difficulties, exhibit extremely challenging anti-social and offending behaviour. They are very difficult to reach and to support effectively because they are often 'lost' by statutory agencies, they do not have a competent and responsible carer to seek help on their behalf, their behaviour cannot be managed by most institutions and they require coordinated multi-agency support at great cost to society and the state.[3]

Many of the children referred to above were troubled and vulnerable youngsters who suffered from mental health problems that are often neither diagnosed nor treated. A study undertaken in 2004 found that one in ten children and young people aged 5–16 had a clinically diagnosed mental disorder, and the incidence of mental disorders rose to 16 per cent in low-income families.[4] This comprehensive study followed another conducted in 1999, which showed very similar results.

Kids Company picked up the slack when local authorities failed to address the needs, including the mental health, of the children in their boroughs. The aim of Kids Company was to provide compassionate companionship. It did this through counselling, therapy and general support for all children and young adults who came to the drop-in centres. When children first arrived they were assessed to determine their needs and given what was deemed to be appropriate help. Kids Company liaised with local authorities; provided specialist therapeutic services for children with complex issues; or referred them to NHS[5] psychiatrists where appropriate. The charity also provided an on-site therapist in schools to allow the attending children to self-refer and receive help. Schools normally made a contribution towards this provision.

As word spread, demand grew and more drop-in centres were opened. Eventually there were 12 spread over three inner London boroughs and Bristol. The schools programme also grew until, on the date when the charity closed, it was present in 34 schools across three London boroughs. Kids Company also expanded its provision to include services such as educational activities; hot meals; holiday outings; Christmas parties; food and travel vouchers; and home visits.

It became obvious from the children's accounts that, in many cases, parents or carers were a significant part of the problem that these youths were facing. The charity began to provide support to parents, sometimes including financial support, and renovations where the home environment was considered unsafe. The 2013 annual report

'We function as substitute parental carers for children who have been devastated by poverty.'

stated, 'We function as substitute parental carers for children who have been devastated by poverty and/or maltreatment. For some children our role is to strengthen their parents so that they can care for their children as they would like to. For others we supplement the care and, sadly, for too many we are substitute parents.'[6]

With the onset of the recession in 2008, local authority budgets were cut, placing additional pressure on social services. At the same time, the demand for local authority children's services was increasing. Nationally, between March 2010 and March 2014, the number of referrals rose by 9 per cent; the number of child-protection enquiries by 60 per cent; the number of children subject to a child-protection plan by 24 per cent; and the number of children in need by 6 per cent, rising to almost 400,000.[7]

An increasing number of children 'without status' began turning up at the drop-in centres. They were from families who had not yet applied for refugee status or had exhausted all avenues to achieve it. With a demand-led ethos, no child was turned away and the charity's finances came under increasing pressure. In 2013, Kids Company opened its first centre in Bristol in an attempt to replicate its model outside London, but this only added to management and financial burdens.

Precarious Funding: Ten Days of Reserves

Kids Company lived a hand-to-mouth existence for most of its 19 years. Cash was spent as soon as it became available, with little attempt to set aside reserves. At the end of 2013, its last year of published accounts, Kids Company's free reserves were only £434,000, a mere ten days' worth of expenditure.

> At the end of 2013, Kids Company's reserves were a mere ten days' worth of expenditure.

Charities should maintain reserves for unexpected costs or falling donations. Although the Charity Commission does not issue specific recommendations as to the amount that should be set aside, it does provide detailed guidance on the factors that a charity should consider when setting its reserves policy. A charity is required to publish its reserves policy in its annual accounts.

A 2012 report on the voluntary sector found that in 2009/2010, operating[8] charities held an average of 7.4 months of free reserves, but 42 per cent of them held no reserves at all.[9] The average level of free reserves for social services and youth clubs was 6.7 months and 5.5 months, respectively. In his evidence to the parliamentary enquiry into the collapse of Kids Company, the partner of the charity's auditor, Kingston Smith, suggested that, given its size and operating model, the charity should have had reserves of around six months of operating expenses.[10] That would have amounted to £8 million at the end of 2013, a far cry from the mere £434,000 of free reserves it actually held.

Kids Company rarely held free reserves of more than a few weeks' worth of running costs. Indeed, it was in deficit during 2010 and 2011. Until 2010, Kids Company aspired to accumulate three to six months of reserves but it never came close to this target.[11] Although the subject of reserves was frequently discussed at trustee meetings, the charity's business model was to spend money according to need. It was also concerned that donors would be reluctant to give if they thought that Kids Company had a cushion of cash. From 2011 it restated its reserves policy to say that it would only build reserves when circumstances allowed. As the charity was demand-led and growing every year, money flowed out as soon as it was available. Little attempt was made to reduce expenditure or build reserves. This proved to be a significant failing of the board of trustees.

Funding: Donations and Government Grants

For the first few years after it was founded, Kids Company relied on donations from individuals and charitable trusts, surviving on around £1.5 million per year. It first gained national recognition in the early 2000s when it attracted interest and donations from Comic Relief and £50,000 from the Big Lottery Fund.[12] In 2002, when it was on the verge of collapse, the government stepped in with a £300,000 rescue package. The following year, Alan Yentob, Creative Director at the BBC, who had been involved with Kids Company since 1997, interceded with the Treasury concerning a £690,000 outstanding tax bill for unpaid employee taxes. The tax office was persuaded to forgive £590,000 of the debt and the remaining £100,000 was settled by a donor. Yentob became the Chairman of Kids Company's board of trustees shortly after. Over the next 13 years, Kids Company received more than £41 million from central government funding and a further £4 million from local government and the Big Lottery Fund.

During its 19 years of existence, the charity was also highly dependent on private funds, raising over £164 million from companies, charitable trusts and individuals. Many were high-profile people such as J. K. Rowling, Damien Hurst and the rock band Coldplay, who donated £10 million over the years. The investment bank Morgan Stanley, and the retailer John Lewis, were among many companies that also gave generously.

Kids Company worked hard to draw media attention, raising its profile to attract private donations. Supporters and visitors to the projects, including Prince Harry, Prince Charles, the Prime Minister David Cameron, Richard Branson and many other celebrity figures featured in media reports praising Kids Company. However, despite the publicity, Kids Company struggled to attract the growing private sector funding it required in an increasingly crowded market. As its success grew and the charity became larger, some longstanding donors started to make noises about wanting to support smaller charities.

Kids Company had come to rely on successful applications for government grants to fill the growing gap between donations and expenditure. The applications were invariably accompanied by a two-pronged attack: letters to ministers threatening possible redundancies, and a media campaign with dire warnings about the effect of reduced services if the money was not forthcoming. The charity frequently made the case for statutory funding from

> Grant applications were invariably accompanied by a two-pronged attack: letters to ministers and a media campaign.

government, stating that it was undertaking work that local councils should have been providing themselves. Statutory funding would have given it a secure base level of resource to work from. However, as the rules stood, it could only receive statutory funding if a client was referred to them by a government agency and, since most of their clients were self-referred, this was not possible.

Between 2007 and 2011, Kids Company submitted several successful bids for central government grant programmes, in each case winning significantly more of the available cash than any other successful bidder. In 2012 its application for further government funds was unsuccessful. The reason given was that it was not offering value for money. Despite this verdict, the Department for Education, the sponsoring government department for these grants, was asked to build a public interest case for continued support of Kids Company. The case recommended support, citing reasons that included the previous support that the government had provided; the quality of its work in helping young people; and 'the reputational damage to the government's wider agenda [...] if it withdrew funding'.[13] Once again, Kids Company's 'unique, privileged and significant access to senior ministers'[14] and its media campaign proved invaluable and the charity was given a further grant for 2013 and 2014 worth a total of £9 million.

> Kids Company had 'unique, privileged and significant access to senior ministers'.

Another cash crisis unfolded towards the end of 2014. Although Kids Company's competitive bid for government funds was again unsuccessful, it did manage to extract a further £4.5 million in discretionary grants. This time it asked for the whole grant to be paid in April 2015 rather than quarterly, as previously, to cope with cash-flow problems. The government set more stringent terms on the 2015 grant, requiring the charity to move to a more sustainable funding structure and to implement a system to measure impact and value for money.

Adverse comments in the press caused difficulties for Kids Company in its efforts to raise funds in 2015, particularly after a critical article appeared in *The Spectator* magazine that February with allegations of financial mismanagement.[15] Despite asking for, and receiving, its entire annual grant of £4.5 million in April of that year, Kids Company wrote requesting more funding the following month. The request was rejected.

In June 2015, Kids Company submitted a restructuring proposal, including redundancies, to put the charity on a sustainable footing, together with a request for a £3 million grant to be matched by the same amount from donors. Civil servants at the Cabinet Office concluded that the funds would not represent value for money, but their judgment was overruled by a ministerial direction and £3 million was paid out on 30 July 2015.

Inadequate Monitoring by Government and Trustees

Once the government began to support Kids Company, it had, in effect, become its shareholder. To take the analogy further, since it was using taxpayers' money to fund its 'investment', it had a duty to taxpayers to ensure that their investment was producing returns.

Throughout the ten-year period that Kids Company received government grants, it repeatedly failed to establish effective performance indicators to measure the outcomes of its work. Even though the 2005 grant required the charity to develop a management information system to record outcomes, this failed to materialise. From 2011 the government relied on unaudited reports from the charity regarding outcomes, which did not always refer to the conditions specified in the grant.[16] Kids Company did submit some external studies of the effects of the charity's work, but these were limited in scope, mostly based on small samples. When the Cabinet Office took over funding decisions for Kids Company in 2013, it commissioned Methods Consulting to monitor and evaluate progress. Methods Consulting verified that Kids Company exceeded the required number of interventions, such as coaching, that its funding required but it failed to measure the value of these interventions.[17] Although efforts were made to create a reliable framework to measure these, the attempts were not wholly successful.

Government officials raised questions on several occasions as to whether Kids Company was delivering value for money. They pointed out that there were other youth charities working with similarly troubled children which had developed effective performance indicators but which attracted much less funding. The government clearly failed in its duty to enforce value for taxpayers' money. Time after time it allowed Kids Company to break its commitment to implement effective measurement frameworks.

The board of trustees also bore responsibility for ensuring that grant conditions were met. Trustees have a duty to ensure that the charity is managing its resources responsibly. This must surely include the establishment of systems to measure the effectiveness of its work. Unfortunately, the trustees repeatedly failed in their responsibility to oversee the establishment of reliable performance indicators.

The grants that Kids Company received came with conditions that required the charity to develop a sustainable form of funding which would not necessitate government grants. Despite being warned on several occasions that the next grant would be the last, the charity continued to receive funding. It was therefore not surprising that it came to believe that cash would always be forthcoming. This may have encouraged the trustees to be more relaxed about the level of reserves.

Financial probity and sustainability should have been easier to monitor. The government was provided with the charity's accounts on an annual basis and it was clear that it had negligible reserves. In 2014 the government commissioned PKF Littlejohn to do an assessment of Kids Company's financial and governance controls. The tender document required the successful bidder to assess the effectiveness of the charity's controls. Littlejohn claimed that the scope of the review was narrowed to establish merely whether or not the controls and procedures in place were appropriate for a charity of Kids Company's size and complexity. Although the report concluded that the existing controls were appropriate, this reassurance had limited benefit. The more important point was whether or not the controls were effective. It appears that the Cabinet Office assumed that the report did provide adequate assurance on this matter. The report also clearly stated that the charity did not have any reserves and was therefore operating in a very precarious manner. This point was ignored by both the government and the board of trustees, who failed to insist that the charity repair its finances.

The House of Commons Committee of Public Accounts investigated the government funding of Kids Company and concluded that, 'despite repeated

> Kids Company showed 'all the warning signs of a failed and expensive experiment'.

warnings and concerns about Kids Company's financial situation and the impact it was achieving, funding to the charity continued and was never seriously questioned, let alone stopped'.[18] The committee said that Kids Company showed 'all the warning signs of a failed and expensive experiment'.

The Trouble with Kids Company

Much of the criticism of Kids Company, in the months before the charity folded, focused on cash payments to large numbers of people and what the media considered to be excessive payments to a few individuals. Kids Company acknowledged that it handed out envelopes every Friday, some containing food vouchers and bus passes, and others including cash lump sums. Cash living allowances handed to children were very small, but families could receive up to £200 per week depending on their needs. Another allegation included a student registered at one of Kids Company's centres who only turned up to receive cash every week, despite claiming state benefits. Yet another centred on an ex-client turned employee who just turned up once a week to collect his pay cheque.[19]

More damaging claims asserted that large sums of money were expended on just a very few, mostly adult, clients. One individual, aged 34, had received help with her rent, clothes and other allowances for years. Although a client of Kids Company from when she was young, and still clearly needing help, it was inappropriate for a children's charity to support her. Another adult client received £73,000 of expenses in payment for private mental hospital fees and a stay at the luxury spa, Champneys, after he was thrown out of the hospital and needed emergency residential care involving a resident doctor and nurse. The charity also spent £5,000 per month on rent for the White House, a luxury five-bedroom art deco house in Hendon. A Kids Company employee stayed there on a permanent basis and the house was used for emergency accommodation for its clients. Batmanghelidjh's driver/general factotum's children received bursaries to attend private schools but also registered as clients with Kids Company to enable them to claim additional support payments.

Kids Company's financial controls stated that all expenditure over £5,000 must be approved by trustees, so all the large expenditures detailed above were presumably sanctioned by them. However, 'such lavish spending was inappropriate, unwise and irresponsible, and did not represent a proper use of charitable funds'.[20] While the expenditure may well have had a positive impact on the individuals concerned, it diverted funds away from other projects that could have helped large numbers of young people.

What Impact did the Charity Actually have?

Kids Company claimed to have helped 36,000 children and young adults every year since 2011 at its drop-in centres and with its schools programme, but this number is misleading. For example, as part of its schools

> Kids Company claimed to have helped 36,000 children every year yet only 1,909 files were turned over to social services when the charity folded.

programme, Kids Company included all children who attended classes with one of the children who had been supported by the charity. Kids Company believed that all children in a class benefit from the improved behaviour of one of its members, so it included all children—those that it 'indirectly' helped as well as those that it had direct contact with. These inflated client numbers would have positively impacted the impression the charity made on donors.

When Kids Company was closed it handed over only 1,909 files on vulnerable children to the relevant local authorities. While the charity dealt with many other clients whose status was not sufficiently serious as to require statutory intervention, there is a significant gap between 1,909 and 36,000. Kids Company did indeed help some vulnerable and damaged children, giving them hope and confidence, and turning them away from a path to self-destruction, but the numbers supported appear to be significantly fewer than claimed.

A Dominant CEO and a Complacent Board?

Batmanghelidjh founded Kids Company and acted as its CEO throughout its short life. The charity had a flat management structure and staff were encouraged to go directly to Batmanghelidjh with any concerns, sometimes bypassing its team of professional managers and trustees. Batmanghelidjh devoted her life to Kids Company and its young people, working long hours fundraising and running the charity, while also leading a team that looked after some of the charity's more challenging clients. Driven by her vision, she dominated the running of the charity. Staff showed a very high job satisfaction rate but senior management sometimes complained that Batmanghelidjh was impinging on their domain.

In November 2014 the charity had a £4 million deficit and £55,000 of self-employed staff invoices outstanding. A potential donor approached Batmanghelidjh offering 'unlimited' funding and 'human resource' towards the charity's projects and to develop its infrastructure. Batmanghelidjh asked for an immediate £1 million cash injection but after the philanthropist requested a day to consider this, Batmanghelidjh rejected the offer of assistance. She said that the donor lacked 'emotional authenticity' and was 'not ready to be genuinely philanthropic'. There is no evidence that the trustees were involved in the decision to turn down the offer of funds[21] which only indicates how unaccountable Batmanghelidjh had become and the extent of her personal power.

Relatively little resource was devoted to administration and monitoring, one reason why a reliable framework to assess the impact of interventions was never fully established. Charities often find it difficult to spend money on administration because donors want their money to go to the front line. It is therefore incumbent on trustees to ensure that sufficient money is spent on infrastructure and systems and to reassure donors of the value of such spending to improve efficiency and sustainability. In July 2015, as the funding crisis deepened at Kids Company, the board of trustees appointed an operations manager without Batmanghelidjh's approval. This may have been one of the rare occasions when the trustees acted contrary to Batmanghelidjh's wishes and was in response to the charity's urgent need to cut back on its expenditure.

Kids Company had a dedicated board of trustees who met at least six times a year while its subcommittees, such as finance and governance, met more than ten times a year. There were between eight and nine trustees: a collection of businessmen and women and philanthropists. Alan Yentob was Chairman of Kids Company from 2003 through to its collapse. He was helped by the Vice-Chairman, Richard Handover, former CEO of WHSmith, the book and stationery retailer. One of the trustees was a former partner at a legal firm, another a partner in a private equity firm and yet another the executive chairman of a recruitment consultancy.

The trustees were clearly committed, one of the trustees worked several days a month pro bono for the charity, funding and organising the warehouse that stored and delivered goods to clients of Kids Company. However, although several of the trustees had significant business experience, none had an extensive knowledge of youth or mental health services, which made it difficult for them to question clinical decisions regarding clients.

Kids Company's demand-led model, based on the principle that no child should be turned away, led to a constant need for funds and significantly increased the risk that the charity would not be able to meet its obligations. Over the years as it expanded and its cash requirements increased, the charity had somehow always managed to come up with the funds. Batmanghelidjh persuaded more donors to give money; the government came through with funding; or the trustees themselves gave loans, many of which were later converted into donations. This situation went on for so many years that it is obvious that the trustees were not addressing the precariousness of the charity's finances, perhaps expecting Batmanghelidjh always somehow to rescue the situation.

And What of Risk Management?

The governance committee of the board was responsible for risk assessment and ensuring that an active risk-management framework was in place. The top three risks that the charity identified were: not taking action to safeguard the children in its care; financial risk, including having insufficient reserves; and reputational risk.[22] However, the trustees did not appear to have seriously considered the links between the separate risks: any damage to the charity's reputation, for example, would affect the flow of cash from donors and thus the financial viability of the charity. When the news broke of child-abuse allegations, it destroyed the reputation of the charity overnight, making it impossible to raise funds. Since it had no reserves, it was unable to ride out the storm.

When the police investigated the allegations, which were of clients being abused by other clients, not by members of staff, they were unable to find evidence to support a criminal prosecution. Most of the reports were third-hand gossip rather than substantive claims. However, the police did not issue its report until 29 January 2016, which was much too late for Kids Company and its clients. If the charity had accumulated six months' reserves, it would have had a good chance of survival.

Duties of Trustees

Although trustees are not paid, their responsibilities are similar to those of company directors. They have a duty of care to act in the charity's best long-term interest. We believe this requires them to act with independence and to ensure a viable strategy, together with a robust framework for the management of risk to protect the organisation's long-term interests.

In the case of Kids Company, its client base expanded, as did the range of services it provided. Given its lack of regular income, this was a risky strategy, compounded by its expansion in 2013 to Bristol. Given the growing demand and limited resources, the trustees needed to be realistic and practical, to use reason to steer passion so as to ensure that the goals of the charity could be met in the long term.[23]

By allowing Batmanghelidjh to remain as CEO of Kids Company despite its growing size and complexity, were the trustees acting in the charity's best interests? The

> Trustees need to be pragmatic and use reason to steer passion.

board had permitted questionable payments and failed to build reserves, both at the behest of Batmanghelidjh. She had a key role as opinion-changer, fundraiser and motivator, but she was no longer an effective manager for the large and complex charity that Kids Company had become. The trustees should have remained independent in their thinking to balance the passion of Batmanghelidjh and her staff. An effective board of trustees would have tackled the difficult task of finding a successor for Batmanghelidjh a few years earlier.

By not insisting on the accumulation of free reserves, the trustees put the charity at risk. They did not manage the charity's resources responsibly. Although the board of trustees had assessed the risks that Kids Company faced, it failed to put contingency plans in place to cope if they materialised. Allowing the charity to spend all available cash may have given the impression that everything possible was being done for the children, but it put the very existence of the charity in jeopardy and, ultimately, it was the children who suffered.

Should the trustees have remained in office for so long? Yentob had been Chairman for 12 years, during which time the charity had grown several times over. Other trustees had also been on the board for considerable lengths of time. Can a trustee remain truly independent after such a long period? The UK corporate governance code advises that an independent company director should serve for no more than nine years.[24] Measured by that yardstick, Yentob was well outside recommended limits and more if his prior commitment and involvement with Kids Company is taken into account. Although admirable, the depth of his, and other directors', commitment appeared to blind them to the faults of the organisation.

Batmanghelidjh had the vision and passion to address an urgent need to rescue disadvantaged children. The trustees shared that vision but failed to rein in her enthusiasm and ensure the long-term sustainability of Kids Company. Ineffective controls, an overambitious strategy and, most egregious of all, a lack of reserves caused the charity's failure. Control of these were all within the remit of the board of trustees. Though well-meaning and supportive, the the trustees ultimately failed Kids Company's employees, donors and the vulnerable young people it served.

A Few Selected Highlights from the Kids Company Story

- *Independent directors and trustees must be prepared to constructively challenge a dominant CEO and replace them if necessary.*

- *Directors and trustees must consider the long-term health of the company and be prepared to challenge conventional wisdom when reviewing and signing off strategy. They need a comprehensive understanding of risk, and effective contingency plans in place to cope with possible outcomes.*

- *While it is valuable for directors to build relationships with management in order to gain a broad picture of the risks and opportunities facing a company, they must retain their independence. Terms should be limited to help ensure this.*

Notes

1. UK Charity Commission, www.gov.uk/guidance/charity-trustee-whats-involved.
2. Now called Place2Be.
3. Kids Company, *Invest to Save Budget Formal Bid*, 2005.
4. Office for National Statistics (2005) *Mental health of children and young people in Great Britain, 2004*, Palgrave Macmillan, 2005.
5. National Health Service—a universal, publicly funded health service.
6. Keeping Kids Company (2013) *Annual Report and Accounts 2013*.
7. Her Majesty's Chief Inspector of Education, Children's Services and Skills (2015), *Ofsted Social Care Report 2013–14*, 10 March 2015.
8. Excluding research-focused charities.

9. UK Civil Society Almanac (2012) *How much does the voluntary sector hold as reserves?* 17 February 2012.

10. Public Administration and Constitutional Affairs Committee (2016) *The collapse of Kids Company: Lessons for charity trustees, professional firms, the Charity Commission, and Whitehall*, HC433, 28 January 2016.

11. Cook, C. (2015) Kids Company—Do the sums add up? *BBC*, 20 October 2015.

12. Comic Relief raises money through entertainment, such as telethons and Red Nose Day, to tackle poverty and social injustice.

13. National Audit Office (2015) *Investigation: The government's funding of Kids Company*, HC566, 29 October 2015.

14. Public Administration and Constitutional Affairs Committee (2016) *The collapse of Kids Company: Lessons for charity trustees, professional firms, the Charity Commission, and Whitehall*, HC433, 28 January 2016.

15. Goslett, M. (2015) The Trouble with Kids Company, *The Spectator*, 14 February 2015.

16. National Audit Office (2015) *Investigation: The government's funding of Kids Company*, HC566, 29 October 2015.

17. National Audit Office (2015) *Investigation: The government's funding of Kids Company*, HC566, 29 October 2015.

18. Public Accounts Committee (2015) *The Government's funding of Kids Company*, HC504, 13 November 2015.

19. Public Administration and Constitutional Affairs Committee (2016) *The collapse of Kids Company: Lessons for charity trustees, professional firms, the Charity Commission, and Whitehall*, HC433, 28 January 2016.

20. Public Administration and Constitutional Affairs Committee, *The collapse of Kids Company: Lessons for charity trustees, professional firms, the Charity Commission, and Whitehall*, HC433, 28 January 2016.

21. Public Administration and Constitutional Affairs Committee, *The collapse of Kids Company: Lessons for charity trustees, professional firms, the Charity Commission, and Whitehall*, HC433, 28 January 2016.

22. Keeping Kids Company (2013) *Annual Report and Accounts 2013*.

23. E-mail from John Moore.

24. Up to 12 years in some countries.

8

China: Land of Opportunity but Beware of Landmines

'For foreign firms, China remains a potential eureka market, fraught with danger and surprises ... China has become the fastest place on earth.' Bill Fischer, Professor of Innovation Management at IMD

The Chinese economic miracle has transformed China from an isolated, poverty-stricken country into a thriving modern economy. More than three decades of stellar growth, at an annual rate of more than 10 per cent, has propelled the country to become the world's second-largest economy and the largest trading nation.[2] From a standing start in 1978, China now produces more than 50 per cent of the world's steel; has constructed the world's longest expressway network up from a mere 147 km in 1988; and has three of the world's top four banks (measured by tier 1 capital).[3]

Business ownership has changed dramatically since Mao's era. State-owned enterprises (SOEs) contributed over 80 per cent of gross national product (GNP) in 1978, but by 2010, corporate or private ownership was responsible for more than half the economic output. However, the state has not relinquished control of key industries; it still fully owns or controls strategic industries such as defence, aviation, oil and communications,

© The Author(s) 2017
A. Micklethwait, P. Dimond, *Driven to the Brink*,
DOI 10.1057/978-1-137-59053-4_8

and it has a strong influence on other pillar sectors, such as information technology, automotive, steel and design.

The vibrant private sector dominates retail and many manufacturing sectors from general machinery to textiles, and it outperforms SOEs with twice the rate of return on net assets. Two new stock exchanges are flourishing, in addition to the well-established Hong Kong stock exchange. While SOEs still receive the lion's share of available financing from large state-owned banks, the combination of equity capital and a growing shadow banking system has allowed the private sector to thrive. Foreign investment has become easier. In the 1980s, foreign investors were required to have a joint venture (JV) with local Chinese people, but today foreigners, in some industries, can set up wholly foreign owned enterprises (WFOEs) without a Chinese partner.

China has done a fantastic job of dragging its citizens out of poverty. The World Bank estimated that 12 per cent of Chinese people were living in extreme poverty in 2010, down from 84 per cent in 1981, and in urban areas extreme poverty has been virtually eliminated.[4] Nonetheless, even after years of supercharged growth, China still has a long way to go: GNP per capita is only a third of the OECD average, measured by purchasing power parity.

Expansion has slowed, even according to China's own statistics, which have long been discounted by economists who believe that the official growth rate of 6.9 per cent for 2015 is overstated by 1 or 2 per cent. The majority of analysts now think that China will slow to a 4 or 5 per cent growth rate by 2018.[5] Yet although some are fearful of the impact of this slowdown, in absolute terms, 5 per cent of $10,360 billion is on a par with the forecast growth for the US economy. This remains a significant opportunity for investors in China.

The Chinese Communist Party (CCP) believes that it needs strong growth to ensure social stability and, ultimately, its own survival. The Chinese public were content with limited freedom and the dominance of the CCP while they were getting richer. Slowing growth and rampant corruption could disrupt this implied contract and cause unrest, so the government is determined to do whatever is necessary to boost the faltering economy and to clamp down on corruption. Interest rates were cut several times in 2015, and major new infrastructure projects are planned. However, liberalising reforms, such as relaxing capital controls and letting zombie[6] state companies fail, are likely to be delayed. China's burgeoning debt, at 282 per cent of GDP in 2014,[7] makes a debt-fuelled expansion dangerous; while a fall in the renminbi has led to capital flight, partly to pay US dollar loans that were taken on when the currency was stronger, but also to escape further currency depreciation.

As China's economy boomed, its governing bureaucracies and institutions had a hard time keeping up. Government agencies, corporate governance, and legal and financial institutions are weak compared with those of most developed countries. Corruption has flourished, building on a culture where political patronage and networks of contacts (*guanxi*) are perceived to be the most important pillars of business success. Both Western and Chinese companies have been hit with corruption scandals. For example, GlaxoSmithKline's salesforce bribed doctors to prescribe Glaxo's drugs. How did the company's culture and remuneration practices enable this corrupt behaviour? In a country where Western-style accounting standards were only introduced in 1993, both accounting knowledge and also an appreciation of the importance of accurate records are limited, contributing to a proliferation of accounting scandals. Could better corporate governance have prevented fraud?

Western companies have found it tough doing business in China. Navigating the complicated licensing system; building trust and personal relationships; and understanding the culture and different needs of the Chinese have made it difficult to develop business. Meanwhile, by listening to their customers, taking lessons from the West and looking to the long term, many Chinese enterprises have developed into giant global companies, such as Alibaba and Haier. Successful Western businesses have also followed this model, but ethical questions arise when value systems conflict: choices that can fundamentally affect the success, or otherwise, of a business.

Google vs LinkedIn

Should Google have censored posts to comply with Chinese censorship regulations? Although it did so from 2007 to 2010, at the bottom of the search page it mentioned the number of results that had been blocked.

It was the only search engine to do this. After suspicion fell on the Chinese government for instigating a cyber-attack on Google in 2010, Google closed its China search engine, and committed to deliver uncensored searches to the Chinese from its servers in Hong Kong. However, Google's servers were then frequently blocked, and by 2014 the company's market share in China had fallen from 30 per cent of Internet searches to less than 2 per cent.

Google had initially bowed to the Chinese government's request for censorship, believing that it was better for users to have some access rather than none. However, after the cyber-attack—an apparent attempt to gather information about dissidents—Google withdrew from China, not prepared to contravene its core values of focusing on the user and 'not doing evil'. Accepting China's censorship rules had upset Google's users, so it was important for Google to reject China's request publicly.

In contrast, when LinkedIn launched a Chinese-language version in 2014, on servers in China, it agreed to censor all politically sensitive posts. It also allowed two local, well-connected partners to take a 7 per cent share in the Chinese operation. LinkedIn's China policy has received many negative comments for contravening its values to put members first. Aside from censoring posts, LinkedIn is required to store Chinese membership data on servers within China and to allow the government access whenever they want. LinkedIn argues that it provides a valuable service to its Chinese members and that doing any censorship is 'gut wrenching'.[8] The jury is still out to decide what harm, if any, this may have on LinkedIn's reputation.

Bribery is Often 'an Unspoken Rule' in China[9]

China has a long-established tradition of bribery and graft, despite frequent purges. In the dying days of the empire, Dr Sun Yat-sen, who would become

> '[An official] must accept bribes in order to pay the bribes exacted of him by his superiors'

the first president of the Republic of China, described how pernicious the practice had become: '[An official] must accept bribes in order to pay the bribes exacted of him by his superiors; and he must connive at all kinds of corruption both in his subordinates and in those who hold higher rank or office than his own.'[10]

During the transition from a planned economy to a mixed one, corruption had its use: loosening up the system by circumventing onerous and complicated regulations. Today however, the costs far outweigh the benefits. Corruption is endemic in China, pervading all levels of government and commerce. From giving gifts to large cash bribes, graft and bribery are omnipresent. The cost is significant: resources are allocated inefficiently; it fosters inequality; it undermines the legitimacy of the CCP; it causes capital flight;[11] and it foments social unrest. Andy Xie, the Shanghai-based economist, estimated that corruption cost China up to ten per cent of its GDP in 2010, a huge expense for the growing economy.[12]

Maoist anti-corruption drives eliminated large-scale manifestations of corruption but other forms soon emerged. In particular, the age-old culture of *guanxi*—networks of personal relationships usually involving reciprocal obligations—flourished in the 1960s and 1970s. People used them to obtain scarce commodities, admission to schools and favours from officials, often in return for gifts. As the economy liberalised and expanded, the opportunities for, and the scale of, corruption grew with it and became entrenched in the governing structure. Graft, bribery, patronage and embezzlement flourished.

Corruption infects all levels of society, and government office. For foreign tourists, not stung for petty bribes by customs officers or police, the scale of bribery is difficult to comprehend. But having a government position was a sure way to riches. For example, public schools in China are free to attend but today, parents are accustomed to paying 'sponsorship fees' to get their children into these top establishments. In Beijing, such fees have reached $16,000, more than double the average annual salary. At the other end of the scale, the multi-billion dollar project to build high-speed railways created phenomenal opportunities for graft and bribery. Ding Shumiao, an illiterate farmer-cum-railway manufacturer, used her connections to make more than $300 million in kickbacks from contractors; railway ministry jobs were bought and sold, and $78 million, set aside to compensate people whose homes had been demolished to make way for the tracks, just vanished.[13]

The Chinese constitution recognises that the CCP's biggest danger is 'separation from the masses', When caused by corruption it can lead to high levels of discontent. In 2012, Xi Jinping, recently elected as President of China and alarmed at the scale of

> Endemic corruption could lead to 'the collapse of the [Chinese Communist] Party and the downfall of the state'.

corruption, gave a speech warning that endemic corruption could lead to 'the collapse of the [Chinese Communist] Party and the downfall of the state'.[14]

Xi instigated a new anti-corruption drive: 'killing tigers and swatting flies', cracking down on corruption of both top-ranking and minor party officials. By all accounts the latest purge has been the most severe yet. More than 400,000 party members have been disciplined by the party and some 200,000 prosecuted in court. The higher echelons of the CCP have not gone unscathed either. Zhou Yongkang, head of the police and secret service, and a member of China's top ruling body, was sentenced to life imprisonment in June 2015 for bribery and leaking state secrets. The investigation spread to include Zhou's family and associates: more than 300 of them were arrested or questioned, and their assets, worth at least $14 billion, were seized.[15]

China watchers suspect that Zhou's prosecution was politically motivated as he appeared to be building a faction in opposition to Xi, but it does seem that the anticorruption drive is also a genuine attempt to reform. Prosecutions have been launched against party cadres and even senior judiciary, but there is a limit to how far the anti-corruption drive can punish the upper echelons of the Party without tearing it apart. As party elder, Chen Yun, said, 'Fight corruption too little and destroy the country; fight it too much and destroy the Party.'[16] However, despite the latest anticorruption drive, China's public sector ranking worsened in

2014, falling to 100th place in the Corruption Perceptions Index, down from 80th place in 2013.[17]

Lack of Systems and Institutions to Keep Corruption in Check

China lacks the systems and institutions present in most developed countries that help to keep corruption in check, such as democracy, a free press and an independent judiciary. Its censorship of the press and the Internet is extreme. Edicts are issued daily, instructing editors which topics to discuss, what not to publish and which stories to remove from the Internet. *China Digital Times*, a website based in the USA, has collected a number of these directives, such as 'all websites are kindly asked to delete the article "180 Countries Ranked in 2013 Press Freedom Index; China at 175th"' and 'all news media outlets must [focus on] strengthening economic propaganda ... [to] promot[e] the discourse on China's bright economic future and the superiority of China's system'.[18]

The Internet is much more difficult to control. China's 'Great Firewall' blocks foreign sites that it disapproves of, such as *The New York Times*, the BBC, Facebook and Wikipedia. Posts are filtered for banned words, and posts and sites are taken down on a regular basis. The effect of this censorship is not only to stifle political debate but also to prevent discussion of any topic potentially critical of the CCP, including corruption. By limiting discussion about corruption because of its fear that it will rebound on the CCP, the Party is blocking one of the mechanisms for exposing bribery and fraud, making it easier for guilty parties to escape detection.

Xi's anticorruption drive has primarily been aimed at reforming the CCP rather than the institutions that should prosecute and control corruption. Some suspect that the clampdown is nothing more than a 'Stalinist' purge to preserve and strengthen the power of the CCP and Xi's position. The recent disappearance of five Hong Kong booksellers—vendors of books critical of the Chinese regime who are now under criminal investigation in China—points to a tightening of Xi's grip on public opinion. On a more positive note, the CCP has recently announced a reform of the judicial system. The courts will remain under the firm control of the CCP but the plan is to reduce the influence of local party cadres.

However, the CCP's 'political and legal' committees, which co-ordinate the work of the police, prosecutors and judiciary at every level, will continue to function, allowing the Party to step in at any point and change direction. Despite the obvious limitations of the proposed changes, they should make it easier to prosecute corruption cases which have no political angle, independent of the influence of the local party. With greater certainty that corruption will be punished, it will hopefully diminish.

Guanxi: You Got My Back, I Got Your Back

In his book *Trust: The Social Virtues and the Creation of Prosperity*, Francis Fukuyama postulates that societies can be divided into low-trust and high-trust.[19] Familial, low-trust societies, such as China, value personal trust, so people are reluctant to enter into business relationships with anyone with whom they have no personal connection. In contrast, people in high-trust societies, with strong institutions, are more willing to extend trust based on professional qualifications or position. *Guanxi* is a practice that evolved in China as a way of building trust outside the family circle in the absence of strong institutions, such as an independent judiciary.

Chinese companies are happier doing business with a company with which they have strong *guanxi* than one where their relationships are weak. People develop *guanxi* over a number of years, giving gifts and other favours to build trust and foster a sense of obligation from the other party, which can be called upon when needed. This is not necessarily corrupt but can be the start of a slippery slope to graft and bribery.

While using *guanxi* to get an introduction to the official responsible for issuing business licences is legitimate, giving lavish gifts to that official in the expectation that he will help to cut through red tape or bypass legislation is not. Unfortunately, for many Chinese companies, this has become an accepted and necessary way of doing business. Success in business is achieved by having the best *guanxi* rather than the best business model. Patronage networks are ubiquitous, often linked to powerful government officials.

Part of Xi Jinping's crusade against corruption has involved a clampdown on conspicuous consumption by CCP officials: a ban on using public funds to stage elaborate galas and banquets; a ban on using official cars for personal use; a ban on giving gifts to visiting officials; and so on. These edicts had an immediate effect on the hotel market and luxury goods market where, for example, the sale of luxury watches declined by 11 per cent in 2013.[20]

GlaxoSmithKline: Doing Business in a 'Connected' Society

The pharmaceutical industry has a chequered history of unduly influencing doctors to buy its drugs. In 2013, one such scandal, involving the British company GlaxoSmithKline, broke in China. A whistleblower sent e-mails to the Glaxo board and senior officers in London, alleging that sales staff had provided doctors with speaking fees, overseas trips, lavish presents and even cash payments in return for prescribing Glaxo's drugs. More e-mails followed, saying that sales staff had submitted inflated expense claims to account for the costs.

Glaxo had experienced trouble before in China due to corruption, firing 30 of its Chinese employees in 2001 after uncovering bribes to officials. In order to keep a lid on potential fraud, Glaxo conducted up to 20 internal audits every year in China. In 2012, more than a sixth of the 312 staff it sacked worldwide for company policy violations were employed by Glaxo China, a number well out of proportion to its revenue.[21] So the company was swift to investigate the new allegations but said that it could find no evidence of bribery.

Glaxo had a significant presence in China, with a 5,000-person sales force and half a dozen factories and research labs. Although Chinese sales only accounted for 3 per cent of global revenue, the company's sales were growing faster there than in its more established Western markets. The market for pharmaceuticals in China was $82 billion in 2012, up more than 18 per cent from a year earlier,[22] and with more double-digit growth forecast the opportunities were huge and very lucrative. Western-manufactured generic drugs sold at high prices in China, yielding above-average margins because of their guaranteed high quality.

The Chinese healthcare system was heavily reliant on patient charges, including payments for drugs. Hospitals earned around 40 per cent of their income from drugs' sales. The scale of fees for operations was set by central government but the price of drugs was more lightly regulated. Hospitals preferred to buy high-price foreign drugs rather than cheaper local generics because they could then earn more profit when sold on to patients at a standard mark-up.

The Chinese healthcare industry suffers from endemic corruption. Doctors are poorly paid and often rely on kickbacks from drugs companies to augment their salaries, while patients are accustomed to 'tipping' the doctor or hospital to get the treatment and drugs they need. An investigation of hospitals in Zhangzhou city in Fujian province discovered that 90 per cent of doctors had been involved in kickbacks.[23] The head of a hospital in Yunnan province is also being investigated for accepting $18 million in bribes related to construction projects, medical device procurement and doctor positions.

> An investigation of hospitals in Zhangzhou city in Fujian province discovered that 90 per cent of doctors had been involved in kickbacks.

With doctors asking for bribes as a matter of course, it is hardly surprising that Glaxo's salesforce saw this as standard practice. Foreign drugs companies were not the worst offenders. Industry analysts and hospital officials say that local generic companies are even more extravagant than foreign companies with bribes and inducements. Higher up the supply chain, pharmaceutical companies need to obtain regulatory approval to licence, import or manufacture their products in China, and they sometimes rely on 'incentive payments' to accelerate the process.[24]

The decentralised nature of the Chinese state has created many layers of bureaucracy which businesses must penetrate. Separate provinces have considerable freedom to issue their own laws and regulations as long as they conform to the general direction of party leadership. This decentralisation of administrative and economic powers has created a complex and opaque licensing system which businesses have to navigate. Companies such as Glaxo which want to operate in China must deal with multiple layers of government agencies, some with competing objectives, which provides endless opportunities for corrupt officials to make a killing.

Glaxo had high ambitions to increase its share of the Chinese market. Sales employees were issued with demanding targets with the promise of bonuses for success of up to 40 per cent of salary.[25] It was part of the job of sales staff to build relationships with doctors in their territory. As pressure increased to hit demanding targets, conference sponsorship turned into all-expenses-paid overseas holidays; a business lunch became a banquet; and, most egregious, doctors were given cash payments linked to the number of prescriptions they issued.

Sales teams for large customers had access to substantial marketing budgets which employees augmented by submitting inflated expense claims using fake receipts that they had purchased, often under instruction from their supervisor. And, despite advice to the contrary, Glaxo advanced cash and reimbursed employees' expenses in cash for those in far-flung territories, increasing the opportunity for fraud.

When the Chinese authorities began their own investigation in June 2013, they discovered that travel agencies had been used to channel inflated expenses through to employees and on to doctors and hospitals. Travel agencies would submit an invoice for running a conference but inflate the number of attendees. 'Some of the extra cash then went directly to one of four senior Chinese Glaxo officers with the rest being used to bribe officials, doctors and hospitals,' said Liang Hong, Glaxo's General Operations Manager in China. Liang also said that the cost of the bribes increased the price of drugs to patients by up to 20 per cent.[26] Liang and three other top Chinese executives were arrested and put on trial, together with Mark Reilly, the British head of Glaxo's Chinese operations.

After a one-day trial, Glaxo was fined £300 million for bribery offences and five of its top executives, including Reilly, were given suspended

> 'Some of the extra cash then went directly to one of four senior Chinese Glaxo officers with the rest being used to bribe officials, doctors and hospitals.'

prison sentences. The authorities in the UK and USA opened their own investigations as the bribery of government officials is illegal under both jurisdictions. Employees are held to the highest standard of jurisdiction regardless of the location where the offence took place. The scandal had an immediate effect on Glaxo's sales in China, which fell by 22 per cent in 2013 to £585 million.

Glaxo was only just recovering from the fallout from a $3 billion settlement with the US authorities, a case which included allegations of bribing doctors. Facing further investigation in Iraq, Jordan and Lebanon, it decided on a radical reform of its marketing policies worldwide. Sales-volume-related pay would be replaced by a broader measure of the quality of information provided to doctors plus a link to overall company performance. Payments to doctors for travel expenses to conferences and speaker fees would be phased out, in line with many other pharmaceutical companies. In a positive indication that staff were taking the policies more seriously, Glaxo received 648 whistleblower reports in 2014, the year following the scandal. This was a 13-fold increase on the previous year.[27]

Glaxo's sales-volume-related bonuses incentivised the salesforce to engage in bribery in order to increase sales and thus their own rewards. However, by changing remuneration practices to reward behaviours which help its ultimate consumer, Glaxo reinforced its core value of focusing on what is right for the patient.

The pharmaceutical industry in China is still corrupt, although the government is trying to make improvements. If Glaxo succeeds in enforcing its policy not to bribe doctors and officials, it will not be operating on a level playing field. Sales may not recover fully in China for some time but, if it can project a truly ethical image, Glaxo should earn a reputation for patient care that could ultimately translate to improved profits.

The problem of false expense claims is equally difficult to address. The sale of fake receipts or *fapiao* is ubiquitous: advertised openly on billboards and via text messages. Since it is normal behaviour to use *fapiao*, it is not easy to prevent the activity. Companies can, and should, verify *fapiao* at local tax bureaus, which may make it possible to expose the majority of false claims.

ChinaWhys: Illegal to Purchase Personal Information

In a sideshow to the bribery allegations, the whistleblower also sent a sex tape involving Mark Reilly to senior Glaxo executives. The tape showed Reilly in bed with his girlfriend, filmed by a covert camera installed in his flat. Reilly commissioned a private investigator, Peter Humphrey and his firm ChinaWhys, a business advisory firm, to investigate the tape and the source of the bribery allegations. He was pointed in the direction of Vivian Shi, Glaxo's former head of government affairs in China. Shi had been let go in 2012 after an investigation into expense manipulation and was at the top of the list of suspects. In a report sent to Glaxo shortly before the Chinese opened their investigation, ChinaWhys concluded that Shi was probably responsible but the suspicions were never substantiated. Shi flatly denied any involvement, she was rehired by Glaxo three years later.

In August 2013, Humphrey and his wife were arrested and charged with illegally purchasing private information. ChinaWhys offered services such as due diligence, employee screening and investigations into corruption.

> Humphreys and his wife were jailed for illegally obtaining items of private information, such as mobile phone numbers.

It also employed third parties to discover information about its targets, a practice that caused the Humphreys' downfall. The couple were charged with illegally obtaining 256 items of private information about Chinese citizens, such as IDs, mobile phone numbers and travel records. Humphrey signed a confession coerced while in detention, allegedly in order to obtain medical treatment for health problems, an accusation that was denied by the Chinese authorities.[28] After a one-day trial, Humphrey and his wife were found guilty and were sentenced to two-and-a-half years' and two years' imprisonment, respectively.

Suspicions arose that during his investigation, Humphrey had offended someone with powerful connections. He and his wife's sentences seem significantly out of line with other convictions for illegally obtaining private information, based on which they should have got away with merely a fine.[29] The court assumed that buying personal information is always illegal. If widely applied, this principle would cause huge problems. For example, any company involved in buying or selling mobile phone numbers for marketing purposes, a practice widespread in China, would be operating illegally. The broad-brush approach of the case also raises serious implications for investigative firms in China and their foreign clients. Foreign businesses will find it ever more difficult to perform the essential due diligence background checks on potential business partners and employees to comply with anti-bribery legislation because, if the principle is taken to its logical conclusion, investigators risk jail if they gather any personal information about Chinese individuals.[30] This is an important governance issue for foreign companies, especially those without a strong network of connections in China.

Fraud and Accounting Scams

Complete and accurate accounts which provide a true picture of a company's financial status are essential for boards and shareholders. It is the board's duty to ensure that it has all the information it requires in order to oversee the company and its management. Unfortunately, in China, accounts cannot always be trusted, which causes a problem for potential investors. Extensive due diligence is essential to reduce the risk of fraud.

After the Second World War, China adopted Soviet-style accounting. Since the state owned all means of production and the concept of profit had been abolished, its main priority was to report on the use of state funds and production quotas. It had little interest in profit measurement or the long-term viability of an enterprise. At one stage, during the Great Leap Forward (1958–1961),[31] accounting records were briefly eliminated entirely with the introduction of 'accounting without books'.

After Deng began his reforms in 1978, accounting standards evolved to cope with the new private enterprises. Western-style accounting was introduced in 1993, and in 2006, China adopted a new set of Accounting

Standards for Business Enterprises, similar to the International Financial Reporting Standards, for all companies listed in China. One important difference is the treatment of related party transactions. Chinese SOEs do not have to declare related party transactions with any company or institution controlled by the state because this might lead to a very long list of related party transactions, mostly of no particular interest to investors.

As China's experience of Western-style accounting is quite recent, the number of quali-fied accountants is still small. In 2006, China had only 70,000 practising accountants, a major-ity with only limited account-

> In 2006, China had only 70,000 practising accountants. If it had the same number per capita as the UK, it would have 5.3 million.

ing experience. Jiang Zemin, China's former president, acknowledged that this was not sufficient and said that the country needed 300,000. Yet if it had the same number per capita as the UK it would have 5.3 million.[32] The lack of professional accountants, combined with poor law enforcement, has led to a profusion of accounting scams.

There was a spate of accounting scandals involving Chinese companies which listed in the USA, Hong Kong and Singapore between 2007 and 2010. In the USA more than $40 billion was wiped off shareholder value as a result of fraud involving Chinese companies listed on its stock exchanges. In a couple of examples of Western-owned Chinese subsidiaries, Caterpillar and Lixil, the parent companies had to write off $560 million and $337 million, respectively, due to negligent accounting and fraud.

From 2007 to early 2010, around 160 Chinese companies gained access to the US stock market by engineering a reverse merger of a listed shell company. This is a inexpensive way to list on an exchange, avoid-ing the costs and more rigorous filing requirements of an initial public offering (IPO). These were mostly small companies, in total represent-ing less than 1 per cent of the market capitalisation of New York-listed Chinese companies.[33] However, they caused a disproportionate amount of upset as company after company was embroiled in accounting scan-dals and accusations of fraud. Eventually 100 Chinese companies were delisted from the NYSE between 2011 and 2012, many because of false accounting, with resultant heavy losses for investors. Most cases were quite simple examples of false accounting: fake bank balances; inflated revenues with the pretence that cash was held by subcontractors; or sale of company assets to related parties without the knowledge of investors. The USA was not the only jurisdiction to suffer: cases also occurred in Canada, Hong Kong and Singapore.

When auditors perform an audit, one of the most important areas to examine is cash balances. This is usually a straightforward exercise of sending a confirmation request to the bank. However, in some countries additional steps are required to gain reassurance that these balances are correct.

Auditors may visit a company's bank directly to view its accounts, as Deloitte did in the egregious case of Longtop Financial Technologies Ltd. When Deloitte went to Longtop's bank in order to verify bank statements, it was told that the confirmation replies that it had previously received were false; that there was no record of certain transactions; and that there were significant loans outstanding that had not been revealed before and that were not in the company's books. As soon as Longtop officers heard of the visit to the bank, they called the bank, denied that Deloitte was their auditor and seized bank documents that Deloitte had copied along with certain of their working papers. A few days later the Longtop chairman phoned Deloitte and said, 'There were fake revenue in the past so there were fake cash recorded on the books' and that 'senior management' was involved.[34] Deloitte had no choice but to resign as company auditor and inform the SEC of what had happened.

Longtop's shares were suspended but the USA was unable to prosecute Longtop's executives because it could not get access to Deloitte's working papers. Auditors based in China are not permitted to give information to a foreign jurisdiction because they are deemed to contain state secrets, so any distribution is forbidden by the Chinese government. It took more than two years for the SEC to persuade the Chinese regulatory agency to give them access to the working papers, and the case against Longtop is still unresolved. The question of access to auditors' papers is still a thorny issue between China and the USA, caused partly by China's insistence on controlling all information relating to Chinese companies and also by the number of different government agencies involved.

Despite lengthy discussions, mostly revolving around which data should be omitted from any accord, no agreement has been reached and every request for information has to be judged separately and at great length. Ultimately, this impasse is not in China's favour: efforts of regulators worldwide should be welcomed in the war against corruption.

Puda Coal Inc accessed the US capital markets in 2005 through a reverse takeover. Its principle asset was a 90 per cent shareholding in Shanxi Puda Coal. In 2009, shortly before Puda raised $166 million in two public offerings, Puda's chairman, with the help of the CEO,

> In 2009, shortly before Puda's public offerings, Puda's chairman, with the help of the CEO, secretly transferred Puda's entire shareholding in Shanxi Coal to himself.

secretly transferred Puda's entire shareholding in Shanxi Coal to himself. He then transferred 49 per cent of the shareholding to CITIC (China International Trust and Investment Corporation) in exchange for shares in a new coal investment trust and pledged the remaining 51 per cent to CITIC as security for a $516 million loan. In China, CITIC marketed its coal investment trust via documents written in Mandarin, extolling the returns it was expecting from its Shanxi Coal assets, while at the same time Puda was raising money in the USA on the back of its supposed ownership of Shanxi Coal.[35] When the asset transfer was discovered, Puda's share price plunged and the company was delisted. In a rare example of successful enforcement, both the chairman and CEO were convicted of securities fraud.

In the case of Puda, a quick web search would have uncovered tales of rampant corruption in the Shanxi coal industry. Aware of this specific risk, potential investors could have insisted on better controls before committing funds.

Lixil and Joyou: Failed Due Diligence

In 2014 the Japanese company Lixil Group, a global supplier of sanitary fittings, came to grief when it acquired the German company Grohe Group for €3 billion, together with its Chinese subsidiary, Joyou AG. A year later, after the discovery of large off-balance-sheet loans at its Chinese operations, Joyou filed for bankruptcy.

Joyou, run by its owner-founder and his son, Jianshe Cai and Jilin Cai, was floated on the Frankfurt Stock Exchange in 2010, raising $105 million. It was one of the biggest bathroom fittings companies in China and the Cais were important businessmen in their home town of Nan'an in Fujian province. Keen to access the Chinese market, by 2013, Grohe had acquired 72 per cent of Joyou through a series of transactions which left the Cai family company owning 13 per cent of Grohe.

Two years before the listing, Joyou reported a 200 per cent increase in sales. A large jump in revenue such as this should act as a red flag to investors, warning of possible fraud. When the scandal broke, this turned out to be the case. Sales had been overstated; false purchase orders and invoices had been created to support the fictional sales; sales expenses had been understated; and loans had not been declared. This was not a one-off event. In order to support the fiction of healthy sales growth, the accounts were falsified on an ongoing basis.

The Cais used cash from Joyou to set up a microcredit company, lending out small amounts at over 20 per cent interest. They borrowed from banks, using Joyou factories as collateral to make more loans into the shadow banking system. Soon after Lixil acquired Grohe, Joyou took out a $300 million credit facility from three of Lixil's banks and used the cash to pay off some of its loans. In October 2014, the collapse of a pyramid lending scheme in south-eastern China caused banks to call loans which resulted in the collapse of the Cais' financial ventures. They managed to keep Joyou afloat with the help of the $300 million credit facility and, in early April 2015, Lixil bought the Cais' 13 per cent shareholding in Grohe for $205 million. Eleven days later, Lixil received a letter from a Chinese bank stating that Joyou had defaulted on a loan. Surprised by the news, Lixil investigated and discovered a whole raft of undeclared loans and false accounting. Joyou filed for bankruptcy and Lixil had to warn shareholders of a $560 million loss.

The information flow coming from Joyou was suspect from the start. The Cais refused to release critical financial information to Grohe and it borrowed money without approval from the supervisory board, which was made up of two Grohe executives and an independent director. Another warning sign was that Joyou, despite apparently having considerable cash on the balance sheet, paid its suppliers late and frequently sought approval for new borrowing. Grohe made attempts to improve the situation by trying to hire Chinese-English bilingual speakers to work at Joyou but it found it difficult to persuade anyone to go to Nan'an. In addition, on two occasions, Grohe hired a new CFO but both times the CFO was unable to gain access to Joyou's financial information. An obvious solution would have been to get rid of the Cais but, as they had complete management control of the company and close relations with customers, suppliers and government officials, that could have been disastrous. Instead, Grohe tried to implement gradual change.

Lixil could only carry out limited due diligence before acquiring Grohe because it was an auction sales process. Its post-closing due diligence was more detailed but again Lixil had trouble getting information from the Cais. Lixil negotiated to buy the Cais' remaining shareholding in Grohe during the due diligence process. To persuade the Cais to sell their shares, the agreement contained only minimal representations and warranties.

The examples above illustrate the potential consequences of inadequate due diligence. As a potential shareholder, can you spot fraudulent accounting? Not always, especially if there is no direct access to question management, but you can be alert to warning signs and, equally important, you can check the corporate governance of the company.

Corporate governance is a relatively new concept for China. It was not until 1993 that the framework for a market-economy-style governance structure was enshrined in the Company Law Act. The Chinese corporate governance code was laid out in 2001, supported by the Companies Law and Securities Law Acts of 2006. Chinese listed companies operate under a two-tier board structure, similar to that in continental Europe. At least one third of the members of the supervisory board must be independent and at least one of those must have an accounting qualification. The definition of 'independent' is that they may not have a position in the company and they should 'have no relationships that prevent them from making an independent and objective judgement'.[36]

The role of independent director has evolved from Western cultures where widely dispersed shareholders need a mechanism to hold management to account and to solve the problem of the separation of ownership and control. In China, most listed companies are former SOEs. Large shareholders, often the state, control both the shareholders' general meeting and the supervisory board. Large shareholders may handpick biddable directors and managers to ensure that the interests of the dominant shareholders are satisfied, to the possible detriment of minority shareholders.

China has recognised the potential problem caused by dominant shareholders when selecting directors. The *Guidelines for Introducing Independent Directors to the Board of Directors of Listed Companies* state that a corporation's top ten shareholders and their families, top five shareholders' employees and their families, all holders of at least 1 per cent outstanding shares, and employees of the holders of at least 5 per cent outstanding shares may not serve as independent directors.[37] However, given China's culture of *guanxi*, it would be easy for dominant shareholders to use their voting power to ensure that the independent directors were favourable to them.

There are several weaknesses in the current Chinese governance code. The supervisory board does not have the power to dismiss directors, nor to sue managers, unless at the behest of shareholders, making it a 'tiger without teeth'. Audit, nomination and remuneration committees, with a majority of independent directors, are not mandatory in China, and few companies have introduced them. Only a very few Chinese listed companies have a majority of independent directors on the supervisory board.

> Only a very few Chinese listed companies have a majority of independent directors on the supervisory board.

A further factor limiting the true independence of directors is that they are usually nominated by the management board, thus management itself decides on who will monitor them. In the past, the quality of independent directors has been a problem, with only a small minority having commercial experience—the majority were civil servants or academics. In China today, independent directors are required to undergo an approved training programme before they are appointed, and to participate in continuing professional training once in office. This should substantially improve the suitability of candidates, although the issue of whether or not they are truly independent still arises.

There is also the matter of possible interference by the state. The CCP maintains control over businesses at the company level. Chairmen of SOEs are CCP members and, by effectively controlling their careers, the CCP ensures that party policy will take precedence over pure commercial objectives. This party presence is also felt in the private sector: more than 50 per cent of privately held companies, including those with foreign ownership, have established party cells to give guidance to management and control the unions. The CCP's goal is to extend cells into every company with more than three employees.

Caveat Emptor—Due Diligence is Vital

Investors in Chinese listed companies should do their own evaluation beyond financial history and forecasts. First, who actually controls the firm: is it the state, a family or an individual entrepreneur, and what motivates them? In the case of a family or individual, is this the only enterprise they own? Do they have other interests that might conflict with, or draw their attention away from, the company? Investors should study the company's corporate governance structure to determine how rigorous it is. Who are the independent directors and do they have any links to management or major shareholders? Is the auditor a top-quality firm? Then they should look at related party transactions and determine whether or not they create value, remembering that in the case of SOEs, these do not have to be reported.

Political connections and exposure to political influence are important factors in China. If the company is private, does it depend on local government for contracts, and if it is state owned, are its goals dictated by government directives rather than aimed at maximising profits?[38] Finally, it is important to be aware of where exactly the company operates, and which set of local laws and regulations are applicable: is it a province committed to reform and what is its reputation for corruption?

A Few Selected Highlights from the China Story

- *Shareholders need to bear the responsibility of assuring themselves that the company they are about to invest in has a responsible board that will represent all shareholders' interests. Extensive due diligence, including an investigation into corporate governance issues, is vital.*

- *Companies should assess the customs and associated risks of new markets and consider what risk-management systems they need to put in place to avoid compromising their value systems.*

- *The board of any company investing abroad should consider the need for in-depth experience of local issues on the board and the local connections necessary to understand and develop the new business.*

Notes

1. Fischer, W. A. (2010) *Improving not inventing: The secret of China's success*, www.management-issues.com/bill-fischer/, 30 March 2010.
2. Romei, V. (2014) China and US battle for trade leadership, *Financial Times*, 10 January 2010.
3. Caplen, B. (2015) Summary of the top 1000 world banks, *The Banker*, 2015.
4. Extreme poverty is defined as an income of less than $1.25 per day.
5. Noble, J. (2015) Doubts rise over China's official GDP growth rate, *Financial Times*, 16 September 2015.
6. Companies that continue to operate even though they are insolvent or near bankruptcy.
7. Dobbs, R., S. Lund, J. Woetzel & M. Mutafchieva (2015) Debt and (not much) deleveraging, *McKinsey Global Institute*, February 2015.

8. Liu, B. (2014) LinkedIn CEO Jeff Warner in interview with Bloomberg TV, www.valuewalk.com/2014/10/linkedin-ceo-jeff-weiner-do-not-prefer-chinese-censorship/ accessed 20 March 2016.

9. Levick, R. (2015) New data: Bribery is often 'an unspoken rule' in China, *Forbes*, 21 January 2015.

10. Dr Sun Yat-Sen (1897) http://www.globalsecurity.org/military/world/china/corruption.htm.

11. $1.25 trillion flowed out of China in illicit outflows between 2003 and 2012 according to the US-based Global Financial Integrity, a research and advisory organisation.

12. Xie, A. (2010) China's foul assets, fouler yet, *Caixin Online*, 13 May 2010.

13. Osnos, Evan (2014) *Age of ambition: Chasing fortune, truth and faith in the new China*, (New York: Farrar, Straus and Giroux).

14. Leung, J. (2015) Xi's corruption clampdown, *Foreign Affairs*, May/June 2015.

15. Lim, B. K. & B. Blanchard (2014) China seizes $14.5 billion assets from family associates of ex-security chief, *Reuters*, 30 March 2014.

16. Osnos, E. (2014) China's fifteen-billion-dollar-purge, *The New Yorker*, 2 April 2014.

17. Transparency International (2014) Corruption Perceptions Index.

18. www.chinadigitaltimes.net.

19. Fukuyama, F. (1995) *Trust: The social virtues and the creation of prosperity* Free Press).

20. Bain & Company (2013) *China Luxury Goods Market Study 2013 Edition: Mainland China Entering an Era of Luxury Cooldown*, Bain & Company, 27 December 2013.

21. Neate, R. & A. Monaghan (2013) GlaxoSmithKline admits some staff in China involved in bribery, *The Guardian*, 22 July 2013.

22. Burkitt, L. & J. Whallen (2013) China targets big pharma, *Wall Street Journal*, 16 July 2013.

23. Martina, M. (2013) More foreign pharmaceutical firms could be probed in China: Xinhua, *Reuters*, 24 July 2013.

24. Kuo, L. (2013) Why bribery is rampant in China's healthcare system, *Quartz*, 17 July 2013.

25. Jourdan, A. & B. Hirschler (2015) GSK in China: Escaping the shadow of a scandal, *Reuters*, 26 November 2015.

26. *China Daily* (2013) *GSK allegedly received sexual services*, www.en.people. cn/90778/8328268.htlml, 16 July 2013.
27. GlaxoSmithKline plc, Annual Report 2014.
28. Roland, D. (2015) British investigator says Chinese officials tried to force confession, *Wall Street Journal*, 18 June 2015.
29. Clarke, D. (2015) *The Peter Humphrey/Yu Yingzeng Case and Business Intelligence in China (draft)*, The George Washington University Law School, 5 August 2015.
30. Clarke, D. (2015) *The Peter Humphrey/Yu Yingzeng Case and Business Intelligence in China (draft)*, The George Washington University Law School, 5 August 2015.
31. A plan to collectivise agriculture and to industrialise China. It is widely believed to have caused the Great Chinese Famine, resulting in the death of tens of millions.
32. Jopson, B. (2006) Perils as well as promise in China accounting switch, *Financial Times*, 3 July 2006.
33. Cogman, D. & G. Orr (2013) How they fell: the collapse of Chinese cross-border listings, *McKinsey & Company*, December 2013.
34. Deloitte Touche Tohmatsu CPA Ltd (2011) *Letter to the audit committee of Longtop Financial Technologies Ltd (copied to the SEC)*, http://www.sec.gov/Archives/edgar/data/1412494/000095012311052882/d82501exv99w2.htm, 22 May 2011.
35. Tan, K. (2011) Chinese giant falls short, *Barron's*, 15 October 2011.
36. OECD (2011) *Corporate governance of listed companies in China: Self-assessment by the China Securities Regulatory Commission*, (Paris: OECD Publishing) http://dx.doi.org./10.1787/9789264119208-en.
37. China Securities Regulatory Commission (2001) *Guidelines for Introducing Independent Directors to the Board of Directors of Listed Companies, Section III*, 16 August 2001.
38. Ying, F. (2014) Corporate governance in China: Risks and opportunities, *China Business Knowledge*, Chinese University of Hong Kong, 3 September 2014.

9

Alibaba: Largest Etailer on the Globe a Mere 15 Years On

You may wonder why we have included Alibaba—one of China's success stories and, at the time of writing, the largest Internet company in the world in a book about corporate failure. Our intention is not to predispose doom, nor to suggest trouble on the horizon. We think that the story of Alibaba and its main founder, Jack Ma, is fascinating: it is a positive illustration of China's traditions in practice, and a large and growing force. We believe there is a lot to learn from its highly productive culture and unusual governance structure.

For a company that exceeded $390 billion in gross merchandise value (GMV)[1] for 2015, has made sales of more than $14.3 billion in one day,[2] is bigger than eBay and Amazon combined and is profitable, one might think that it is an old and well-established business. Yet the Alibaba Group, in relative terms, is still an early-stage operation. Launched in 1999 by Jack Ma, the Alibaba Group will celebrate a mere 17 years in existence in 2016. But its dreams are large and its vision long term:

© The Author(s) 2017
A. Micklethwait, P. Dimond, *Driven to the Brink*,
DOI 10.1057/978-1-137-59053-4_9

'We aim to build the future infrastructure of commerce. We envision that our customers will meet, work and live at Alibaba, and that we will be a company that lasts at least 102 years.'[3]

China may have been slow to enter the Internet economy. However, with a population of more than 1.3 billion, the high cost of property, the relatively low cost of delivery and a nation of entrepreneurs and small businesses, it is a fertile environment for the Internet and Alibaba's explosive growth. Today, China is the world's biggest e-commerce market, estimated to be greater than $500 billion, and it will be double the size of the US e-commerce market by 2018. The Alibaba Group is the dominant online marketplace. In 2013 it accounted for 80 per cent of China's e-commerce revenues.

Alibaba is an ecosystem for small businesses throughout China. It is a trading platform for business to business (B2B) products and services as well as the largest e-commerce marketplace for business

> 'We aim to build the future infrastructure of commerce.'

to consumer (B2C) and consumer to consumer (C2C) trading. Initially a business driven through personal computer access, the group quickly extended its platform to include mobile devices. Some thought this might create a hiccup or cause the company to falter, but the rate and success of this transition was impressive. Today more than 30 per cent of its transactions are mobile led and it is the dominant m-commerce provider in China.[4] In 2014, iResearch asserted that 80 per cent of all m-commerce in China took place on Alibaba's mobile platforms.[5] Its success is commonly attributed to its corporate culture, which is fierce and nimble.

In September 2014, Alibaba was the largest Initial Public Offering (IPO) in history, raising approximately $25 billion. After release, the share price jumped by almost 30 per cent, allowing the company to issue more shares. The business at the time of its IPO was valued at over $230 billion,[6] moving it directly to the position of the 11th largest company on the Standard & Poor's 500 by market capitalisation. It launched with an unusual share structure for a company of its size: one that separates ownership and control. The board is elected by a small group of founders and partners rather than its larger shareholders, which was a major factor in its decision to launch on a US stock exchange rather than on Hong Kong's. This structure supports Alibaba's corporate ethos: one that puts the customer first, the employee second and the investor last.

The Alibaba Group is not without a whisper of scandal. The authenticity of some of the brands sold on its marketplace have been questioned, as well as the centralised control that its founder and chairman allegedly has. Indeed, it has a structure that does not represent the rights of all classes of shareholders equally, and more recently it has reported some questionable acquisitions. Yet it continues to grow at a staggering pace. *How did its culture and governance structure contribute to the phenomenal growth it has achieved? Will the pressures of shareholders, US capital markets and its now slowing growth rate erode its culture or alter its long-term approach? What impact will be felt when Ma, its dominant founder, steps down?*

Building the World's Biggest Internet Company: Alibaba's Explosive Growth

The Alibaba Group was founded in 1999 by Jack Ma and 17 others, a rather large group for a start-up, from Ma's apartment in Hangzhou, China. Ma had been inspired by a trip to the USA where

> A long-term approach: Alibaba believed that its customers will meet, work and live at Alibaba, and that its business would last at least 102 years.

he received a brief introduction to the Internet. He returned to China believing that the Internet would provide small businesses with the necessary scale to trade domestically and internationally. So Alibaba's first Internet business, alibaba.com, was launched: a global wholesale marketplace with an English-language platform. The group inherited its name from the fable. Ma believed that Alibaba is a globally recognised story which conjures up images of small businesses saying 'open sesame' to new treasures and opportunities through the Internet.[7]

This business was shortly followed by the launch of 1688.com, a Chinese marketplace for the domestic wholesale trade, allowing it to raise $5 million from a consortium of small investors. From here it grew at an exponential pace without any apparent difficulty in finding funding. In January 2000, Ma attracted an investment of $20 million from a group led by Softbank, a Japanese conglomerate in the information and mobile communications industry, which would become Alibaba's long-term partner. During the next two to three years, the business hit a number of critical milestones: more than 1 million registered users and a positive cash-flow status.

At the same time, Ma became interested in eBay and its business model. He formed a small team that locked itself in his apartment to build and launch Taobao, translated as 'search for treasure'. This business was based on the principles of eBay: to serve the growing middle class and allow consumers to sell to each other. However, he had an advantage: as a Chinese national, he had a better understanding of the Chinese customer and culture which translated into a more relevant customer experience than the site that had inspired it. Taobao embraced the challenge that a formidable competitor such as eBay represented; it was a David and Goliath story.

> 'Customer ethos: Believe in your dreams, find good people and make sure the customer is happy.'[8]

The Spirit of *Guanxi*: Strong Relationships Accelerated Alibaba's Growth

A JV was set up with Softbank to develop Taobao, and together they devoted $50 million to a series of investments. Ma believed in the need to keep his Chinese customer happy so offered the platform without cost for its first three years. Ultimately this policy would cripple eBay. On Taobao's launch in May 2003, eBay China owned 79 per cent of the Chinese market, but within two years, Alibaba's Taobao had taken almost 60 per cent of the market while eBay's share slid to less than 40 per cent. Although Meg Whitman, eBay's then CEO, believed that China could have been eBay's largest market on a global basis, this was not to be—the US model was unable to compete with Taobao. eBay's failure to understand its Chinese customers and its lack of a local partner would contribute to its struggle. Eventually, eBay faced a humiliating retreat from China.

During 2004, Alibaba celebrated its five-year anniversary; raised $82 million through a private equity commitment; developed a personal messaging and videoconferencing tool on Taobao; and launched Alipay, an independent third-party online payment platform. This platform was developed in response to the security fears and lack of trust that Chinese consumers had surrounding online payments. Understanding this fear, Ma developed a platform that releases payments to the seller only after the customer has acknowledged and is satisfied with the delivery. Alibaba's principle: suppliers do not get paid until you, the customer, say you are happy with the merchandise. This was a feature that eBay would later copy. Not surprisingly, Alipay would set the standards for, and has gone on to become, China's largest online payment service provider.

> A code of ethics should include trustworthiness: respect for customers, employees and others.

In 2005, Yahoo and Alibaba entered into a strategic partnership. Yahoo invested $1 billion in cash and contributed Yahoo China to the Alibaba Group. In exchange it received just over 40 per cent of the equity, valuing the group at $4 billion. The result for Alibaba: C2C, B2C and B2B marketplaces joined forces with a search engine and a significant war chest of cash to spend on development. And for Yahoo, it entered a necessary and relatively low-risk partnership. Alibaba went on to become its most valuable asset.

Yahoo was one of the first US Internet companies to enter Asia, and it had learnt from its mistakes; little of what was understood or successful in the USA could be transferred to China. However, it had experienced success in Japan by giving its Japanese partner, Softbank, local autonomy for operating decisions. Yahoo's union with Alibaba was symbiotic: they shared a common partner in Softbank, and Yahoo's co-founder, Taiwanese-American Jerry Yang, was a good fit with Jack Ma. During the period of its investment, Yahoo would be well rewarded for the faith it had placed in the growth of the group. Yahoo US had received more than $20 billion in cash from Alibaba by 2015. At the same time its remaining investment was valued at over $30 billion.

Much of Alibaba's Growth was Organic or Came from Small Acquisitions

During its first ten years, Alibaba built its ecosystem, completing a network of Internet business services for its buyers and sellers which is the source of much of its success today. The trading platforms were complimented by the introduction of Taobao University, which was launched to provide e-commerce education to its members. In 2007, Alimama, a marketing technology platform, was launched to offer sellers online marketing services for both personal computers and mobile devices. And Alisoft, a computer software program, was released to handle finances, inventories and customer information for the Alibaba subscribers.

To complete the trading platforms for B2B and C2C, in 2008, Alibaba launched Tmall, a B2C platform. Similar to Amazon, Tmall is a dedicated platform for businesses to sell to consumers, and it gives Chinese consumers access to branded products and a premium shopping experience. Tmall's unique selling point was the online 'mall' experience it provided where brands set up their own website. Brands commonly have more than one website: their own dedicated site and one within the mall. They paid a deposit to list on the site and then paid commission on the goods sold. Its level of success is similar to that of Taobao. In 2012, Tmall accounted for over 50 per cent of China's B2C online sales. In contrast, Amazon has an approximately 20 per cent share of the US market.[9]

In 2009, Alibaba announced its acquisition of HiChina, the leading Internet infrastructure provider, and cloud computing was founded in China. Originally it was developed to cope with the large volume of transactions from its trading platforms. However, it also serviced related businesses—its payment platforms—and generated revenues from its sellers. Sellers within its marketplaces were given access to cloud computing, significant computing power and scalability during periods when traffic spiked.

So during its first ten years, Alibaba effectively launched an ecosystem around three trading platforms, creating China's version of eBay and Amazon with annual revenues greater than $500 million and approximately 48 million registered users. During the next five years, from 2010 until its IPO in 2014, Alibaba continued to grow at a relentless pace: revenues hit $7.5 billion on sales of over $240 billion. Much of Alibaba's growth has been organic, from launches or from small acquisitions of mainly Chinese businesses, which has allowed it to keep its culture intact. Some highlights are listed below:

March 2010:	Taobao introduces online group, buying marketplace Juhuasuan
April 2010:	AliExpress launched; Chinese exporters to transact with global consumers
July and August 2010:	Vendio and Auctivae acquired: e-commerce solutions
August 2010:	The Mobile Taobao app is launched
November 2010:	OneTouch acquired: one-stop services for Chinese exporters
June 2011:	Tmall.com is spun off as an independent platform
October 2011:	Juhuasuan is spun off as an independent platform
September 2011:	Initial repurchase of shares from Yahoo
July 2013:	Alibaba Group unveils the Alibaba Smart TV operating system
September 2013:	Laiwag launched: mobile social networking app
February 2014:	Tmall Global launched: international brands offer products direct to Chinese consumers in China
June 2014:	UCWeb acquired: mobile browser company; mobile virtual network operators services in China; 60 per cent acquisition of ChinaVision: movie and television programme producer
July, 2014:	JV established with Intime to develop an O2O business in China; investment in AutoNavi: digital mapping company

In September 2014 the Alibaba Group went public on the New York Stock Exchange (NYSE). It was the largest technology launch in history at a time when China had become the largest e-commerce market in the world. Ma, through Alibaba, had created a complex ecosystem of business services, payment systems and leading marketplaces: B2B, C2C and B2C platforms that facilitated global trading, enabling a huge community of Chinese entrepreneurs, small and mid-size businesses, to build their business, trade and make money. By allowing so many to prosper, Ma has created a brand worth over $200 billion and a 'rock star' status for himself in the global online world.

> Alibaba is a globally recognised story which conjures up images of small businesses saying 'open sesame' to new treasures and opportunities.

Culture is Often a Profound Illustration of the Values of Its Founder(s)

Jack Ma: 'We will win, we will make it because we are young, and we never give up'[10]

As we discussed in the previous chapter, China has a long established culture of *guanxi*; a social network of contacts and relationships which form part of China's social fabric. Good *guanxi* is a network of mutually beneficial relationships often formed from social interactions. It is based on the notions of obligation and loyalty. These ideas are evident in Alibaba's culture.

It is often said that Alibaba's biggest asset is its founder—Jack Ma, described as a great storyteller, charismatic, direct-speaking and accessible. He displays a great respect for Chinese tradition and Western experience. Once an English teacher, his passion for learning no doubt contributed significantly to the company's reputation for agility, adaptability, continuous learning and evolving. His behaviours toward his customers and employees are illustrations of the *guanxi* tradition. Ma and his co-founders have built a business culture which is cited to be fundamentally responsible for its successes. The management have acted in the spirit of partnership with an owner mentality: long-term and incentivised to do the right thing.

Ma had big dreams and founded a business driven by purpose, with the happiness of the customer at its core: he wanted to empower small companies and to make it easy to do business anywhere. Moreover, he wanted Alibaba to be a partner to all business people and, specifically, small businesses. He believed that, in Asia, commerce is dominated by 'the shrimp'. Alibaba went 'after the shrimp because it was easy to catch a shrimp, but if you tried to catch a whale you might get hurt'.[11] He recognised that the Internet could put e-commerce back in the hands of small businesses.

Self-professed, Ma knew little of technology but he was consumed by the customer experience: 'I'm 100 per cent "made in China"',[12] he learnt English himself and knew nothing about technology. He was acutely aware that the founders were explorers with passion and big dreams in a world where they had little background or experience. To compensate, he would later bring together an executive team of international managers with blue chip backgrounds from world-class institutions: universities, consulting firms and investment banks. He said,

> Almost all my co-founders back in Hangzhou have no business experience. So I told my founders that they shouldn't expect to be the senior managers in the company. We need to find those experts who have real business experience to take the company to the next level. You see, I was trained as an English teacher. So I know nothing about running a company. And after four years I will resign as CEO and hand over the company to a new generation of managers.[13]

Ma did not resign four years on, but it was clear that he recognised the importance of talent and experience.

No Matter how Big, it will Always be a Start-Up with a Customer-Centric Approach

In the company's early days the benefits of Alibaba's marketplaces accrued almost entirely to its customers; it was many years before Alibaba would share in the revenues. Ma was often quoted as saying that 'you have to suffer', 'once our members make money we will make money' and, famously, 'right now we are running too fast for revenues'.[14] Complementing this low-revenue environment was a frugal, waste-no-renminbi culture, a state of constant chaos with no strategy, no stated priorities nor organisation chart—a common story among start-ups. Although structure would be imposed and chaos somewhat tamed, Ma believed that the company needed to maintain its start-up mentality:

> The company will remain a "start-up" no matter how long it has been in existence. Whatever has been stable, I will disrupt that stability. The company needs to continue to innovate and grow. I want the employees to believe that we are a small company, no matter how big we get. I believe we can create a system and culture to perpetuate this culture of entrepreneurial and start-up spirit.[15]

Part of the spirit of a successful start-up is the ability to embrace competition, to allow competition to make an organisation stronger and better. Alibaba has been referred to as fierce and nimble. This description was well earned when Ma 'waged war' on eBay by developing and launching Taobao. He recognised that in this equation, Alibaba was the shrimp. Yet the organisation was not intimidated; it was energised. However, Ma would never let the battle get too intense: he acknowledged that it was a game, a sport, and that the company was lucky to have a big competitor like eBay. To him it was like having the chance to play basketball against Michael Jordan.

Culture is Shaped through Behaviours that are Reinforced through Acceptance

Alibaba documented its mission, vision and values early in its evolution. Its mission was to make it easy to do business any-

> Alibaba's values: customer first, passion, teamwork, embracing change, commitment and integrity.

where; it vision to build the future infrastructure of commerce; and its values included customer first, passion and teamwork. Today these values also include embracing change, commitment and integrity. Although documented, values also need to be observed and rewarded to take hold. Alibaba's values were guiding principles in the recruiting process and in employee performance evaluation: 50 per cent on performance against objectives and 50 per cent against corporate values. These principles formed the foundation of the group's culture.

Alibaba's long-term view and owner mentality, together with the notions of obligation and loyalty, are evident in its relationship with employees—treating them as founders with its policies on the distribution and ownership of shares. Share ownership is a very important component of Alibaba's compensation, and there are many illustrations of just how important it is. Employees are given company shares in the form of stock options or restricted shares. In some cases they have been encouraged to hold on to them even after they leave. When Alibaba was faced with its first experience of laying off employees, after it moved too quickly to the USA, it allowed the employees affected to keep share options in the hope that one day they would be in a position to return to the company. Another example of this was when Alipay was rolled out of Alibaba into a newly formed structure. Ma stated that he would ensure that employees owned a significant percentage of the newly founded company and that he would not benefit. Furthermore, when Alibaba was floated on the NYSE, a portion of the shares were held aside for employees and partners, only to be released to the general public if they did not take up the offer. Importantly, one of the requirements to be part of the partnership is a meaningful holding of company stock. Indeed, Alibaba has made many employees rich, subsequently requesting that they invest responsibly and start their own businesses.

Being Accountable for the Outcomes of a Company's Actions and Inactions

It has been said that it is our reaction to adversity, rather than the adversity itself, which is a display of the level of our integrity. As the number of Alibaba's suppliers increased, its ability to monitor the quality of goods became a significant risk. The readily acknowledged and rampant occurrence of fraud and knock-offs in China escalated this risk. If the consumer could not trust the Alibaba platforms to facilitate the exchange of authentic merchandise, the damage to the brand could be irreversible. So the online scandal that hit the media in 2011 was highly visible on a global scale and provided some insight into the character of Alibaba's leader.

Online Scandal in China: Alibaba and the 2,236 Thieves[16]

In a filing with the Hong Kong Stock Exchange, Alibaba revealed that it had granted what it referred to as 'gold status'—a mark of quality—to more than 2,000 undeserving business that later went on to defraud customers. A gold subscriber pays a fee and is subject to third-party checks. Alibaba by many accounts handled this issue with transparency and speed: when made aware of the issue it launched an investigation and was forthcoming in publishing details.

Alibaba published a report that stated that a number of sales staff and internal individuals were directly responsible either intentionally or negligently, and it attributed the fraud to 'the pursuit of short term financial gains at all costs'.

> The Firm will 'only prosper by holding on to our ideals and our principles'.

Those involved were let go. Ma then issued a letter stating that the firm would only prosper by 'holding on to our ideals and our principles'.[17] Interestingly, eBay had also had to deal with this accusation of 'knockoffs' sold as authentic merchandise, yet it was eBay that reportedly instigated much of the negative press against Alibaba.

The Alibaba Group's Corporate Governance and Control

Corporate governance—the framework of rights, roles and responsibilities of various groups—has a relatively common meaning in Western economies. A board should be put in place to act in the best interests of shareholders; and the board and its committees should be structured to act independently of management and individuals who have control over management. However, China and its ownership policies result in structures that are not aligned with these concepts. The corporate governance under which Alibaba has operated, its ownership structure, how it is controlled and its board are different. To date, these differences may have contributed to its successful growth. Indeed, they did not act as a deterrent to raise capital in the USA. But will these differences prove to be problematic for the capital markets, and specifically for some classes of shareholders, in the future?

The SINA Structure, Getting Around Chinese Regulation on Foreign Ownership

Common among Chinese companies listed in the USA is an ownership structure called a SINA model, a structure first introduced when SINA, a Chinese online media company, went public.[18] This structure was born out of necessity: to navigate the ownership restrictions imposed on local Chinese and foreign entities. Effectively it requires three entities. First is a variable interest entity (VIE). This is owned and run by a Chinese national. It owns the assets but transfers the profits, by agreement, to a second entity. The second is a foreign-owned company registered in China but owned by a third entity, an 'offshore' company typically having its domain in tax havens such as the Cayman Islands. The foreign-owned company then transfers profits to the offshore company.

In China the Internet is considered a sensitive, key industry and is therefore heavily regulated. The government does not allow direct foreign ownership. The Alibaba Group, like many Chinese Internet companies, employs the SINA structure.

Jack Ma, the founder and chairman, and a Chinese national, has the majority ownership of the material VIEs, and he retains shareholder control. Separately, the shareholders and their foreign partners established a WFOE in China. The VIE and the WFOE are bound through contractual agreements. Alibaba's WFOE is wholly owned by a firm registered in the Cayman Islands.[19] Effectively the shareholders in the Cayman Islands have ownership of the revenue and earnings stream of the VIE, located in China, but they do not have a claim on its assets. This ownership of revenues is through legal agreements rather than through shares.

This structure still has significant controversy surrounding it because it exists to allow Chinese companies to get round government sanctions on foreign ownership and gain access to foreign capital. At the time of Alibaba's IPO announcement in the USA, some members of the US Senate raised concerns about VIE structures. Reviews were initiated but no actions were taken; the Securities and Exchange Commission's (SEC) stated priority was that investors are adequately warned of the risk. Yet the level of risk it posed was unclear. At that time the Chinese government had not stepped in to interfere or reverse the practice, and it had not made a public statement about what was acceptable. In effect, China had turned a blind eye to the practice. However, in 2015 a law was newly proposed suggesting that VIEs would be rendered illegal, specifically those companies not controlled by a Chinese national. Fortunately, this law will not affect the VIEs in Alibaba's case because they are owned by Ma.

A Structure that Leaves Shareholders Vulnerable

In 2011, Alibaba's SINA structure allowed Ma to move a valuable asset—its payment platform, Alipay—out of the group and into a local Chinese company controlled by him and owned by a sister financial firm, Ant Financial. This move became public when Yahoo, one of Alibaba's largest shareholders with 40 per cent equity, announced that it was unaware of, and very unhappy that this move had taken place.

Ma's response was to insist that it was a board decision. Yahoo had a representative on the board who had full knowledge of the move and, indeed, Yahoo had received compensation. Ma explained that the move was necessary because the Chinese government would never allow a Chinese payment platform to have foreign ownership, so this was a necessary move prior to an IPO. Fortunately the decision appeared to have been in the long-term interest of shareholders. Yahoo may in fact have been aware of the rollout prior to its happening, but, even as the largest shareholder, it would not have had any right to stop it. This transaction was a good illustration of how vulnerable the SINA structure leaves the foreign shareholder.

Increasing Shareholder Risk, Separation of Ownership and Control

When the Alibaba Group was ready to announce an IPO, it looked to the USA because it is home to the majority of public companies that give proportionately greater rights to different classes of shares, effectively allowing ownership and control to be separated. Hong Kong, perhaps the more natural place for Alibaba's listing—since it was there that it floated in 2007 and subsequently reprivatised—rejected the IPO, insisting that shareholders should have a say about management. It is interesting to note that recently the Financial Conduct Authority in the UK has issued a formal ban on shares listed on the London Stock Exchange's main market with different voting structures.

With an IPO in sight but yet unannounced, Alibaba made a series of acquisitions and cleaned up its share structure. In September 2011, Yahoo received a payment to reduce its overall holdings to 23 per cent, and it agreed to sell many of the remaining shares that it held when Alibaba floated. As an aside, even after the float, more than 90 per cent of Yahoo's market cap ($36 billion in December 2015) would be represented by its ownership of Alibaba shares.

Alibaba's structure, which has come under scrutiny on a number of occasions, holds its investors at risk. First is the risk of a SINA structure—separating the ownership of assets and revenues. Second is the separation of ownership and control—control of Alibaba is held by its partnership, a small group of founders and partners led by Ma, with the power to control the board into perpetuity without owning a majority of its shares. Third is the location of its owner's domain: the Cayman Islands. The prospectus, when Alibaba floated, stated that given the ownership of a Cayman Island company, the ability for an investor to protect their rights through the US Federal courts might be limited.

Yet, even with all of these risks, investors flooded in. The IPO effectively raised 10 per cent of its current capital. Today the profits of Alibaba Group, including the majority of its subsidiaries other than Alipay, are owned by the Cayman Island company, Alibaba Group Holdings. The approximate ownership breakdown of the Cayman Island company is 10 per cent via public shares, more than 40 per cent by Softbank Japan, 28 per cent by Jack Ma and family, and the balance distributed to Yahoo, employees and partners.

What About the Quality of Board Oversight?

The board of directors is elected by a partnership group which effectively controls the business. The partnership had 30 members at the time of the IPO: 25 within the management of the group and 5 within its affiliates. The partners are elected annually, must have a minimum of five years' tenure with Alibaba prior to election and are required to maintain a meaningful level of equity interest. The partnership operates on a one partner, one vote basis and has the power to elect a simple majority of the board of directors. Although this election is subject to shareholder approval, the largest shareholders—Yahoo and Softbank—are required to vote in favour of the Alibaba partnership nominees for as long as they remain material shareholders.

At the time of the Alibaba Group IPO, its board of directors would not have passed the scrutiny of a diversity lens: with one exception—Michael

Evans—all of its directors were Asian men. The proposed board of directors included nine members: five executives led by Jack Ma, the lead founder and Executive Chairman; and four further longstanding directors. The four non-executive directors included Jerry Yang, the co-founder of Yahoo and a significant shareholder, as well as Chee Hwa Tung, the Vice Chairman of the Twelfth National Committee of the Chinese People's Political Consultative Conference of the People's Republic of China.

What was the role of the board? It appeared to lack genuine independence, so was it able and willing to provide constructive challenge? During 2015, some progress was made in both areas of diversity and independence: Alibaba's board welcomed Ms Wan Ling Martello, a long-term Nestlé employee, and Borje E. Ekholm, a Swedish national.

Alibaba's Performance since the IPO

Included in the risks outlined in Alibaba's IPO prospectus is the risk that it may not be able to keep its culture intact. Certainly, if growth is pursued through acquisition, this might be difficult, and given a reported $38 billion war chest for acquisitions, it is a possibility.[20] Yet if this is not the case, and if the behaviours representing the company's values continue to be rewarded and observed in the actions of its senior executives and board, there is no reason to think it will be diluted. However, given the very dominant influence of its lead founder, perhaps the greatest risk to its culture and future success is the loss of Jack Ma. How much of the company's culture is tied up in him? Are the behaviours of the senior team; the organisational structure and its reporting lines; its compensation and incentive systems; strong enough to sustain its culture if Ma is replaced?

Alibaba has gone on to fund a shopping spree of acquisitions. Since January 2015, 22 deals have been reported. Some areas of investment are not obviously within its ecosystem, such as video, movie production and sports. To some it sounds like the right thing to do as Alibaba continues to pursue growth and understand new trends and technologies. Others have expressed concern about whether the company has carried out sufficient due diligence on the companies it has targeted. In 2014, Alibaba disclosed accounting irregularities in one of the operations it had purchased, a film production unit, to the tune of $800 million. A Chinese football club was another purchase rumoured to be the result of a night's drinking with the club's owner.[21]

The Chinese e-commerce prize is large because the penetration in China is still low relative to developed market standards. By 2020, China's e-commerce market is projected to hit $600 billion. Maintaining its current

> 'We must be as quick as a jack rabbit and as patient as a turtle.'
> Jack Ma in an interview with Fortune magazine

market share could see a doubling of Alibaba's revenues. However, that would produce a compounded average growth rate of only 15 per cent, which hardly stacks up to its previous annual gains of over 50 per cent prior to the IPO. As its international commerce revenues are less than 10 per cent of its total revenues, perhaps this is where it will find much of its future growth.

Alibaba's fiscal year end, March 2015, indicated the end of a very successful year, with revenues up 45 per cent, delivering a profit margin of 42 per cent. Yet its market capitalisation dropped by 20 per cent from a high of $250 billion not long after its IPO. This fall presumably reflects slowing revenues.[22] A year on from its record-breaking IPO, its quarterly results show a cumulative nine-month slowdown, with only a 27 per cent growth rate for the three months ending September.

Is a Strong Ethical Culture Enough to Protect Shareholders?

We have included Alibaba in this book because we think it has a fascinating story and is a positive illustration of China's traditions in practice. The company's success to date is attributed to its management team's 'owner mentality', a clear sense of mission, a long-term focus and a commitment to values.

This is a story about a company that has embraced and profited from the universal values of respect for customers, employees and others and accountability for its actions and inactions. It is a great illustration of a productive and ethical culture. The actions and behaviours of its leadership team illustrate its values and set the company standard.

An ethical culture is an essential element of a risk-management strategy, but is it enough to protect shareholders? So much of the protection and control that shareholders normally seek through Western-style corporate governance practices are not present here. Alibaba's share structure, with different classes of shares, leaves many shareholders vulnerable. And it is unclear how much independence the board actually has or exerts.

We believe that corporate governance, board leadership and culture all matter. In its current form, Alibaba's board is not adding its greatest value: independent thinking.

A Few Selected Highlights from the Alibaba Story

* *Culture is shaped through the actions, behaviours and values of the leadership team. The board's behaviours and the decisions it takes should reflect the values and ethics that it wishes to inspire.*

* *Companies should adopt universal values of respect for the customer, employee and others. It should be accountable for the outcome of its actions and inactions. Incentive systems should inspire behaviour that supports these values.*

* *Robust corporate governance practices and structures should include a majority of independent non-executive directors and classes of shares that protect the rights of all shareholders. When these are not present, caveat emptor.*

Notes

1. GMV refers to revenues at the retail level.
2. This was Singles Day, the day when the single digits align: (11 November) 11, 11. Alibaba has designed an e-commerce marketing event around this day.
3. www.alibabagroup.com, Alibaba's Vision Statement.

4. M-commerce: using a wireless device such as a mobile phone for a commercial transaction.

5. www.iresearchchina.com, iResearch Consulting, 2014.

6. Davidson, L. (2014) In five charts: How Alibaba pulled off the largest IPO ever, The Telegraph, 22 September 2014.

7. Erisman, Porter (2015) *Alibaba's World: How a Remarkable Chinese Company is Changing the Face of Global Business,* (Macmillan).

8. Erisman, Porter (2015) *Taobao World: how a remarkable Chinese company is changing the face of global business,* (Macmillan).

9. KPMG, China 360, (2014) E-commerce in China: Driving a new Consumer Culture, January 2014.

10. D'Onfro, Jullian (2016), 15 quotes that show the strange relentless genius of billionaire Alibaba founder Jack Ma, www.uk.businessinsider.com.

11. Erisman, Porter, *Alibaba's World: How a Remarkable Chinese Company is Changing the Face of Global Business,* (Macmillan) Publishers.

12. Rose, Charlie (2015), Entrepreneurial masterclass: Alibaba founder Jack Ma interview, www.biznews.com.

13. Erisman, Porter, *Alibaba's World: How a Remarkable Chinese Company is Changing the Face of Global Business,* (Macmillan) Publishers.

14. Erisman, Porter, *Alibaba's World: How a Remarkable Chinese Company is Changing the Face of Global Business,* (Macmillan) Publishers.

15. Fischer, B. (2013) China Needs a New Generation of Dreamers, *Harvard Business Review*, 15 November 2013.

16. *The Economist* (2011) Alibaba and the 2,236 thieves, *The Economist*, 24 February 2011.

17. *The Economist* (2011) Alibaba and the 2,236 thieves, *The Economist*, 24 February 2011.

18. Looking at Chinese VIE's, Forbes, October, 2012.

19. Alibaba's prospectus filed with the SEC, September, 2014.

20. Slater-Robins, M. (2015) *Chinese internet giant Alibaba could spend up to $38 billion on acquisitions in 2016*, 11 December 2015.

21. *The Economist* (2014) After the Float, *The Economist*, 6 September 2014.

22. Orbis database, Company report of Alibaba Group Holdings Limited.

10

Conclusion

In the preceding chapters we have illustrated how shortcomings in corporate governance and the prevailing culture within a company have driven companies close to, and sometimes beyond, the brink of disaster. While we acknowledge that other factors also contribute to failure, we contend that effective board oversight and a productive ethical culture will, if not always prevent, at least mitigate the consequences of poor decisions and external shocks.

Again and again we have seen the devastating consequences of an ill-chosen and poorly informed board. In the case of Olympus, the lack of independent directors prevented discovery of the cover-up. Other cases, such as the Co-op, the banks, Enron and Kids Company, illustrate how nominally independent directors failed to hold CEOs to account due to complacency, inexperience or sheer reluctance to challenge the status quo. Without independence and the willingness to challenge conventional wisdom, risk was not well understood and risk management, a core board responsibility, was woefully supervised, thereby magnifying the detrimental effects of poor decisions.

We have also witnessed the devastating impact of a flawed culture. When a company's culture is corrupt, the long-term viability of the

© The Author(s) 2017
A. Micklethwait, P. Dimond, *Driven to the Brink*,
DOI 10.1057/978-1-137-59053-4_10

organisation is placed in peril. A culture of deference and excessive loy-alty to superiors blinded the directors of Olympus to even the possibility that one of their own was committing fraud. A culture focused on profit, regardless of risk, and at the expense of customers, led to the LIBOR and FX scandals, as well as the banking crisis of 2008.

Some Progress has been Made

In the aftermath of the 2008 crisis, governments instigated numerous reviews and introduced regulations aimed at preventing a future crash. Although most of this was directed towards the structure and oversight of banks, there was also an element of corporate governance reform. The Dodd–Frank Act in the USA, while primarily concerned with the stricter regulation of financial firms, also included clauses about compensation and shareholder rights. The UK changed the regulatory regime for banks and also revised the UK corporate governance code in 2010 and 2012, putting more emphasis on implementing the spirit of the code rather than just box-ticking.

Japan's new corporate governance code, introduced in 2015 in response to the Olympus and Toshiba scandals, is a huge step forward in increasing the board's accountability to shareholders, and improving governance and transparency. Although it only mandates a minimum of two independent directors on the board, once Japanese companies realise that external scrutiny will not prove to be disruptive but can make their companies stronger, we expect that the code will gradually converge with that of other countries. Many other countries have issued revised corporate governance codes over the past few years and we expect further revisions in future. Development of these codes has become an iterative process, with countries gradually adopting best practices from elsewhere.

The majority of these codes are principles-based and include a 'comply or explain' provision: if a company does not feel that it is appropriate to comply with any provision, it has to explain, in some detail, why this is the case rather than just state the deviation from the code of practice. The flaw in this approach is that, in Hector Sants' memorable phrase, 'a principles-based approach does not work with individuals who have no principles'.[1] Integrity is an essential trait in a leadership team if one is to ensure that core values are not overridden by self-interest. US companies have to comply with mandated rules, as set out by individual stock exchanges and relevant legislation. Both systems have their merits. While a rules-based approach leaves little room for ambiguity and is easier to enforce than a principles-based approach, it can become just another box-ticking exercise and is less able to cope with rapid changes in the business environment.

A whole raft of legislation has been passed, or is being developed, to address problems related specifically to banking, as discussed in Chapter 3. However, many of these have still not been implemented fully. The Basel III accord, aimed at strengthening the banks' balance sheets, is not due for completion until 2019. The UK Senior Managers and Certification Regime, designed to increase the personal responsibility and accountability of senior managers, is coming into effect in early 2016 but it will be a year before it is fully in place. The Group of Seven (G7) is pushing the International Financial Stability Board to develop a voluntary code of conduct which could be applied to all bankers.

Fines and compensation paid by banks since 2008 totalled a mind-boggling $235 billion by May 2015, with more forecast to come.[2] Unfortunately, it appears that some banks regard such fines merely as a cost of doing business so the effect on their behaviour is limited. It is also the case that the cost of fines has been borne disproportionately by shareholders rather than by the perpetrators themselves. Cognisant of this, regulators are trying to increase the personal responsibility of individuals through legislation and new codes of conduct. Yet banks are fighting back against new regulations, in some cases removing unworkable rules but also watering down others before they are adopted.

In any event, rules and regulations can only go so far. The banks themselves need to support these initiatives with a framework of control and governance based on a value system that rewards personal integrity.

At the time of writing, in a regrettable move, the Financial Conduct Authority (FCA) had abandoned its planned review of banking culture and incentive structures in favour of discussing actions with individual banks directly. A review such as the one that the FCA originally planned would have been publicly available, allowing interested parties and the general public insights into banking culture and efforts to change it. While we agree that it is time to stop 'banker bashing', we hope that this decision will be reversed and a thorough review undertaken to remove the suspicion that the banks are being let off lightly and that it is back to business as usual.

Shareholders have a Role to Play

Shareholders take a risk whenever they invest in a company, a risk that the company will not perform as expected or even that it will fail. As we stated earlier, before investing, shareholders bear the responsibility of carrying out due diligence to assure themselves that the company they are about to invest in has a responsible board that will represent their interests. If a company that offers double-digit returns but has weak corporate governance meets disaster, passive shareholders should bear some responsibility for their own losses—a case of greed overcoming caution.

The influence of shareholders is not limited to the annual general meeting but can play a vital role in forcing through change at other times. We believe that this is best done through conversations with the board. As we have seen, unreasonable shareholder expectations, unrestrained by the board, will damage the long-term health of a company. Working together, shareholders and the board need to establish a healthy ongoing dialogue to manage expectations of performance. However, at times, particularly in relation to the composition of the board, shareholders may be required to become more vocal. The threat that a large shareholder may divest its holding, with the consequent hit to the share price, might be required to focus directors' minds on its concerns.

In the case of Olympus, the silence of Japanese institutional investors was shameful in contrast with the intervention of Western fund managers, which helped to force through an independent enquiry. Although the Japanese government has imposed some corporate governance changes, it is only through shareholder pressure that significant reforms will be implemented.

We have seen a case where shareholders' influence can be restricted in share structures that have different classes of shares. This structure gives some groups of shareholders undue influence over the governance structure, a system that is open to abuse. Minority shareholders can promote their own interests, including the election of directors who are favourable to them at the expense of the majority.

In the case of Alibaba, with its different classes of shares, its culture and influential board have, so far, kept the company focused on its core strategy. Whether this continues over the long term as Jack Ma reduces his involvement is to be seen.

Independence in a Director is a Valuable Trait

In the examples we have used, the board has failed in its responsibilities to shareholders and other stakeholders. While in most cases the board had a majority of so-called independent directors, Olympus' 15-man board had only three. Although this complies with the recently introduced Japanese corporate governance code, we believe that independent directors should form a majority on the board. Where directors are in a minority, they risk being sidelined and ignored by the majority insider directors who have a more in-depth knowledge of the company and strong connections with each other.

> Independent thinking, the greatest value a board can add.

As we indicated in our introduction (Chapter 1), to be truly independent, board members must have the necessary business experience and expertise to feel competent to question management and to make proper decisions. If this is lacking they are more likely to defer to management. However, historically, the selection of directors has been far from ideal. All too often, directors have been chosen on the basis of long service or cronyism, while others have been mere figureheads; they have not had the necessary knowledge or specific industry experience required to make an effective contribution. In the case of the banks, a lack of relevant experience, particularly as it related to risk, meant that boards failed to understand the dangers of the new derivative products they were dealing in or to put in place adequate risk-management systems to limit the risk.

The 2003 Higgs review of UK non-executive directors found that nearly half were recruited through personal contacts or friendships.[3] After Higgs' recommendations on the hiring process for directors were adopted, efforts increased to recruit from a wider field, but much more could have been done: the example of the Co-op provides a case in point. Today the Co-op has made considerable progress in improving

> Independence requires relevant experience or board directors are likely to defer to management.

its corporate governance. The board has been reduced to a more optimal number, from 20 members to nine, of which a majority are independent. All of these directors have relevant experience, and member-nominated directors are screened for their commercial acumen before being put forward for election.

Much of the problem is that directors have been chosen from too small a gene pool. As J. B. Kassarjian said, 'the lack of genetic variety in top management blinds organisations to painful current realities and to emerging new opportunities'.[4] On a positive note, this pool has grown over the last ten years, helped by governments' encouragement to increase female and minority representation on boards. Sadly, in countries such as China, there is still a lack of well-qualified directors.

The nomination committee is responsible for choosing new board members. While in many countries it is a requirement for the committee to have at least a majority of independent directors, Japanese companies have no such obligation and, indeed, are deeply suspicious of any attempt to force the involvement of outsiders in the choice of directors or executive pay. We strongly believe that this is a mistake and that Japanese companies, and their shareholders, are missing out on the valuable contribution that experienced outsiders can offer.

When identifying qualified directors, a good nomination committee will understand the existing and missing skills, and the knowledge and experience of the board and, in light of this, specify the criteria for a candidate director. It should also assess an individual's ability and willingness to challenge in a constructive manner. An independent third party, such as a recruitment agency, should be employed to undertake a rigorous and unbiased search. It should consider the views of the CEO but also retain its independence and avoid undue influence from executives.

Equally, any prospective director must undertake due diligence to understand the true state of affairs within the company and whether they are prepared to accept the risks and obligations of the post, including dedicating what may be a significant amount of time to the role. Directors on a board have a responsibility for the activities of the company that they oversee and are accountable for their actions and inactions. Whereas in years past a directorship was seen as a useful earner and part-time occupation for retired executives, it is now a professional position. The responsibilities and risks have a much higher profile. Busy executives are less likely to be able to handle this additional responsibility—it is not for those who are heavily committed elsewhere. This is equally true for the trustees of charities.

Training also has a place in improving the effectiveness of the board. Directors not only need instruction to understand their rights and duties but also training in issues specific to the company. Training as a board allows directors to develop a better understanding of one another and it can help them to develop interactions that encourage constructive challenge. Some codes require ongoing training for directors, and we hope that this practice will grow in future.

Independence is Essential to Discharge the Duties of the Director

There is an inherent information asymmetry between executive and non-executive directors. Non-executives rely on information provided to them by the company in order to perform their duties. They must have information in time to prepare properly for board meetings. Receiving papers on the day of the meeting and having to return them the same day, as in the case of Olympus, gives directors neither the time to assess the issues and prepare questions for the meeting, nor the opportunity to review the subject later. Non-executive directors must insist on receiving the appropriate amount of information in a timely manner to adequately understand the financial position and risks facing the company.

It is also vital for the board to be given the opportunity, and resources, to engage independent third parties to investigate issues that are important to the company and to provide the information needed in order to

take informed decisions. Directors need to be careful to choose independent advisors if possible. When the directors of Olympus asked a consultancy to value the three small companies that the operation was proposing
to buy, they used the same consultancy that Olympus managers had used
themselves. Since there was almost no chance that they would receive an
alternative valuation, the exercise provided no additional transparency on
the proposal, leaving the directors no better informed.

Suitable qualifications and experience are necessary, but not sufficient, criteria for an effective,
independent board member. As
Warren Buffett said, truly independent directors are rare. In our
view, true independence is a state of
mind: the willingness to ask tough
questions and get answers, and to

> Independence is a state of
> mind: the willingness to ask
> tough questions, challenge
> conventional wisdom and
> walk away if not satisfied.

walk away if not satisfied. All too often, directors will either not challenge
executives or will accept their answers too readily. The board of the Royal
Bank of Scotland (RBS), perhaps accustomed to the strong management
style of the CEO, Fred Goodwin, and confident in his undoubted abili-
ties, were persuaded to accept his logic for RBS's untimely cash offer to
buy ABN-AMRO.

We believe that directors have an obligation to dissent. This does not
mean that they should be continually disruptive but rather positively disruptive. If directors disagree on a point at issue, they have a duty to see it
through and not to desist until they receive a satisfactory answer. If this
became the norm then board behaviour would take a turn for the better.

The nuclear option of resigning, rarely taken by directors, is one that
can bring about change when discussion fails. It also takes a significant
amount of courage. Although it is better to stay at the table to work it out,
if this is not possible and it is an issue that could jeopardise the long-term
sustainability of an organisation, resigning may be the only option. Trying
to explain the sudden departure of a board member causes problems for
companies, so the mere threat of resignation should make executives think
twice about ignoring the concerns of the independent directors.

We strongly recommend, as is already the case in some jurisdictions, that the board appoints a Senior Independent Director (SID) to check the concentration of power on the board. This director acts as a sounding board for the chairman and as a conduit for other directors and shareholders to express their concerns if they do not want to approach the chairman or executives. It is a crucial role in a company which has an executive chairman, as is common in the USA. It is important for independent directors to meet alone on a regular basis without the presence of any executive officers and also, on occasion, without the chairman. In this environment, led by the SID, directors can discuss issues which may be critical of the CEO or the company's strategy without awkwardness. After all, it is not easy to chat informally with the CEO one minute and then shortly after question his/her proposed pay rise.

Discussing issues of this nature away from executives allows independent directors to adopt a balanced view and a united front to subsequently speak with one voice. It also gives independent directors the opportunity to discuss the performance of the chairman and, if necessary, take corrective action.

Avoid the Pitfalls of a Dominant CEO

Even where there has been a majority of independent directors, in many cases they have allowed themselves to be dominated by the CEO. This is partly due to the long experience and achievements of the CEO, but also to complacency on the part of board members and a reluctance to challenge the status quo. This is wrong. The CEO is employed by the shareholders and board, not the other way round. In an ideal situation, the board will work as a team of equals, supportive of management but prepared to constructively challenge accepted norms or decisions that are in conflict with the company's values or put operations at risk.

As part of a necessary system of checks and balances, we believe that the roles of chairman and CEO should be separate in all cases. This has been the case for some time in the UK and, under the dual-board system, common in continental Europe. The USA is a notable exception. However, even there, 40 per cent of Standard & Poor's 500 companies had split the roles in 2012, up from 25 per cent in 2004.[5] Each has a separate and distinct contribution to make.

We further believe that a retiring CEO should not normally step up to the chairman's post. It is a difficult transition for a CEO to become the non-executive chairman of the same company. While continuity of knowledge and experience can be extremely useful, there are significant drawbacks to such a move. As one CEO who became a non-executive director of his company said, 'The chairman should allow the CEO to shine, so if you've been the CEO previously you're still seen as the person in the spotlight … you'll know all the details of what the CEO does so it [is] very difficult to [be] challenging without sounding a bit defensive.'[6] The presence of a CEO-turned-chairman risks undermining the new CEO, particularly if the chairman is someone with a strong personality who has found it difficult to step back from day-to-day operations. As was the case with Olympus, it can also prevent or delay the exposure and correction of past errors.

Risk Management is a Primary Responsibility of the Board

With the increasing complexity of business transactions, shorter product lifecycles, technological advances, globalisation and the overall pace of change, there is a burgeoning need for more, and better, risk management. In our examples there have been failings in internal controls and risk oversight. Any organisation serious about managing risk must award it sufficient attention and resource. All too often, compliance and risk officers are regarded as second-class citizens, with the disastrous results of which we have written. Value should be awarded to risk management by giving it prominence in the company's organisation and remuneration structures.

> Risk management is the responsibility of ALL board members.

One of the primary duties of the board is to ensure that a comprehensive risk-management framework is in place and adequately monitored. The board requires a structure that includes appropriate risk-management and governance committees led by board directors with strengths in risk management. However, risk management must not be left solely to this committee. It is the overall responsibility of the board to ensure that an adequate risk framework is in place. All directors need to have sufficient knowledge and experience to understand the risks that the company faces, and to accept responsibility for managing and containing these risks. Where industries face considerable or complex risks, it is advisable for the chief risk officer to be a board director. Such an appointment will raise the profile and authority of risk management.

The board must discuss and clarify the risk appetite of the company. These discussions should not be confined to the boardroom. Building effective communications with senior management ensures that the board is better informed to build a broad picture of the risks that the company is facing. It is then in a better position to understand how to manage these risks effectively. While improving communications is important, directors must remain independent so that their ability to challenge is not compromised.

> Any organisation serious about risk management must award it sufficient profile, attention and resource.

Directors need to understand the risks underpinning a given strategy and take decisions based on acceptable tolerance levels. For example, it is unlikely that some of the board directors at Enron understood the increased risks they were bearing as the company changed from a staid utility to an aggressive trader. Unacceptable risks do not necessarily mean that a strategy has to be abandoned completely. Excessive risks can be mitigated or transferred out through insurance products, for example, but they must be well understood. The banks thought that they had transferred risk away by issuing credit default swaps. However, they did not fully understand that the insurance they had bought was only as strong as the insurance companies themselves, and that part of their risk-management process should have involved assessing the viability of their counterparties. Ultimately, some risks should be rejected entirely and the strategy may need to change as a consequence.

The board needs to ensure that adequate resources are allocated to manage and monitor risks. Key risks should be identified and brought to the attention of the board. Risk reports should not only identify dangers but also pinpoint their root causes, and how they may interact and even amplify one another. Activities that involve inherently high risks, such as trading, should be supervised accordingly. The risk-management plan should not only estimate the probability of risks but also determine how the company plans to cope if such a threat materialises. The board is responsible for discussing and assessing the risk-management plan on a regular basis.

A risk oversight strategy must also include a process for whistleblowers to report their concerns. A survey by the Association of Certified Fraud Examiners highlighted the vital role of people who are willing to stand up and be heard. It found that more than 42 per cent of corporate frauds are uncovered by tip-offs, compared with 30 per cent by internal audit or management review. By contrast, external auditing uncovered fewer than half of the frauds that were discovered by accident (6.8 per cent).[7] The whistleblower's lot is a lonely one: tainted with a hint of betrayal, often dismissed and then sometimes unemployable, these people need strong moral incentives to speak up. The Securities and Exchange Commission (SEC) has a whistleblower award programme where an informer whose case is proven can be awarded between 10 and 30 per cent of the fine collected. However, generally their most important desire is to be taken seriously and to be protected from losing their job.

Many companies have whistleblowers' policies, but these are not always effective. Someone who is willing to come forward needs to be able to report any misgivings to an independent person, usually to the board audit committee where anonymity should be preserved whenever possible. Concerns should not be routinely dismissed if the informant refuses to disclose their identity, as happened at Olympus.

A Productive Ethical Culture is an Important Part of a Risk-Management Strategy

A company's culture develops through a process of successful adaptation. Its values and code of ethics often depend on the industry it operates in and the values of the society it is immersed in, but, as discussed in Chapter 1, there are a few universal values that all companies can subscribe to, such as trustworthiness; respect for customers, employees and others; and responsibility for the outcomes of a company's actions or inactions.

These values should be elaborated on to make it clear how they apply to the company's day-to-day operations. However, a lengthy code of ethics (remember Enron's 64-page code) is more likely to be filed and forgotten than a short outline of

> It is the board's responsibility to ensure an ethical culture as a tenet of a risk-management framework.

the main principles. Most importantly, these ethics and values must be observed in the actions of the board of directors and its senior executives.

Banks have recently been sending employees on training courses in corporate culture and values. However, training such as this will only increase scepticism and cynicism if the company's incentive systems do not support its espoused values. Corporate values must be observable because actions speak louder than words. If a bank's values include respect for its customers as a priority, but at the same time it sends out a letter saying that salespeople are allowed to add undeclared commission to trades, it is really saying that profit comes first, not the customer.

Remuneration and Organisational Structure Drive Behaviours

A company's organisational structures, its reward systems and the way it measures and tracks performance influences behaviours. Recognition by promotion, or genuinely increasing the stature of a role within the organisational structure, is visible acknowledgement of the worth of a function or individual. Behaviours that result in the award of a bonus tend to become the norm. For example, the chief risk officer should have the same status as business heads, as well as appropriate remuneration. This would be observable evidence that the role is valued, and those working within risk management and compliance would have a clear career path to follow with a route to the top.

The senior management team, responsible for developing and managing the company's risk strategy and internal controls, needs to have incentives which match the company's long-term objectives. Its incentive scheme should be aligned with the risk appetite of the company, measuring performance in light of any risks incurred.

> A company's organisation structure, its reward systems, and the way it measures and tracks performance all influence behaviours.

Share option packages awarded to bankers were a one-way bet and had the effect of increasing the incentive to take risks. Some banks, such as Crédit Suisse, now award restrictive shares, rather than options, which vest over several years and whose value can go down as well as up. This practice should be more widely adopted. Regulators have insisted on claw-back clauses in employment contracts in order to introduce a measure of accountability for mistakes, but it is still uncertain how easy it will be to enforce them in practice. Although this measure is directed purely at the financial service industry, it is our opinion that it should apply in other situations.

Boards are required to approve executive compensation packages, which should be designed to encourage long-term thinking and to focus on long-term achievement, with some penalty for poor performance. A bonus system focused solely on rewarding increased revenue will encourage risk-taking, to the probable detriment of future earnings. Glaxo's Chinese salespeople, awarded bonuses purely on the basis of sales, felt justified in bribing doctors to buy their products. Changing its reward system to include metrics of the provision of good-quality information to doctors, a measure of respect for customers, should start to change their behaviour.

Executive compensation periodically receives a lot of media attention. The OECD and the American Federation of Unions calculated the ratio of executive pay to that of the average worker. They estimated that

> The actions and decisions of the board should reflect the culture it wishes to inspire.

US executives were paid 354 times the average worker in 2012.[8] We are not debating the rights and wrongs of the level of executive compensation but we do note that it is a contentious subject and one where boards have the final decision. As such, boards must have an understanding of the impact of remuneration on behaviour and culture. Remuneration committee members should be robust enough to challenge proposed pay packages even when supported by remuneration consultants.

While it is not possible to eliminate all bad behaviour through well-structured compensation packages, aligning remuneration with sustainable performance should reduce the incentive to increase short-term earnings at the expense of the long-term health of the company. For example, it might act as a curb on making reckless acquisitions: an acquisition would need to deliver the promised performance before the CEO could benefit.

Bad Behaviours Need to be Identified and Addressed

While rewards are an essential tool to reinforce 'good' behaviours, the use of 'sticks' is another important way to change culture. Zero tolerance for small infractions, rooting out 'bad apples', and a 'no-blame' process for self-reporting mistakes are some of the methods that companies can use to alter behaviour.

As indicated in Chapter 1, there have been many studies which have shown that negative words or actions have a disproportionate effect compared with positive ones: one bad customer experience will far outweigh several positive ones; and a

> Bad behaviours need to be stopped before they become normalised through acceptance.

personal criticism will be recalled long after a glowing report has faded into distant memory. The same is true of employees who treat customers or fellow employees with disrespect or otherwise ignore company values. It is advisable to identify and retrain or remove these employees so that they cease to demoralise or corrupt others.

Minor infractions that are ignored on the basis that they have no serious impact can become habitual. Employees who feel that they are not being held accountable may see no obstacle to committing more serious breaches. One of the issues highlighted by the LIBOR/FX scandals was the widespread acceptance that these aberrant activities were in fact acceptable because so many people were involved. There was a strong sense of self-justification: 'everybody does it', 'we have always done it so why stop now', 'if I don't do it someone else will' and 'nobody will notice and nobody is hurt'. However, the perpetrators warned each other to keep quiet about what was going on and wanted to hide their activities from compliance. In other words, they knew they were doing something wrong. The company should have a zero-tolerance disciplinary policy, one that is tough but fair; not tolerating infractions but still treating those who commit breaches with dignity and respect.

A style of management that may seem to contradict the zero-tolerance method is the no-blame culture where staff can report mistakes without fear of blame or dismissal. However, stamping down on unreported infractions is different from encouraging employees to come forward to report their mistakes. There is growing evidence that praising staff to report errors rather than blaming them allows companies to learn what the problems are and then to correct them. Rewarding this kind of behaviour can help an organisation to learn and evolve.

The aviation industry has an enviable safety record due, in no small part, to the compulsory system of reporting and investigating errors whether they are near misses in the air or mechanical faults. Hospitals are experimenting with no-fault reporting of errors and have found that it leads to much improved patient outcomes. No-fault reporting on Toyota's production line has made continuous improvement possible.

The evidence is overwhelming: a supportive culture like this where employees can ask naïve or uncomfortable questions without being belittled or ignored is a step towards becoming a learning organisation. It should also have a channel for staff to report ethical dilemmas before any decision is taken. Ethical questions are not always clear-cut. A well-defined organisational structure with a clear route to seek guidance allows individuals an opportunity to resolve issues in a timely manner, aligned with corporate values.

Final Word

We have identified what we believe are the root causes of corporate disasters: poor corporate governance and a corporate culture lacking integrity. A culture of excessive risk-taking combined with corporate governance failings in risk management played a significant part in the stories we have told. We have outlined some actions that can be taken to influence culture and improve corporate governance, but the list is by no means exhaustive.

A story that had not fully emerged by the time this book went to print is the scandal at Volkswagen (VW). Although the enquiries have yet to report, it seems certain that there were serious failings in corporate governance and culture at the company. Aggressive growth targets relied on boosting sales of diesel cars in the USA, but, as environmental regulations are stricter there than in Europe, this required design changes to the engine. VW engineers knew that this would not be possible within the tight time schedule that had been set. Rather than report their failure to management, they designed a 'defeat device'—a software patch that would detect when a car was being tested and change its operation so that it could pass the test. As a result of this revelation, VW has suffered great damage to its reputation of engineering excellence and reliability. The financial damage is as yet unknown but will likely run to several billion euros.[9]

It is clear that VW suffered from several flaws in its culture: a general acceptance that it was okay to break the rules; fear of admitting mistakes; and a focus on profit to the detriment of the customer. It has long been known that, in Europe, stated engine performance, as achieved under test conditions, is significantly better than that experienced under normal driving conditions. This is true not only of VW but for most, if not all, car manufacturers. The ways in which manufacturers manage the test results is currently legal but undoubtedly deceives the customer. Behaviour against customers' interests has been normalised and accepted as 'everyone does it, so why shouldn't we'. One could speculate that the VW engineers, accustomed to ideal test conditions, took this just one step further and actually changed the operation of the car's emission controls to enhance performance under these specific conditions.

It has been reported that the engineers were scared to tell top management that they could not achieve the target set and that this culture was common throughout VW. Although when the scandal first broke, blame was placed on just a few 'rogue' engineers, it seems clear today that the 'defeat device' was common knowledge within the department. The fear of accountability was widespread: VW's CEO, Martin Winterkorn, was blamed for fostering a climate of fear and authoritarianism.

VW's board must surely be held at least partly responsible for the failure. It agreed VW's strategy and growth targets; appointed the CEO; allowed the environment that bred fear to persist; and failed to oversee effectively the management of risks and internal controls. The structure of the supervisory board reflects large block shareholdings in VW, and German law specifying that half of the members must be labour representatives. Of the 20-person board, only one is truly independent; the others are either worker representatives or represent the three large shareholders: the Porsche/Piech families, Qatar and the German State of Lower Saxony. Outside shareholders have only 12 per cent of the votes, although they own more than 30 per cent of the capital, so they have little influence on appointments. The board is severely lacking in expertise and experience. For example, despite VW's global market, 17 members (85 percent) of the supervisory board are German or Austrian.

Once again, weak corporate governance, and an environment that bred fear and normalised aberrant behaviour have led a company to the brink. VW will not go bankrupt as a result of the scandal but the consequences of its actions will be widespread and severe. This is not the last scandal to be uncovered: new tales of fraud and mismanagement will doubtless emerge.

Improvements in corporate governance are not a universal panacea: disasters can still occur. However, we believe that much of the disaster we have written about could have been avoided with the appropriate level of board oversight. The board represents the interests of shareholders and large stakeholders. Collectively, directors are responsible for ensuring the long-term health of an organisation.

A board's greatest value comes from its ability to remain independent and objective, to provide challenge against conventional wisdom in its duty to sign off strategy, to monitor performance and to oversee the management of risk. Indeed, it is responsible for ensuring the evolution of a productive ethical culture as a critical part of a risk-management strategy.

Notes

1. Sants, H. (2009) *Delivering Intensive Supervision and Credible Deterrence*, Speech delivered to the Reuters Newsmakers Event, 12 March 2009.
2. Slater, S. (2015) Misconduct bill tops $235 billion as banks struggle to shake off past sins, *Reuters*, 21 May 2015.
3. Higgs, D. (2003) Review of the role and effectiveness of non-executive directors, *Department of Trade and Industry*, January 2003.
4. Professor J. B. M. Kassarjian, Professor of Management at Babson College, Emeritus Professor of Strategy and Organization at IMD (2016), e-mail correspondence.
5. Ferracone, R. (2014) Combined Chairman/CEO roles: You think, *Forbes Magazine*, 5 March 2015.
6. Making the switch from CEO to Chairman, *Criticaleye*.
7. *The Economist* (2015) The Age of the Whistleblower, *The Economist*, 5 December 2015.
8. Ferdman, R. (2014) The pay gap between CEOs and workers is much worse than you realize, *The Washington Post*, 25 September 2014.
9. Edwards, J. & G. Prodhan (2016) VW faces billions in fines as U.S. sues for environmental violations, *Reuters*, 5 January 2016.

Glossary

Asset-backed commercial paper A short-term debt (with a typical maturity ranging between 30 and 180 days) that is collateralised by other financial assets.

Asset light Refers to a strategy adopted with the aim of generating profits from a small fixed asset base. Certain industries, such as banking and financial services, are by nature asset light.

Asset securitisation A process whereby debt instruments (e.g. loan paper or accounts receivable originated by banks or credit-card companies) are aggregated in a pool and new securities then issued backed by the pool.

Bank covenant A restriction on a borrower imposed by the lending bank. For example, it could be a requirement placed on a company to achieve and maintain specified targets, such as levels of cash flow and/or balance sheet ratios and/or specified capital expenditure levels in order to retain financing facilities.

Bank of International Settlements An international organisation which fosters cooperation between central banks and other agencies in pursuit of monetary and financial stability. Its banking services are provided exclusively to central banks and international organisations.

Basel III accord A comprehensive set of reform measures designed to improve regulation, supervision and risk management within the banking sector. The first version of Basel III was published in late 2009. Largely in response to the credit crisis, banks are required to maintain proper leverage ratios and meet certain capital requirements.

© The Author(s) 2017
A. Micklethwait, P. Dimond, *Driven to the Brink*,
DOI 10.1057/978-1-137-59053-4

Benchmark rate (see Reference rate).

Big Bang The name for the introduction in 1986, in the UK, of major changes in trading on the stock exchange, principally involving widening of membership, relaxation of rules for brokers, and computerisation.

Bull market A market in which prices are generally rising.

Capital structure The mix of a company's long-term debt, specific short-term debt, common equity and preferred equity. The capital structure is how a firm finances its overall operations and growth by using different sources of funds.

Chapter 11 bankruptcy In the USA, bankruptcy is the state of insolvency of an individual or an organisation. Under US law, Chapter 11 provides that, unless the court rules otherwise, the debtor remains in possession of the business and in control of its operation. It also makes possible the negotiation of payment schedules, the restructuring of debt and even the granting of loans by the creditors to the debtor. (The UK equivalent term is 'administration'.)

Collateral A specific property that a borrower pledges to a lender in order to secure repayment of a loan.

Collateralised Debt Obligation A type of structured asset-backed security. It can be thought of as a promise to pay investors in a prescribed sequence, based on the cash flow the CDO collects from the pool of mortgages or other assets it owns. It is 'sliced' into 'tranches', which 'catch' the cash flow of interest and principal payments in sequence, based on seniority. If some loans default and the cash collected by the CDO is insufficient to pay all of its investors, those in the lowest, most 'junior' tranches suffer losses first. The last to lose payment from default are the safest, most senior tranches. Consequently, coupon payments (and interest rates) vary by tranche with the safest/most senior tranches receiving the lowest rates and the lowest tranches receiving the highest rates to compensate for the higher default risk.

Commercial paper Short-term obligations with maturities ranging from 2 to 270 days issued by banks, corporations and other borrowers to investors with temporarily idle cash.

Compliance department The department or unit within a brokerage firm, bank or financial institution that ensures compliance with all applicable laws, rules and regulations. It generally has a range of roles and responsibilities within a firm.

Co-operative A business or other organisation which is owned and run jointly by its members, who share the profits or benefits.

Counter-party exposure The risk borne by one party involved in a transaction in the event that the other party is unable to fulfil its side of the contract/agreement/transaction.

Credit default swap A financial swap agreement that the seller of the CDS will compensate the buyer (usually the creditor of the reference loan) in the event of a loan default (by the debtor) or other credit event. That is to say that the seller of the CDS insures the buyer against some reference loan defaulting. The buyer makes a series of payments (the CDS 'fee' or 'spread') to the seller and, in exchange, receives a pay-off if the loan defaults.

Credit ratings (see **Ratings**).

Dark pool trading Private exchanges or forums for trading securities. Unlike stock exchanges, dark pools are not accessible by the investing public. They are so named for their complete lack of transparency.

Debt capital Capital raised by the issuance of debt securities, usually bonds.

Delinquent mortgage A mortgage on which the borrower has failed to make the required payments.

Derivative A derivative instrument is a contract that derives its value from the price of an underlying asset, an interest rate or an index. Examples of derivatives are forward contracts, futures contracts and options. Derivatives usually cost a fraction of the underlying asset, making them highly geared. Equity derivatives are based on the underlying value of equities.

Due diligence This is (1) the obligation on a securities firm contemplating a new issue of securities to explain the new issue to prospective investors; and (2), in mergers and acquisitions, the process of reviewing the condition of a company in detail.

Earnings per share The total profits of the company after tax divided by the number of issued shares.

Equity capital Any issued share capital entitled to a share in both the distribution of dividends on capital and proceeds on wind-up of a company. However, it usually means ordinary shares only, so that the 'equity interest' is that part of the business which belongs to the ordinary shareholders.

Financial Conduct Authority UK financial regulatory authority formed in 2013. It regulates financial firms providing services to consumers and maintains the integrity of the UK's financial markets. It operates alongside the Prudential Regulatory Authority which is responsible for the prudential regulation and supervision of banks, building societies, credit unions, insurers and major investment firms. Together, the two authorities are successors to the Financial Services Authority.

Financial Services Authority This was a UK regulatory body responsible for the regulation of the financial services industry in the UK between 2001 and 2013. It was succeeded by the Financial Conduct Authority and the Prudential Regulatory Authority in 2013.

Foreclosure In the case of a mortgage, a foreclosure occurs when the mortgage holder (home owner) cannot pay the mortgage loan payments and the bank repossesses the home.

Forward contract In a forward contract the parties agree to exchange assets in the future. It specifies the assets to be exchanged, the date of the exchange and a price. The terms of the contract are tailored to the needs of the counter parties.

Freddie Mac and Fannie Mae US government-sponsored enterprises with the objective of expanding the secondary market for mortgages. They buy mortgages on the secondary market, pool them and sell them as mortgage-backed securities to investors on the open market. This secondary mortgage market increases the supply of money available for mortgage lending and increases the money available for new home purchases. They are only permitted to buy conforming loans with strict lending criteria. These were relaxed in the run-up to the banking crisis.

Free reserves (charity) Money set aside to protect a charity against a drop in income or to allow it to take advantage of new opportunities. The money can be spent on any of its aims.

Futures contract A highly standardised forward contract traded on organised exchanges. Financial futures mainly relate to bonds, exchange rates and equity market indices. The size of traded units is standardised, as are the dates of exchange.

Goodwill The excess of going-concern value of a business over net asset value, generally understood to represent the value of a well-respected business name, good customer relations, high employee morale and other such factors expected to translate into greater than normal earning power.

Guanxi The Chinese system of social networks and influential relationships which facilitate business and other dealings.

Hedging Action taken to offset or reduce possible adverse changes in the value of assets or the cost of liabilities currently held or expected to be held at some future date.

Index fund A portfolio of investments that are weighted the same as a stock-exchange index in order to mirror its performance (also called an index tracker).

Initial public offering A corporation's first offering of shares (stock) to the public.

Interbank lending market A market in which banks extend loans to one another for a specified term. Most interbank loans are for maturities of one week or less, the majority being overnight. Such loans are made at the interbank rate.

Investment grade Securities rated Baa or above by Moody's or BBB or above by Standard & Poor's are known as investment grade (see also **Ratings**).

Junk bond A bond with a credit rating of BB or lower by rating agencies is a junk bond. They are issued by companies without long track records of sales and earnings, or by those with questionable credit strength. Since they are more volatile and pay higher yields than investment-grade bonds, many risk-oriented investors specialise in trading them.

Leverage The proportion of a company's long-term debt and preference share capital to its ordinary equity share capital. High leverage means that prior charges and/or debt capital are high in proportion to ordinary shares. Low leverage means the reverse. High leverage can enable ordinary shareholders to benefit from higher-than-average levels of profitability through the use of loan stock, but it works to a company's disadvantage during times of declining profitability because fixed interest costs must be met in full regardless of profits. (The UK equivalent term is 'gearing'.)

Limited liability partnership A legal entity structure often used as a fixed-life investment vehicle. It consists of a general partner (the management firm, which has unlimited liability) and limited partners (the investors, who have limited liability and are not involved with the day-to-day operations). A partnership agreement covers terms, fees, structures and other items between the limited partners and the general partner.

Mark-to-market accounting The adjustment of the price of a security or other position to reflect its market value, a process which gives rise to unrealised profits or losses.

Market maker A broker-dealer firm that accepts the risk of holding a certain number of shares of a particular security in order to facilitate trading in that security.

Merchant assets Assets purchased for investment purposes but considered to be held for later sale by a company rather than as a longer-term investment. The assets are generally held at fair value or market value rather than historical cost.

Minority interest A non-controlling ownership of less than 50 per cent of a company's voting shares by either an investor or another company.

Money market A segment of the financial market in which financial instruments with high liquidity and very short maturities are traded.

Montecarlo simulation A type of spreadsheet simulation which randomly and repeatedly generates values for uncertain variables to simulate a real-life model.

Mortgage-backed securities A type of asset-backed security that is secured by a mortgage or a collection of mortgages.

Net present value The value of a future income stream discounted—using an appropriate interest rate—to take account of the time value of money.

Nikkei 225 An index based on the 225 leading Japanese stocks traded on the TSE.

Non-prime (see **subprime**).

Non-recourse A non-recourse debt is a type of loan that is secured by collateral, which is usually property. If the borrower defaults, the issuer can seize the collateral but cannot seek out the borrower for any further compensation, even if the collateral does not cover the full value of the defaulted amount. This is one instance where the borrower does not have personal liability for the loan.

Off-balance sheet Financing which results in neither the debt nor the asset appearing on the company's balance sheet. Under such financing, the financial ratios which may be used to determine borrowing capacity are not affected.

Originate and hold A situation when lenders make loans with the intention of holding them through maturity, as opposed to selling them to other financial institutions and/or investors.

Originate and trade A situation when lenders make loans with the intention of selling them to other institutions and/or investors, as opposed to holding the loans through maturity.

Over the counter A market which is outside a formal stock exchange where transactions are completed directly by dealers acting as principals rather than agents, using the telephone, telex or computer.

Payment protection insurance This insurance is sold alongside credit cards, mortgages and other finance agreements to ensure that payments are made if the borrower is unable to make them due to sickness or unemployment.

Position An investor's stake in a particular security or market. A long position equals the number of financial instruments owned. A short position equals the number of financial instruments owed.

Preferred share A share which entitles the holder to a fixed dividend, the payment of which takes priority over that of ordinary share dividends.

Private equity The equity securities of unlisted companies.

Pyramid lending scheme An illegal investment scam based on a hierarchical set-up. New recruits make up the base of the pyramid and provide the funding, or so-called returns, given to the earlier investors/recruits above them.

Ratings An evaluation of the creditworthiness of a specific securities issue or borrower, made by an agency in the USA, such as Standard & Poor's or Moody's. The gradings are assigned from AAA for the most creditworthy to DDD for the least. Ratings shift as the borrower's financial position changes.

Reference rate A rate that determines pay-offs in a financial contract and is outside the control of the parties to the contract. Examples include LIBOR, EURIBOR, WMR and ECB exchange rate fixes.

Related party transactions Interaction between two parties, one of which can exercise control or significant influence over the operating policies of the other. As the parties may apparently act independently, in most countries listed companies are required to make certain disclosures concerning related parties and any transactions between them.

Reverse takeover This is (1) when a private company acquires a public company, effectively bypassing the usually lengthy and complex process of going public (also referred to as a *reverse merger*); (2) when a smaller company buys out a larger company; and (3) when a target company takes over the prospective bidder instead of the opposite.

Securities and Exchange Commission The US government commission that regulates the securities markets and protects investors. In addition to regulation and protection, it also monitors corporate takeovers in the USA.

Securities and Futures Authority The UK regulatory body responsible for authorising and monitoring firms which carry out investment business. It was replaced by the FSA in 2000.

Senior independent director A senior independent director serves as a sounding board for the chairman and acts as an intermediary for the other directors. They are responsible for holding annual meetings with non-executives, without the chairman present, to appraise the chairman's performance. They would also be expected to meet with the non-executives on other occasions when necessary.

Shadow banking This comprises a diverse set of institutions and markets that, collectively, carry out traditional banking functions, but do so outside, or in ways only loosely linked to, the traditional system of regulated depository institutions. They include money-market funds, hedge funds, private equity funds, mortgage companies, structured investment vehicles and some operations of investment banks.

Short-term paper (see **Commercial paper**).

SINA structure (see **Variable Interest Entity structure**). This was originally named after a company called SINA.com, which was listed on NASDAQ in 2000.

Special purpose entity A company formed for a single purpose, usually to hold assets or receive cash flows in a financial transaction. Often such vehicles are not formally owned by the company which benefits from the financing transaction and are not therefore consolidated in the financial statements.

Structured finance This refers to any non-standard means of raising funds, where the lender may tailor the financing to meet the specific client's needs. Generally this involves highly complex financial transactions.

Subprime (non-prime) This is a classification of borrowers with a tarnished or limited credit history. Lenders will use a credit-scoring system to determine which loans a borrower qualifies for. Subprime loans carry more credit risk and as such will carry higher interest rates as well.

Swap contract This describes (1) an interest rate swap, which is an agreement by which two parties agree to pay each other interest on a notional amount over a defined period but calculated according to different interest bases; and (2) a currency swaps, which is an agreement between two parties to sell agreed amounts of specified currencies to each other on a future date at an exchange rate established at the outset.

Tobashi Japanese for 'flying away', this describes the practice where external investment firms typically sell or otherwise take loss-bearing investments off the books of one client company at their near-cost valuation to conceal investment losses from the clients' financial statements. In that sense the losses are made to disappear, or 'fly away'.

Tokkin In Japan, this is a type of short-term corporate investment fund managed by a trust bank, providing a reduction of tax liability and other financial advantages.

Trading book Financial instrument or commodity held either with the intent to trade or in order to hedge other positions of the trading book. Each trading book consists of positions in a similar category of instrument or commodity so that an institution often has a significant number of different trading books.

Value at risk A model used to estimate the market risk of a trading portfolio. It is widely used by banks, securities firms, commodity and energy merchants, and other trading organisations.

Variable interest entity structure A solution to getting an overseas public listing for a Chinese company which normally would not be permitted to do so.

The solution has been to create a domestic vehicle that contains the restricted businesses and is owned by a Chinese individual (the VIE). However, through a series of legal agreements, as opposed to share ownership, the economic interest is transferred to a domestic vehicle (the **WFOE**), which in turn is owned by a foreign-listed company. As the economic interest ultimately lies with the foreign company, it is able to consolidate the VIE.

Volumetric production payment A financing mechanism whereby a gas producer enters into a long-term contract for the supply of a fixed volume of gas at a fixed price in return for an upfront payment.

Wholly Foreign Owned Enterprise (see **VIE**) Limited liability company for mainland-China based business financed by foreign funds. It does not require the involvement of a Chinese investor but is not permitted to engage in certain restricted business activities.

List of Abbreviations

ABCP	asset-backed commercial paper
ACCA	Association of Chartered Certified Accountants
ACFE	Association of Certified Fraud Examiners
ASBE	Accounting Standards for Business Enterprises
B2B	business to business
B2C	business to consumer
BaFin	Bundesanstalt für Finanzdienstleistungsaufsicht (Federal Financial Supervisory Authority)
BBA	British Bankers Association
BBC	British Broadcasting Company
CalPERS	California Public Employees Retirement Scheme
C2C	consumer to consumer
CCP	Chinese Communist Party
CDO	Collateralised Debt Obligation
CDS	Credit Default Swap
CEO	Chief Executive Officer
CET	Central European time
CFA	Chartered Financial Analyst
CFA Institute	Institute of Chartered Financial Analysts

© The Author(s) 2017
A. Micklethwait, P. Dimond, *Driven to the Brink*,
DOI 10.1057/978-1-137-59053-4

CFO	Chief Financial Officer
CFS	Co-operative Financial Services
CFTC	Commodity Futures Trading Commission
CIBC	Canadian Imperial Bank of Commerce
CITIC	China International Trust and Investment Corporation
CMHC	Canadian Mortgage and Housing Corporation
COO	Chief Operating Officer
CP	Commercial Paper
CPA	Certified Public Accountant
CWS	Co-operative Wholesale Society
E&Y	Ernst & Young ShinNihon LLC
EBS	Enron Broadband Services
ECB	European Central Bank
EPS	earnings per share
EURIBOR	Euro Interbank Offered Rate
FBI	Federal Bureau of Investigation
FCA	Financial Conduct Authority
FSA	Financial Services Authority
FSB	Financial Stability Board
FSU	Family Support Unit
FX	foreign exchange
G-5	Group of Five
G-7	Group of Seven
GMV	Gross Merchandise Value
GNP	gross national product
HBOS	Halifax Bank Of Scotland
ICE	Intercontinental Exchange group
IFRS	International Financial Reporting Standards
IMD	International Institute for Management Development
IMF	International Monetary Fund
IMM	International Money Market
IMPP	Insured Mortgage Purchase Program
IPO	initial public offering
IRS	Internal Revenue Service
JEDI	Joint Energy Development Investment
JV	joint venture

LIBOR	London Interbank Offered Rate
LLP	limited liability partnership
MIT	Massachusetts Institute of Technology
M&A	Mergers and Acquisitions
MBS	mortgaged-backed security
NED	non-executive director
NHS	National Health Service
NINJA	no income, no job, no assets
NPV	net present value
NYPA	New York Power Authority
NYSE	New York Stock Exchange
OECD	Organisation for Economic Co-operation and Development
OIS	overnight indexed swap (rate)
OTC	over-the-counter (market)
PACAC	Public Administration and Constitutional Affairs Committee
PIRC	Pensions & Investment Research Consultants
PPI	payment protection insurance
PPP	purchasing power parity
PRC	People's Republic of China
PwC	PricewaterhouseCoopers
RBS	Royal Bank of Scotland
SEC	Securities and Exchange Commission
SFO	Serious Fraud Office
SID	senior independent director
SOE	state-owned enterprise
SPE	special purpose entity
STIR	short-term interest rate
TARP	Troubled Asset Relief Programme
TSE	Tokyo Stock Exchange
VAR	Value At Risk
VIE	variable interest entity
VPP	volumetric production payment
VW	Volkswagen
WFOE	Wholly Foreign Owned Enterprise
WMR	World Markets/Reuters

Index

© The Author(s) 2017
A. Micklethwait, P. Dimond, *Driven to the Brink*,
DOI 10.1057/978-1-137-59053-4

Printed by Printforce, the Netherlands